Amazon Town TV

Joe R. and Teresa Lozano Long Series in
Latin American and Latino Art and Culture

Amazon Town TV

An Audience Ethnography in Gurupá, Brazil

RICHARD PACE AND BRIAN P. HINOTE

University of Texas Press ◄► *Austin*

Chapters 1, 5, and 6 contain material based in part on Pace's previously published article "Television's Interpellation: Heeding, Missing, Ignoring, and Resisting the Call for Pan-National Identity in the Brazilian Amazon, *American Anthropologist* 111(4):407–419. Chapter 3 is based in part on material previously published in Pace's book *The Struggle for Amazon Town: Gurupá Revisited* (Boulder, CO: Lynne Rienner Publishers, 1998). Chapter 4 is based in part on material previously published by Pace as "First-Time Televiewing in Amazônia: Television Acculturation in Gurupá, Brazil," *Ethnology* Vol. XXXII, No. 2:187–205.

Requests for permission to reproduce material from this work should be sent to:
    Permissions
    University of Texas Press
    P.O. Box 7819
    Austin, TX 78713-7819
    utpress.utexas.edu/index.php/rp-form

♾ The paper used in this book meets the minimum requirements of ANSI/NISO Z39.48-1992 (R1997) (Permanence of Paper).

Library of Congress Cataloging-in-Publication Data
Pace, Richard, 1956–
Amazon town tv : an audience ethnography in Gurupá, Brazil / by Richard Pace and Brian P. Hinote.
        p.   cm. — (Joe R. and Teresa Lozano Long series in Latin American and Latino art and culture)
Includes bibliographical references and index.
ISBN 978-0-292-76204-6
1. Ethnology—Brazil—Gurupá (Pará) 2. Television and culture—Brazil—Gurupá (Pará) 3. Television and families—Brazil—Gurupá (Pará) 4. Television in popular culture—History. 5. Social change—Brazil—Gurupá (Pará) 6. Gurupá (Pará, Brazil)—Social life and customs. I. Hinote, Brian P., 1976– II. Title.
GN564.B6P33 2013
302.23′4—dc23
                                                            2012031507

doi:10:7560/745179

First paperback edition, 2014

Contents

Preface

Amazon Town TV began in 1983 as I was in the final stages of dissertation research preparation at the University of Florida. I had received funding to conduct a restudy of Gurupá, an Amazonian community studied by my mentor, Charles (Chuck) Wagley, thirty-five years earlier (*Amazon Town*, 1976, 1968, 1953). Chuck introduced me to his son-in-law, Conrad Kottak, of the University of Michigan, who had just received a large grant to study the social impact of television in rural Brazil. Conrad wanted to include Gurupá in his study and asked me to join the research team.

Conrad's project called for yearlong audience ethnographies of communities previously studied by anthropologists. The project was to be the first multisite study of television in anthropology, the first ethnographic study of television in Brazil, and the first television study anywhere incorporating quantitative methods (statistical analysis of over one thousand interview schedules) with yearlong qualitative methods in multiple sites. It was to be one of the first ethnographies focusing on the role of media in the imagination of new social vistas and the construction and maintenance of imagined communities (Askew 2002: 7). The results of this research are found in *Prime-Time Society* (Kottak 2009, 1990 [hereafter referred to as *PTS*]).

The timing was perfect, and I accepted. Yet in the back of my mind reservations lingered. Like many anthropologists in the early 1980s, I was not quite certain this "media anthropology" trend would ever be of genuine academic interest. I worried that spending too much time studying television might prove a distraction from "essential" research in the discipline—in my case, political ecology (examining resource use, land disputes, and incipient social movements struggling to enfranchise agricultural workers in the Amazon). Even more insidious, I envisioned tele-

vision as a potential threat to the cultural integrity of my research site—
a form of cultural imperialism exerting unknown corruptive forces on
noncorrupted peoples. I recalled reacting with a measure of contempt
when I spotted the first TV antenna in Gurupá, even though I had agreed
to study television's impact in the community.

Twenty-five years later much had changed. Television had not destroyed the cultural integrity of Gurupá, nor was television research an
intellectual dead end. In fact, I had just published an article in the *American Anthropologist* that documented the ongoing impact of television in
Gurupá (Pace 2009), media anthropology was clearly of academic interest
and had become a booming subfield specialty, and I was even calling myself a media anthropologist. Reflecting on the happenstance that brought
me to that point in my career, I realized that if not for Conrad's pioneering
foray into television studies I would have missed (by ignoring) an incred-
ibly rare opportunity to watch and record the introduction and spread of
television in a non-Western setting.

Continuing the research initiated by *PTS* over the years, however,
has not been an easy task. By the late 1990s most anthropological and
ethnographic-based studies of media fell within the domain of cultural
studies in which researchers employed symbolic/interpretive approaches
tempered by poststructural/postmodern concerns (see Couldry 2010:
36). The approach used in *PTS*, which my coauthor, Brian P. Hinote,
and I have continued to use ever since, is a positivistic approach centered
on television's *influence* and viewers' ability to mediate it. For example,
in *Amazon Town TV* we ask questions such as what television does to
people and cultures and what people do in response. We count and analyze things, behaviors, and opinions through surveys and present our findings in tables. Most cultural studies approaches, almost by default, frown
on, if not outright renounce, such research as discredited scientism or
simplistic "effects" research and then largely ignore it. We beg to differ, of
course, as we present our data and arguments. Nonetheless, *Amazon Town
TV* treads into hostile environs.

Over the years I have returned fourteen times to Gurupá and spent a
total of two years in the community. All along I have combined my media
research with the study of political economy and political ecology. Gurupá has had much to offer, being the site of a very successful politico-
environmental movement informed by social Catholicism (liberation
theology) and organized by an activist rural workers' union. With the
assistance of an innovative nongovernmental organization named Federação de Órgãos para Assistência Social e Educacional (FASE; Federation of

Agencies for Social and Educational Assistance), it has had important successes in regularizing landownership and establishing sustainable development projects, extractive reserves, and *quilombos* (former slave refuges; see Pace 2004, 1998, 1992). I have also studied gender roles (Pace 1995) and concepts of race and ethnicity (Pace 2006). By combining a host of previous and later studies of the community (see Chapter 1), Brian and I have been able to place the impact of television in a historical, localized cultural context and greatly strengthen the findings of this work.

In 2009 Brian joined the project. As he describes below, he is a sociologist with interests in health and medicine, political economy, and social change. He traveled to Gurupá in summer 2009 and has been working ever since on the project's data analysis, which in many ways forms the backbone of this study. He has also applied his editorial skills to improve the writing of this book.

My family has also been essential to the completion of this work. My wife, Olga, has accompanied me on most of the trips to Gurupá and assisted in building rapport, systematic observations, and informal interviews. Her understanding of Latin American culture has opened my eyes to events, practices, attitudes, and feelings I otherwise would have missed and greatly enriched my anthropological expertise. Our two daughters, Cynthia and Annie, have likewise accompanied us to Gurupá. Cynthia has conducted her own research on the community's public health system and will include Gurupá in her doctoral research in applied medical anthropology. Annie, a journalism graduate, has filmed in Gurupá in the preparation of several documentaries. A number of her photographs appear in this book.

As mentioned above, my introduction to Gurupá was through Chuck Wagley. Always curious to know what was new in Gurupá, he provided support and guidance that were indispensable to the research. In the 1980s I was able to converse with some of his original consultants from the 1940s. His good name always facilitated rapport building, and I quickly became known as the student of Seu Charles (Senhor Charles) who was in town to write another book. In recent years his daughter, Isabel (Betty) Wagley Kottak, has graciously shared stories about the "Gurupá years." She has also provided scores of photographs taken in the community during the 1940s and 1960s by her father; these are now treasured in Gurupá as important historical documents.

Many others have been important in the formation of this work. Marianne Schmink patiently guided me through the early stages of research, Samuel Sá steadfastly assisted me in my research endeavors throughout the decades, Paulo H. R. Oliveira offered invaluable comparative research findings from his work on social conflict and union organization, FASE provided much institutional support and graciously opened its archives to a decade of sustainable development research, the Sindicato Trabalhadores Rurais (Rural Workers' Union) of Gurupá gave much appreciated logistic support, and Pedro Alves provided valuable insight into the local sociopolitical processes. I wish to also thank Middle Tennessee State University and the Faculty Research and Creative Activities Committee (FRCAC) for various grants to conduct research over the years, as well as the Fulbright Commission for financing both the 1984–1985 and 2011 research. In Belém, the Programa de Pos-Graduação de Ciências Sociais (Post-Graduate Program for Social Sciences) of the Federal University of Pará has provided much-valued academic support during the Fulbright grant.

Conrad Kottak deserves most of the credit for directing me toward media studies. Over the years he has provided much support for this re-search—financial, methodological, and theoretical. Much of what is written here demonstrates his foresight regarding what media anthropology can be.

Richard Pace

Richard Pace introduced me to the Brazilian Amazon and to Gurupá in 2009. As a sociologist working in the United States, I focused much of my previous research on the countries of the former Soviet Union (a large part of my doctoral work under the tutelage of William Cockerham) and on sociological, health, and policy issues in the United States. Eagerly anticipating new experiences and always open to collaborating on interesting research questions in different parts of the world, I jumped at the chance to play a role in this project.

In addition to many individuals and organizations that assisted in this and previous research in Gurupá (noted above), I too wish to thank Middle Tennessee State University and the FRCAC for grant support to assist in completing this project, as well as the College of Liberal Arts and the Department of Sociology and Anthropology for other valuable research support. I also wish to thank my family, an important part of this and all my research, especially my wife, Tyne, who has always provided valuable encouragement and has supported me in every way imaginable.

Unlike Richard's experience, this work is my first venture into Brazil and into media studies. It was by some measure of chance or luck that I found myself in the Amazon at all, traveling by boat toward Gurupá while reading Wagley's original *Amazon Town* and others' work as we approached this small town in the rain forest—my first glimpse only a distant point of light beneath more stars than I had ever seen. But much of my contribution to this book took place in the comfort of my office in the heart of Middle Tennessee, crunching numbers and taking care of the numerous loose ends that always come up during the course of research.

Brian P. Hinote

Amazon Town TV

CHAPTER I

Cross-Cultural Television Studies

In the darkness of the Amazon night, afloat on a small tributary of the Amazon River, I sat in the middle of a wooden canoe as it glided gracefully through the blackened waters.[1] Moonlight showed the way, but just barely. Despite the tropical humidity the night air felt cool on the skin. The only sounds were the background buzz of insects along the bank, an occasional cry from some nocturnal creature in the rain forest canopy, and the plopping of the paddles as they dipped into slow-moving water. Paddling behind me was my friend and consultant, Benedito,[2] a forty-year-old subsistence farmer and timber extractor who lived in the rural interior of the municipality of Gurupá. Paddling in front of me was his teenage son, João. We were on the way back to Benedito's house after visiting his brother-in-law who lived about twenty minutes downstream. We had stayed later than usual—well into the darkness—caught up in a documentary about the Amazon River and rain forest broadcast on his brother-in-law's new television set. It was a special treat for all to see, made even more so because it was a foreign production about their home. Benedito pitched in to pay the fuel for the diesel motor needed to power the television, since the house was far into the interior where no electric lines ran. He did this periodically to see important soccer matches, catch up on the news, enjoy a heralded movie, or watch parts of really good *telenovelas*—popular, prime-time melodrama series akin to soap operas.

As we proceeded upstream, I asked Benedito and João a favorite research question of mine: "What do you think of television?" Benedito responded between paddle strokes that it is very interesting and that he really likes learning about the world beyond his home. João added that he loves watching kung fu movies and Formula One racing, pausing as he paddled hard to maneuver the canoe around a partially submerged tree

Figure I.I. Interior home with satellite dish. Photograph by A. Pace, 2011.

branch. Once clear of the debris, he said that he also likes cartoons and soccer matches.

I next asked about all the time and effort expended just to watch TV programs—paddling to the brother-in-law's house, sometimes returning after dark. João exclaimed he would do it every day if his father would permit him. Benedito chuckled that his son would probably spend all day in front of the television if he could—but then no work would get done and everyone would go hungry. He added that the paddling, paying for fuel for the diesel motor, and the time away from work is worthwhile for some shows. He told a story about how, a few years back, in 2002, João and he had gotten up in the middle of the night to paddle to his brother-in-law's house to watch live broadcasts of the World Cup soccer matches in Japan. He said, "I never imagined what it would feel like to see Brazil win games on the other side of the world. We watched them cheer in Japan, then in São Paulo and Rio de Janeiro. So we cheered—yelling into the rain forest—all at the same time as the rest of the world!"

About this time, without warning, there was a loud splash in the darkness to the side of the canoe. In a startled voice Benedito muttered, "Boto" (freshwater dolphin), while João squealed, "Cobra grande" (giant anaconda); neither is a welcome guest to the canoeist. In unison they paddled close to the riverbank for safety. With all signs of danger past—real or imaginary—Benedito continued to talk about television. His mood had shifted somewhat as he commented on the documentary we had just seen. He was disappointed with the way the narrator had besmirched the notion of botos and cobra grandes having supernatural powers. All his life he had heard stories of botos transforming into human form and bedeviling the unwary, and personally he was sure he had seen the glowing red eyes of the monstrous snake while out night fishing, more than once. João agreed, saying he too had seen the mysterious snake in the darkness and was scared to death that it might capsize his canoe one day.

We finally reached Benedito's home. João tied the canoe to a crooked pole emerging from the dark water as we climbed up a narrow, water-worn ladder to their house set upon stilts. In the dim light of an oil lamp that Benedito's wife had left for us, I hung up my hammock next to João's in the front room. As I climbed into the hammock to sleep away the rest of the night, I heard Benedito say as he walked to his room in the back of the house, "Television has surely gotten it wrong."

On another Amazonian night in the small town of Gurupá, not far away, I recorded a different assessment of television. Socorro, a nineteen-year-old clerk in a small clothing store, sat down with her family and mine

Figure I.2. Canoeing on the Amazon River. Photograph by A. Pace, 2011.

on a Friday night at the riverfront *praça* (plaza or square). We were seated on white plastic chairs around a white plastic table. At our backs, ten meters below the rocky rise on which the town sits, flowed the Amazon River. It appeared to stretch endlessly into the darkness (actually it is five kilometers wide as it passes Gurupá). To the front, several hundred towns-folk mingled, spread throughout the praça up to the row of pastel-painted homes, all flush with the street and joined together to form the entire block. The townsfolk stood in small clusters, telling stories, gossiping, flirting, or simply watching others as they shared bottles of regional beer and nibbled on pizza, popcorn, or mayonnaise-covered fries. *Brega* (a regional music) blared from a nearby bar, filling any pauses in conversation.

As we all talked I managed to shift the conversation to the local impression of television. Socorro, without hesitation, began complaining how boring the 9:00 telenovela was. The program was about a wealthy family from Rio de Janeiro. After watching it for two weeks, she wasn't interested anymore. So tonight she simply turned it off just after it started, deciding it would be more entertaining to come to the praça to socialize.

Socorro's mother, looking puzzled as she glanced at her watch, questioned where her daughter had been in the intervening time, since the telenovela had ended quite some time ago. Socorro responded defensively, saying she had actually walked about halfway to the praça when she remembered a crime report she had just heard on the evening news. A criminal in the faraway city of São Paulo had slipped through an unlocked door while a family was out and then waited until their return to assault them. She stopped in her tracks, returned home, closed all the shutters, found the key to the door left inside on a nail in the wall, and securely locked it. Feeling safe, she left the house a second time. Socorro's mother frowned at this sequence of events, telling her daughter that there is so little crime in town that her actions seemed excessive.

Undaunted, Socorro continued her defense. As she walked toward the praça, in house after house, so many people were peering out their front windows or sitting in the door stoops. Turning to me, she commented that nobody in town watches that dreadful telenovela. Turning back to her mother, Socorro insisted she had to stop and greet most of them since they were her relatives, *padrinhos* (godparents), coworkers, or friends. Next she noticed a friend out in the street with a new pair of high heels, very similar to the ones worn by the star of the telenovela she had just turned off, so she had to stop and ask her where she had bought them. Socorro explained to her mother that she had saved enough money so that on her next trip to the large city of Belém at the end of the month she

Figure I.3. Town square. Photograph by R. Pace, 2011.

might be able to buy the shoes, if she knew where to find them. Continuing on her way, she finally reached the riverside praça, at which point she spent some time trying to find her family in the crowd.

Socorro paused as her mother nodded in acceptance of the explanation. Socorro then returned to my question, telling me people here are not interested in watching television. They prefer to watch the local nightlife.

With the global spread of television, people in some of the most isolated regions of the world now routinely watch programs about events, peoples, places, and technologies far removed from their quotidian lives. Through engagement with the medium they are presented with novel concepts, exotic situations, and curious explanations that are challenging and puzzling, occasionally boring and senseless, but most frequently entertaining and educational. The potential for sociocultural change inspired by this informational barrage is tremendous. What that change might actually be, however, is far from obvious or predictable.

For example, why do some people go out of their way to enjoy television, as in the case of Benedito above, eagerly absorbing information about distant places and events but openly skeptical of messages that touch close to home? Why do others, like Socorro, talk as if they are disinterested in television programming but nonetheless alter their behavior to consume products displayed in programming or to guard against unlikely threats suggested by the medium? In a more general sense, why do viewers sometimes heed television's messages—changing or maintaining beliefs and behavior in compliance with the suggested identities, roles, and behaviors exhibited in programming—but at other times miss, ignore, alter, reject, subvert, or resist messages? What role does culture play in this interaction? Are there patterns to viewers' responses, or are reactions infinitely varied? If patterns exist, can they be delineated, observed, and measured, or must they only be assumed and never proven?

These are some of the critical questions currently driving research and debate in media studies. The responses from researchers, however, are fractious, with a significant rift between those prioritizing media influence (e.g., the power of messages incorporated in the text of the medium to influence viewers) and those emphasizing active audiences (e.g., viewers' ability to mediate messages; Kitzinger 2004: 24; Corner 2000: 383). This rift has led to a paradigmatic impasse, with researchers in the various camps typically ignoring or disparaging the work of the other camps (see, e.g., Rajagopal 2001 or Hobert 2005 and 2010 vs. Sparks 2006). Likewise, there is a considerable gap in methodological and epistemological approaches, characterized by quantitative and positivistic approaches (e.g., effects research) typical in American mass communication research versus qualitative and poststructural or humanistic/interpretive approaches (e.g., cultural studies) characteristic of European and Latin American research and American anthropology (Kitzinger 2004: 25; Lozano, Frankenberg, and Jacks 2009). There is also a geographic imbalance, with a relative abundance of studies on wealthy nations and a paucity of studies on non-Western nations, particularly rural areas.

In addition, there exists tremendous variation in the subject matter researched, with some studies documenting broad societal changes created by the absorption of information over many years, some examining changes produced by specific program genres (e.g., news, soap operas, children's programs), and others focusing on the immediate impacts of singular texts, such as a reaction to a movie or news program. Some studies observe viewers' social interactions during televiewing, some focus on widely ranging practices associated with or oriented toward television and other media as part of people's daily routines, and others try to place behavioral changes and worldview shifts in a greater sociocultural context (Kitzinger 2004: 24–25; Couldry 2010: 36). The result of these various approaches to different subject matters is a theoretical and methodological jumble, with no agreement on the appropriate focus of study but much criticism of competing research (see Peterson 2003, for an attempt to present a common rubric for research).

This book joins the contentious discussion on media influence and audience engagement, offering detailed documentation of the multiple changes emanating from the introduction of television into a small rural community in the Brazilian Amazon. What the work brings to the litigious debates is fourfold: a cross-cultural focus from a little-studied part of the world, which is crucial for comparative purposes; an ethnographic approach that also uses quantitative findings from interview schedules administered in 1986, 1999, and 2009; a longitudinal span of twenty-eight years during which the authors were given the unique opportunity to witness, firsthand, the introduction and spread of the medium; and a theoretical "middle ground" approach that attempts to bridge the theoretical impasse by gauging the relative strength of television influence vis-à-vis viewers' ability to mediate it.

The Value of Cross-Cultural, Ethnographic, and Long-Term Studies

Most social science approaches to television over the past few decades have presumed that the North American and Western European patterns of media adoption and engagement are intrinsically normal, natural, and inevitable, meaning that models based on this experience can logically be extended across the globe in a fairly uncritical manner (Ginsburg 2005: 19–20; Peterson 2003: 10). These claims to the normalcy, naturalness, and, hence, universality of Western behaviors, however, are infrequently tested in cross-cultural settings, leading to suspect propositions that may be tainted by cultural bias.[3] Cross-cultural research, in these cases, plays an essential role in uncovering the cultural boundedness of particular assumptions. In the case of television studies, it serves as an important check on current theory, potentially providing data to decenter the West as the default norm or basic model for all human thought and behavior (Peterson 2003: 11). This is crucial to communication theory, particularly since the non-West has typically been understudied or ignored by media researchers, at least until recently. Our case study of Gurupá, therefore, provides an important cross-cultural test whereby ideas of universalism based on Western models of culture and society can be assessed.

In addition to challenging ethnocentric notions, cross-cultural research contributes valuable information on the variations and complexities of message dissemination and viewer responses. For example, as television programs cross cultural spaces—national, ethnic, regional, or class—they are inevitably transformed. Canclini (1988, 1997) labels this process hybridization. Straubhaar (2007: 3) describes hybridization as "becoming part of the ongoing history[,] . . . interacting with previous forces, and becoming localized, enacted, and received by local people with their own identities, histories, and agendas" (see also Kraidy 2005; Canclini 1997). Appadurai (1990, 1996) likewise calls attention to how media messages can be significantly transformed, or indigenized, by different populations, particularly in the articulation of the national and transnational through local processes.

Within cross-cultural settings, ethnography is an essential tool for observing, contextualizing, and understanding the complexity of media engagement. Ethnography is an intensive, firsthand study of a group of people. Traditionally it is a long-term (i.e., a year or more), site-specific approach involving data gathering techniques of participant-observation, unstructured and structured interviews, and, in our case, the administration of interview schedules. From this base the ethnographer can interpret media's impact as situated in daily life, building up layers of detail from a wide web of social interactions, placed within a sociohistoric framework (see Descartes and Kottak 2009: 5; La Pastina 1999: 80). Doing ethnography results in the ability to observe community and social changes missed, or even unperceivable, by other methodologies (La Pastina 2005: 142). The result is a clearer picture of the role of the media in the processes of social and cultural transformation (Peterson 2003: 8–9; Tufte 2000: 31).

Many studies of media have defined their approaches as ethnographic without fulfilling these prerequisites. Hirsch (1989) commented that "ethnographic" becomes a gloss for qualitative techniques (usually interviews), without recognizing that ethnographies are the product of particular procedures, both methodological and epistemological. Peterson (2003: 126) writes that much of what is considered "ethnographic" by media scholars is primarily an attempt to "read" an audience as one would read a text. This is a technique borrowed from the structuralist studies of Hebdige (1979), which has little to do with ethnography as practiced by anthropologists. Nightingale (1993) points out that what has been lacking in many audience ethnographies is attention to cultural differences, close observations and descriptive detail, consideration of the contiguity of the subject matter to the broader aspects of social process, and reflexive engagement with the multiple, often dissenting voices of those studied.

For this study we have spent two years conducting ethnographic research on-site in Gurupá, stretched over a twenty-eight-year period. We have also embedded our media research in a broader project that analyzes long-term sociocultural changes in the community and region. In this regard, we have studied divergent topics such as social movements, religion, gender, politics, ethnic identity, public health, nutrition, and folklore, as well as television.[4] As a result we are able to add many layers of sociocultural detail to the analysis of television's impact. We have also been privileged to observe and record the initial phasing in of television and subsequent changes as the medium has spread throughout the community. This, in and of itself, is a rarity for television studies.

Also greatly beneficial to our study is the considerable historical and social science literature on Gurupá that provides a rich context with which to assess changes emerging from the introduction of television. Initial ethnographic research was conducted in 1948 (see Wagley [1953, 1968] 1976; Galvão 1955) and has continued until the present. I have been conducting research in the community since 1983, including participation in a 1984–1986 multiregional study of television's impact in Brazil directed by Conrad Kottak ([1990] 2009). Additional researchers have worked in Gurupá on topics such as historical demography, environmental changes, medicinal plants, social movements, gender roles, racial identity, land tenure, communication technology, child labor, and education (see Miller 1974, 1976; Kelly 1984; Magee 1986; P. Oliveira 1991; FASE 1997a, 1997b, 2002; Royer 2003; Barroso 2006; Soares 2004; Treccani 2006; Hendrickson 2006; Santos 2008). There are also many reports and journal entries from government census takers, travelers, and clergymen dating to the early seventeenth century that mention Gurupá. Collectively, these works provide a unique long-term view within which to situate the multiple changes created by the introduction of television.

The Theoretical Middle Ground

The debate that exists in media studies over the influence of television in people's lives revolves around the following questions: What power does it have to change behavior, to shape, mold, or even determine people's worldviews and social identities? At the same time, how proficient are viewers in teasing out social, political, and cultural constructions embedded in programming, if such messages are not overly polysemic or incoherent? Do viewers readily or reticently accept, reject, ignore, or subvert all or parts of television's messages? Does this change behavior? Do the messages simply go unnoticed? Or can we at best only describe what people do and say in "relation" to media and drop all pretense of offering causal explanations?

To answer these questions, we use an approach that seeks to gauge the relative strength of television influence vis-à-vis viewers' ability to mediate it. Our approach is similar to what Kitzinger (2004: 1, 16, 193) has called the "New Media Influence Research," which seeks to examine both the extent and the limits of media influence over time (5). It is a hybrid assemblage of studies researching the interface between media's representations of reality and how viewers talk, think, and behave in response (192). Key components of the approach are the agenda-setting paradigm (e.g., McCombs and Shaw 1972, 1993), which explores how information presented through the media helps define the terms of public debate, and various framing, priming, and branding approaches (e.g., Goffman 1974; Chibnall 1977), which study how media accounts implicitly reproduce given assumptions while marginalizing others as well as make certain themes prominent through media exposure. Through these processes, preferred messages are embedded in the televisual texts and are repeatedly presented to viewers.

Simultaneously, and just as critical, the approach accounts for viewers' ability to reinterpret, filter out, or subvert messages using culture and personal experiences (Kitzinger 2004: 14–15; Corner 2000: 384). It explicitly takes the position that audiences are active participants in the creation of meaning, which significantly contextualizes the manner in which media power functions. For our study, we divide viewer response to televisual texts into four categories: heeding, missing, ignoring, and resisting. These categories are based on Hall's (1981) tripartite classification of textual reading (preferred, negotiated, oppositional—also see Wilk 2002b: 289–290), adapted to the cultural context of the Amazon. *Heeding*, or accepting, the preferred messages embedded in programming typically occurs when the program producers and audiences share a basic cultural framework. The intended message is decoded by viewers with negligible alteration. That is, the viewers get the implied or preferred meaning. In the case of *missing* the preferred message, viewers lack the required background and familiarity with content to recognize and understand what is being communicated. The messages simply go unnoticed. In the third response, *ignoring*, messages are noticed but interpreted as uninteresting, unintelligible, or plainly false. Finally, in the case of *resisting*, messages are understood as false, as misleading, or as a threat to the preferred or accepted worldview. Instead of ignoring these messages, viewers subvert them by articulating alternative viewpoints. These viewpoints are constructed from other sources of available information such as churches, political parties, unions, family members, and friends.

As a note of caution, these four categories of responses are intended to serve as heuristic devices. They are suggested ways to delineate and order viewers' engagement with television programming. This is an important caveat as the categories are not always mutually exclusive. For example, a group of viewers may have different responses to the same messages. Likewise, a single viewer may heed part of a message but miss, ignore, or resist other parts of the same message (see Straubhaar 2007: 213; Mankekar 1999: 27). Viewers can also change their perspectives on the text over time, negating their original interpretation.

In addition, the placement of viewer responses in one or another of four categories can prove problematic. We may classify a response as heeding, but the amount of reworking the viewer performs on the original message may lead one to think the category of resisting is more appropriate. The same could be said for the other categories. Because of these difficulties, we use the four-part classification as a starting point to understand the process of viewer interaction with the text. Concerns about placement of responses and exactness of fit are less important than establishing a way to conceptualize and structure the range of viewer responses.

Another helpful concept to gauge viewer response to televisual messages is Bourdieu's (1984) notion of cultural capital. This concept refers to people's knowledge and experiences that allow them to navigate the social order, particularly in terms of being included or excluded in social groupings such as class, ethnicity, region, or religion. It is based on an individual's level of education, type of employment experiences, engagement with political and religious entities, personal networks, family background, ethnicity, travel opportunities, and so forth. When the concept of cultural capital is applied to televiewing, it also includes knowledge of narrative structures and strategies of programs, genre rules, and familiarity with different types of images and characters commonly used in programming. It is expressed through "a series of identifiable factors that people use when deciding what they want to watch on television and how they interpret what they watch . . . specific things like humor, gender images, dress, style, lifestyle, ethnic types, religion, values and knowledge about other lifestyles" (La Pastina 2004: 306).

The type and amount of capital that viewers possess will influence their ability to read and interpret a televisual text. This ability is also referred to as media literacy (Kilborn 1992). The idea of cultural proximity (Straubhaar 2003: 85; 2007: 203) is a related concept. Viewers' abilities to decode and interpret texts may depend on how recognizable are the visual elements (e.g., the landscape, clothing styles), verbal elements (including regionalism, historical references), and other distinctive features associated with a particular national, regional, local, or class culture. Straubhaar (2007: 203) states that cultural similarities or affinities produce forms of cultural capital that inform cultural proximity. He continues:

> [Cultural] affinities may be specific factors such as linguistic commonalities, shared religious histories, gender roles, moral values, common aspirations, common histories with colonialism, shared art forms, shared music forms, similar forms of dress, character types and stereotypes, and ideas about genre, storytelling, and pacing. Perceived cultural similarities also might include ethnic types, gender types, dress, style, gestures, body language, and lifestyle. Perceived cultural relevance seems to include news and discussion topics, definitions of humor, familiar stars and actors, and audience knowledge about other lifestyles. Images and values include perceptions of other countries and peoples, opinions or evaluations of them, and values about marriage, family relationships, importance of material goods, work, and ideas about where and how to live. (206)

The four categories of audience response, shaped by the cultural capital possessed by viewers and cultural proximity of the text, set the stage for a wide range of viewer interpretations of television messages. Yet, despite this potential, viewers are still responding to heavy barrages of repeated messages shaped and disseminated through agenda-setting, branding, framing, and priming. Responses tend not to be limitless. On the contrary, as we show, viewer responses can in fact be highly patterned.

The approach we use here tries to capture this interplay between media power and active audience readings. It is a nuanced approach attempting to weigh media power through the understanding of viewers' responses as "products of time and place, embedded in power structures, shaped by patterns of everyday life, conventions, common sense and language" (Kitzinger 2004: 189). Accordingly, this approach does not conceptualize audience activity and TV effects as opposing models (Creeber 2006: 95).

Socialization

In our approach we prioritize television's role as an agent of socialization. We focus on the impact of long-term exposure to the medium and how this interaction successfully, or unsuccessfully, molds or cultivates viewers' opinions, values, and worldviews, as well as affects behavior. This approach builds on cultivation analysis, pioneered in the 1960s by George Gerbner (1967), in which television is viewed as a major socializing agent on par with family, schools, peers, community, and churches. In this approach television does not necessarily tell viewers what to think, but it is very successful in telling them what to think about (Comstock et al. 1978), thereby directing attention toward some things and away from others (Gerbner and Gross 1976; Hood 1987). Much of the research in this approach has focused on the link between heavy television viewing (six hours or more a day) and distorted views of the "real world" (Gerbner et al. 1977, 1979, 1980, 1986). In particular, researchers have examined the impact of violent content in programming on an audience's perception of the world, as well as personal behavior (see Gerbner and Gross 1976; Gerbner et al. 1980).

Ideology—Interpellation

We combine the focus on television's long-term socialization influence with a critical approach to the ideological messages embedded in media texts. Though there is much debate over the meaning and importance of ideological approaches to television studies (see Hall 1982, 1981; Abercrombie et al. 1980; Barker 1999; Fairclough 1995; Abu-Lughod 2005; Mankekar 1999: 26), the various approaches have been commonly employed since the 1930s to uncover the implicit political and economic nature of television and the means by which social identities are reflected and articulated (Creeber 2006: 51). By "ideology," we refer to the ideas and beliefs whereby people understand the world and their place in it. In stratified societies it is linked to the ruling class, such that ideology typically normalizes and naturalizes systems of dominance and subordination. Particularly through ideological state apparatuses—such as those found in education, politics, religion, law, family, culture, and media—ideological messages hail, call out, recruit, or interpellate individuals (Althusser 1971).

According to Althusser (1971: 173–176), interpellation denotes the point at which an outside voice calls an individual, who by acknowledging or responding to the call becomes a subject, in a sense being defined by the call. Althusser gives the example of a police officer calling out, "Hey, you there!" to gain the attention of a passerby. By recognizing that she or he is being hailed by the police officer and turning around in response, the passerby is brought into existence as a subject. In the case of television, viewing the media is the act that brings the audience into existence as a subject, and interpellation describes how ideological messages in programming catch the viewers' attention and how that process can influence the viewers' thoughts and behaviors.

Interpellation involves a relationship between ideology and subjectivity in which individuals are "always-already subjects" receptive to a dominant, naturalized, and therefore invisible ideology in society (Althusser 1971: 172). As an individual responds by "turning around" or "tuning in" and by being defined by the hailing process, he or she is guaranteed identity as a "concrete, individual, distinguishable and (naturally) irreplaceable subject" (172). At the same time interpellation creates conditions leading to shared identity, expressed through class, gender, and ethnic/race associations, as well as regionalism, nationalism, and other forms of imagined communities.

Althusser continues, "The existence of ideology and the hailing or interpellation of individuals as subjects are one and the same thing" (163). Television viewers, in this sense, are preprogrammed or cultivated (through socialization) to receive dominant or preferred messages broadcasted by the medium. Through the act of watching television they are defined by it, both as unique individuals and as members of imagined communities. That is not to say that interpellation always works. Interpellation is an action that can "regularly miss its mark" (Butler 1997: 33), as we show in Chapter 6.

Polysemy

Contested components of ideological approaches in media studies include viewpoints that challenge the belief that preferred messages in television texts actually exist or are coherent and that they can be effectively understood by viewers. By "preferred messages," we refer to socially and politically motivated representations of reality (Hall 1981), generated by a power elite and an associated cadre of writers and producers, no matter how fractious, who are generally supportive and sympathetic to the powers in control. If writers, producers, and viewers share a basic cultural framework and political worldview, then viewers are likely to decode the intended message without much alteration. That is, viewers heed the implied or preferred meaning.

Critics of this approach point out that television's messages/texts cannot be seen as closed or privileged sites of meaning that affect audiences in a one-directional manner (i.e., not amenable to alternative understandings). Instead, the messages are conceived as polysemic, open-ended with multiple meanings, or sites of contestation. They might guide the viewer, but they cannot determine or fix the meanings emerging from the interplay between the text and the viewer's imagination. Countless interpretations are therefore possible, depending on the sociocultural background or cultural capital of the audience. In terms of the general critique of textual analysis, some hold that any analysis attempting to identify a preferred text offers little more than idiosyncratic interpretations since texts can be read in so many ways (i.e., there is no textual determinism). Others, using discourse analysis, seek to understand how different sociocultural discourses compete for meaning, at the same time pointing out textual inconsistencies, contradictions, and ambiguities existing in programming (Creeber 2006: 35).

Reacting to these criticisms, proponents of ideological approaches to media continue to point out the existence of power relations embedded in messages, although typically acknowledging that ideology forms a dialogue (Volosinov 1973; see also Barker 1999) between text and reader in which the reader can negotiate or reject meanings. In a more direct rebuke, Kitzinger (2004: 190–191) warns against using the "mantra of polysemy" to deny viewers' potential to decode messages. She maintains that the framing, priming, branding, and agenda-setting of messages, even when entangled in intentionally polysemic texts (e.g., point and counterpoint exchanges in news reporting), can effectively communicate preferred messages.

In our research we set out to test these assumptions. We start with the view that media power, media effects, and active audience readings of texts are not mutually exclusive processes. Instead, they are elements in a complex and likely uneven process of influence, negotiation, and subversion. In some cases viewers accept, identify with, and heed ideological themes in programming, particularly when program creators or producers and program viewers share similar backgrounds (Creeber 2006: 95; Kitzinger 2004: 186–187, 190). In cases in which they do not, the interesting questions that arise are why viewers sometimes still heed messages but at other times miss, ignore, and resist them.

Although our approach is designed to weigh viewers' responses visà-vis textual influence, by far the bulk of our research focuses on viewer reception. What we do in terms of textual analysis is present the findings of other Brazilian and Brazilianist scholars, extrapolating from their collective findings the principal messages repeatedly transmitted over the decades. We then observe which messages influence viewers in our research setting and which ones are missed, ignored, or resisted. By comparing results collected over three decades and placing them in an ethnographic context dating to the 1940s, we are able to identify broad trends and hypothesize television's impact. Within this general approach we occasionally analyze the impact of particular genres of programs (e.g., telenovelas, news, cartoons) or even specific shows to highlight key components of our analysis. Yet the main focus is on broad trends in viewer reception over the decades.

Media Engagement

We devote considerable attention to audience engagement with and use of television. Here the focus is on media interaction as sets of ritualistic behaviors (Peterson 2003: 133), or what Armbrust (1998: 413) calls "habits of spectatorship." The idea is that constructed meanings and associated behavioral changes must be understood in the context of the routines of daily life and all its constraints (Bird 2010; Barker 1999: 110; Fiske 1987; Lull 1986). Research focuses on the sites of reception (e.g., home, restaurants, public squares) and the functions of media consumption. Peterson (2003: 137–138) comments on this approach, noting that the "analysis of sites of reception is useful not only for its capacity to open our eyes to social dimensions of media use that go beyond engagement with the text, but also offer us the capacity to *situate* acts of interpretation" (original emphasis). Researchers study the ways in which sociality is constructed during televiewing, how power relations among viewers are acted out, and how audiences experiment with new forms of social behavior (Peterson 2003: 137).

Interest in media engagement, media consumption, and habits of spectatorship has led to a methodological shift within media studies to the ethnography of televiewing audiences. An early example of this approach is David Morley's (1980, 1981, 1986) analysis of televiewing in Britain. By focusing on family viewing practices, he is able to examine the ways in which televiewing interrelates with other social dynamics such as domination and subordination within the family. For example, he identifies gendered viewing practices where masculine influence is the key in negotiating everything from program choice to viewing styles.

In a study conducted in China, Lull (1986: 601) examines the varying ways people engage with television. He constructs a long list that demonstrates the complexity and richness of Chinese habits of spectatorship. For example, he finds that people used television for background noise, companionship, entertainment, punctuation of time and activity, regulation of talk patterns, experiencing illustration, establishment of common ground, and entering into conversations. He finds that television is used to reduce anxiety, clarify values, provide an agenda for talk, create patterns of physical and verbal contact and neglect, increase family solidarity, reduce conflict, and maintain relationships. Television also is an aid in decision making, behavior modeling, problem solving, value transmission across generations, opinion legitimization, and information dissemination. In addition, television is used for substitute schooling, role enactment, role reinforcement, substitute role portrayal, intellectual validation, exercise of authority, gatekeeping, and the facilitation of arguments.

Recent research in media practice theory on the centrality of viewer engagement with and use of television and other media in everyday life overlaps with our study's focus (see Bräuchler and Postill 2010). Practice theory is a fairly eclectic approach that seeks middle ground between methodological individualism and holism. According to Postill (2010: 6–7) the approach builds on the work of Bourdieu, Giddens, Foucault, Ortner, and others in an attempt "to liberate agency—the human ability to act upon and change the world—from the constrictions of structuralist and systemic models while avoiding the trap of methodological individualism." Our approach differs from the parts of practice theory concerned with media influence in everyday life in that we accept positivistic epistemology as a valid and useful tool to identify, isolate, and, at times, measure television's impact. The actual data gathered from practice theory's ethnographic findings are rich and illuminate our work.

Cross-Cultural Studies: A Selective Review

Despite the jumble of methodological and theoretical approaches to cross-cultural studies of television's impact, there is a growing body of research that allows us to delineate certain types of changes associated with the medium's introduction. Below we review a few such studies—although the review is hardly exhaustive. It is important to note that while the overall changes are unique to each individual cultural site, there are many parallels to the changes we describe for Gurupá in the chapters that follow.

One of the first, and now-classic, studies of the cross-cultural reception of a particular show is Liebes and Katz's (1991) study of the series *Dallas*. By focusing on cross-cultural readings, the authors find that viewers from different cultural backgrounds have alternative, sometimes oppositional readings of the program. For example, U.S. audiences assume that the program has no themes or ideology, whereas Russian viewers focus on the politics of biased representations of the capitalist lifestyle and Arab audiences point out the Western moral degeneracy displayed. In each case cultural identity mediates or filters the decoding of the program.

Kottak's ([1990] 2009) study of television in Brazil is one of the earliest examples of a cross-cultural media ethnography. It is also unique in that it utilizes extensive quantitative data obtained from interview schedules. Kottak's study is a team project that examines television's reception and impact in six Brazilian communities. My participation in the project involved conducting research in Gurupá, one of the study sites. We measured responses to television by length of site exposure, length of individual exposure, and current viewing habits (i.e., Gerbner's light, medium, and heavy viewing). One key finding is the strong correlation between TV exposure and "liberal" views on gender issues. Heavier viewers and longer-exposed viewers are significantly more tolerant in their opinions on such matters as whether women should work outside the home, frequent bars, and consider divorce; whether men should do domestic chores; and whether parents should talk to their children about sex.

Another interesting finding is the identification of a five-stage model of TV impact (described in more detail in Chapter 3). Stage I is the arrival of television in a community. The medium is novel and strange, and people are captivated by their sets. Basically the medium, rather than the message, is the mesmerizer. In Stage II people become more accustomed to television and begin a process of more selective acceptance and rejection, interpretation, and reworking of TV messages. Many statistical correlations between viewing and other factors are obvious. Stage III is the saturation point as nearly everyone has access to television. The medium loses its novelty, dismissive comments about the medium increase, and its influence is more difficult to measure statistically. In Stage IV there is life-long viewing, and television becomes a powerful national agent of mass enculturation. The more profound and long-term sociocultural effects of television become discernible. Stage V involves the proliferation and diversification of media technology, which transforms television and associated media from agents of mass enculturation into technologies of segmental appeal.

In a study similar to that of Liebes and Katz, Miller (1992, 1995) finds alternative readings of the U.S. soap opera *The Young and the Restless* in Trinidad, maintaining that viewers "localize," make sense of, and absorb the program's messages into local practices and meanings. Audiences pay close attention to the gossip and scandal in the program, relating it to the concept of Bacchanal (a folk concept that joins confusion, gossip, scandal, and truth). The program becomes the subject of much discussion (e.g., TV-talk), creating a backdrop for deliberations about local events and/or interactions, which when contrasted with the foreign content become an important element in the formation and maintenance of Trinidad identity. In another study, conducted in Britain, Gillespie (1995) also examines TV-talk in her analysis of audience reception of the show *Neighbours* among British Asians in London. She finds that the character portrayals of assertive women, particularly in romance, create a great deal of discussion about gender identities. This allows British Asian girls an outlet to discuss, ponder, and imagine topics normally taboo in their culture.

Abu-Lughod's (2005, 2002) study of working-class women in Cairo and villagers in Upper Egypt finds selective readings of television dramas. She suggests that these viewers subvert and elude the dominant messages of programming (in this case, modernity), not because they are traditional and ignorant, but because the distance between the "realities" dramatized in the serials and the lives they live is so vast. The ability to read and understand the versions of modernity depicted (primarily that of urban middle-class professionals) depends on viewers' class positions and the accessibility of certain kinds of educational and career opportunities (in other words, Bourdieu's cultural capital and Straubhaar's cultural proximity). The viewers simply ignore or suspend judgment on aspects of programming that are not part of their personal experiences. Abu-Lughod maintains that television creates its own world, a sphere unto itself.

Mankekar's (1999) study of television reception in a northern Indian city also shows how class, community, gender, age, and household position mediate viewers' interactions with television texts. She notes that the Indian state has attempted to use television to construct a pan-Indian culture based on urban, middle-class experiences. Even though the viewers she studied are far removed from the televised worlds, she was astonished to find that they frequently linked their favorite serials with their own lives. It becomes an easy way for many to not only discuss what they watch but also to contextualize their own experiences.

At the same time that viewers might strongly identify with characters on television (which provoke strong emotional responses), they are also able to draw back and criticize what they view. Mankekar notes that televiewing is becoming an opportune setting for group discussions and criticisms about government power. She cautions, however, against the assumption that a critical awareness means that viewers are straightforwardly resisting the dominant discourses of programming or that they are beyond the reach of the state. In her research she finds that viewers often submit to one of the multiple messages in a serial but use another one to criticize the government. She maintains that resistance to and compliance with television's messages are not mutually exclusive categories.

Wilk (2002a, 2002b) examines the way in which television stimulates discourses on national culture in Belize. He reports that television programming has presented viewers with an objectified "other" with which to contrast Belizean cultural traditions. Viewers develop a common language from televiewing (i.e., a discourse community) that allows them to define foreign otherness and Belizean sameness on topics such as ethnicity, gender roles, social welfare, and youth problems. Wilk maintains that since the arrival of television people have become more aware of the autonomy of local culture (e.g., music, cooking, dance, language) and can talk about Belizean culture in ways not possible before. Wilk (2002a: 182) finds that as a result local culture has become a symbol of identity and pride as it represents familiarity, security, and continuity with the past. It is understood as a form of resistance and opposition to the foreign rather than as a symbol of backwardness, ignorance, or isolation.

Finally, although not a cross-cultural study, Descartes and Kottak's (2009: 2–3) work on the American middle class examines the ways that parents receive, interpret, process, use, avoid, and/or resist media messages regarding work and family, relative to choices within their own work and family lives. Parents, in fact, process a large amount of media content pertaining to work and family and are able to critically discuss the various depictions of men's and women's roles. Various messages arouse concern among parents that the media inaccurately portrays real-life American families, and those in his study group usually favored content that reflects their own opinions and life choices. For this group of parents, the media fulfills several social functions. First, it provides a basis of social comparison with which to evaluate themselves and their families relative to others. Second, it offers a connection to the world beyond the local community—a connection that some resist and some embrace. Third, it represents a body of shared knowledge or "social cement" that serves as a common ground for families exposed to similar content. In summary, Descartes and Kottak (2009: 157) write that the mass media provides "scripts" or cultural models that are perceived, evaluated, and used to understand and evaluate individual and group identities, situations, decisions, and life possibilities in the social world.

8

18

The Brazilian Context

Researchers focusing on Brazil have applied a variety of approaches to the study of television. Sodré (1977: 128–129), for example, following generally the media power approach with a focus on the ideological messages embedded in programming (also known as the cultural industry approach, as proposed by Horkheimer and Adorno [1947] 1969), asserts that Brazilian television is a powerful creator of hegemonic cultural views. The medium accomplishes this feat by defining Brazilianness and normalcy through the process of "the esthetics of the grotesque." Sodré writes that in the 1960s and 1970s Brazilian television helped define and then identify with the nonelite sectors of society being excluded by the economic and political policies of rapid modernization. By assimilating and then repacking regional and minority cultural traits in a patronizing and distorted manner, the medium appeared to champion the nonelite sectors while actually exerting a predatory influence on true popular culture and values. To Sodré, the authentic cultural values of Brazil are transformed into exotic-picturesque clichés that have the effect of neutralizing possibilities of popular expression.

Along the same lines, Hoineff (1996: 28–29) maintains that Brazilian television has transformed programming from a representation of reality to an expression of reality. Hoineff argues that the polarization of wealth in Brazil, joined with the widespread illiteracy and high quality of television production, creates a situation in which television defines reality. He goes on to criticize networks' abuse of power through their fabrication of public opinion and their influence over the audience (Hoineff 1996: 32).

Much television research in Brazil has focused on the impact of viewing telenovelas, which though akin to American soap operas are uniquely Latin American in form and content. Among the findings are data suggesting that telenovelas may have an impact on the decline in fertility by exposing audiences to family planning (Faria and Potter 1999), they may influence the electoral process (Lima 1993; Porto 1994), and they may encourage new lifestyles (Kottak 1991, [1990] 2009). Contrary to assertions of television's hegemonic power over audiences, some media scholars suggest that television may be a force for the emancipation of the oppressed by occasionally providing counterhegemonic discourses challenging stratification and inequality (Vink 1988: 130). Telenovela discourses can be subversive to the social order in that they offer views that denaturalize the status quo and, in particular, present class structure and gender roles as unnatural and changeable (Vink 1988: 247; Straubhaar 2007: 151).

Researchers in Brazil have observed that telenovela themes offer a vocabulary and a set of references for discussion—the material from which a discursive community can be created (see Chapter 5). Lopes (2009: 2) likens the telenovela to a national narrative that becomes a communicative resource for disseminating cultural representations that act to include variant sectors of society. Prado (1987) observes that messages encoded in the telenovela text bring to one's consciousness certain key issues, for example, social tensions surrounding landownership in a telenovela with a rural theme or conflicts/concerns over race and sexuality in a telenovela with an urban theme. Tufte (2000) writes that viewers find it easier to talk about feelings of class and racial prejudice when actors in telenovelas portray these struggles. Leal (1986) notes that female viewers find it easier to discuss their emotional relationships when actors in telenovelas are doing the same.

Faria and Potter (1999) suggest that viewing telenovelas might lead to the questioning of gender relations and challenges to the established patriarchal order. Watching women take on nontraditional roles in the programs provides new information for women in their push for change (also see Vink 1988: 206–212). Kottak ([1990] 2009) likewise finds a statistical correlation between the amount of televiewing and "liberal" (i.e., nontraditional) views on gender roles. On the other hand, Afonso (2005: 136–140, 239–240) finds parallel messages in telenovela story lines that stereotypically represent women as less capable than men in the public and professional spheres. Women are portrayed as fragile, vain, and objects of beauty at the same time that they are shown with greater power to conquer new spaces.

Machado-Borges (2003) speculates that telenovelas and related information (i.e., the telenovela flow) has an impact on Brazilian society in three ways. First, they encourage national identity through the audience's collective consumption of images of Brazilianness. Included in this category are Brazilian bodies (e.g., actors, actresses), Brazilian lifestyles, Brazilian landscapes, and consumer items—the consumption of which serves as the basis for a collective identity (Machado-Borges 2003: 119; see also Lopes 2009: 5). Second, telenovelas reinforce social hierarchies by presenting them as unremarkable. Third, they present viewers with different ways of symbolizing and personifying their own positionality in those hierarchies (as suggested by Tufte, Leal, Faria, Potter, and Kottak above). Viewers can recognize, scrutinize, question, and challenge hierarchies such as race, class, and gender through media engagement (Machado-Borges 2003: 121, 139).

Researchers in Brazil also comment on the limitations of television's impact. Lins da Silva (1985), in his study of two working-class communities (Paicara along the coast of São Paulo and Lagoa Seca in Rio Grande do Norte), analyzes viewers' decoding of news presented by the program *Jornal Nacional* (National News). He concludes that other sources of information, such as churches, unions, political parties, radio, newspapers, and interpersonal contact supply information to the public that may contradict the messages provided by television. Lins da Silva suggests that in many cases other sources of news are taken more seriously and may be more influential than television. He also finds that previous knowledge of an issue presented in the news plays an important role in the decoding of messages. In the case of news from abroad, of which audiences normally have little to no knowledge, viewers accept the information at face value. By contrast, viewers tend to challenge local and national news when presented on *Jornal Nacional*. These findings show that members of a community can develop a critical reading of the information provided by television, as long as they have access to other sources of information.

La Pastina (1999, 2001, 2004), looking at the relationship between televiewing and such topics as national identity, gender, consumption, and politics in the northeastern community of Macambira, finds that the relative isolation of the community—radio and television are the main sources of information about the outside world—restrict the cultural capital of viewers. This limitation complicates the audience's understanding of telenovelas, in particular, the intertextuality of current news and plots in the telenovelas. The lack of cultural capital also restructures viewers' understanding of consumer themes. Despite these drawbacks, viewers try to emulate the pan-Brazilian attitudes and behaviors shown in the programming as a way to participate vicariously in national urban culture. La Pastina finds that the telenovela influences language, fashion, behavior, ideas, and aspirations. He finds that teenagers use the subject matter of programs to challenge established local norms. He finds cases in which televiewing leads males to confront their own reality, in addition to giving women an array of role models that strengthen perceptions of their rights. At the same time, televiewing reinforces the perception of isolation, of being on the periphery, of belonging to a different reality from the Brazil depicted on television. La Pastina (1999: 194–195) writes, "This gap . . . did not seem to reduce the sense of belonging to the nation as a political entity, but rather created a sense of injustice and inequality. It also created a perception of a cross-cultural conflict, in which the values, morals and attitudes of those from the South were distinct from the viewers in Macambira, even though they continuously invaded the local reality through the medium."

Reis's (2000, 1998) study of Pirabus, Pará—an Amazonian community similar in many ways to Gurupá—discusses several changes accompanying the introduction of television, including new ways of conceptualizing time and space, new patterns of consumerism stimulated by advertisements, shifts in expectations toward life and toward the community, and an increased distrust of authority and politics. Concerning the latter, he notes a number of recent electoral defeats of local political oligarchies by leftist newcomers. Reis (2000: 261) writes, "Television did not do it; but it is arguable that the access to news and information . . . played a major role in the way that particular political process occurred."

The Research Setting: Why Gurupá?

The setting for this research is the Amazon community of Gurupá. One may ask how this particular case study of a small community aids the social science endeavor to understand television. Why pick Gurupá out of all the possibilities in the region, the country, or the planet? There are several responses to this query. The first is the aforementioned longitudinal research in the community by numerous scholars. Kemper and Royce (2002) have commented on the unparalleled opportunity long-term research provides to study firsthand the trends of cultural transformation and stability; the unique ability of other researchers or community members to use the data collected to ask new questions; and, most important, the depth, breadth, quality, and variety of understandings achievable. In our case in Gurupá, the long-term research conducted by multiple scholars has resulted in a detailed, well-rounded study of change. It serves as an important point of departure, or a basis for comparison, with which to ground, interpret, and measure the multitude of changes occurring over time, such as those introduced by television.

Second, there are only a few published studies that focus specifically on television's impact in the Brazilian Amazon (Dutra 2005; Roberts 1995) and only one incorporating ethnographic methods (Reis 2000). To put this in perspective, the geographic expanse of the Amazon is roughly the size of the continental United States. The associated cultural region of concern here, sometimes referred to as Amazônida culture, includes populations of indigenous peasants or agro-extractivists, other rural workers, and urban populations who share elements of the regional culture. Collectively, they number over two million people, which is one-half of the rural population (Hall 1997: 70). In other words, the region is seriously understudied, and nearly any study will carry substantial weight in providing cross-cultural information on the nature of television encounters and engagement. This case study of Gurupá, therefore, should provide significant cross-cultural information from a little-studied part of the world.

An additional characteristic of Gurupá that makes it an intriguing site for television research is its long isolation from the rest of Brazil, both geographically and culturally (a feature common to many Amazonian communities). This isolation means that only in the past few decades has there been much exposure to pan-Brazilian culture. Only through radio in the 1950s and then television beginning in the 1980s have most people in the community been able to learn details about life in the rest of Brazil. Low levels of literacy in the community also pose an interesting question: Without the ability to read about the rest of Brazil, and the world, has television's impact been even more powerful?

Methods

The findings presented in this book are based on two years of fieldwork in the community of Gurupá spread out over fourteen visits between 1983 and 2011. The field methods utilized for this research are the standard ethnographic techniques of participant observation, structured and unstructured observations, formal and informal interviewing, and collection of life histories both in the town of Gurupá and in its rural countryside. In addition, a locally recruited research assistant, Edson Palheta Teixeira, and I administered interview schedules between 1984 and 1985 to a 9 percent random sample of homes in the town of Gurupá (n = 69). In 1999 a second research assistant, Milton Dias, and I administered a follow-up interview schedule to an 8 percent random sample of homes in town (n = 99). We conducted a third interview schedule with a 7 percent random sample of homes between 2007 and 2009 (n = 101).

Our study, employing a longitudinal, mixed-method approach, fits what Creswell (2009) describes as a concurrent triangulation strategy. In this design we analyze both quantitative and qualitative ethnographic data in order to examine convergent or divergent trends and insights between data sources. Other researchers (e.g., Greene, Caracelli, and Graham 1989) describe these comparative functions as confirmation, disconfirmation, cross-validation, or corroboration. This design more specifically permits us to use different types of data and analysis to inform, confirm, or elaborate the insights derived from our other data sources. Our approach extends this methodology further by considering multiple data types at multiple points in time, thus providing a very useful set of successive waves of comprehensive, concurrent measurements and observations.

Clearly there are advantages to this methodological approach, despite the difficulties often encountered in its implementation (e.g., time, funding, access, coordination of resources). For example, if one data type or collection method possesses inherent weaknesses, approaches like ours help to offset such deficiencies by providing alternative information. Conversely, if one or more data types possess some intrinsic strength, our approach maximizes these strengths by bringing them together, generating well-validated and substantiated findings (Creswell 2009: 213). Finally, validity and reliability issues are directly addressed in the application of a comprehensive triangulated research approach (Frankfort-Nachmias and Nachmias 2000; Singleton and Straits 1999). In short, our approach in the chapters that follow is methodologically integrative, representing an appropriate set of tools to help us decipher the enigmatic role that television has played in Amazon communities and the lives of their citizens.

Organization of the Book

Chapter 2 explores the history of network television in Brazil, including a description of the types of programs commonly found. We identify key preferred messages that are repeated in Brazilian programming, utilizing the work of Brazilian and Brazilianist media scholars. Chapter 3 describes the research setting, from environmental adaptation to religious beliefs in the community. Special attention is paid to regional cultural formation throughout the community's prehistory and history. Chapter 4 explores the arrival of television in Gurupá. It focuses on behavioral changes stemming from the new habits of spectatorship that arise and the impact they have on traditional patterns of social interaction, including alterations in the use of time and space. Chapter 5 focuses on the positive responses to television's interpellation in Gurupá. Chapter 6 describes the areas where viewers miss, ignore, or resist the preferred messages of television. Chapter 7 concludes the study and then returns to address the general theoretical questions and issues raised in this first chapter.

CHAPTER 2

Brazilian Television

In terms of delivering messages to the largest number of people possible, television is by far the most accessible, most widely consumed, and most influential of all the forms of mass media in Brazil. The nation's largest television network, Globo, has reached over 99 percent of the national territory since the 1990s (Mader 1993: 67). In 2000 census takers estimated that 87 percent of households in Brazil have at least one TV set, adding up to some 39 million television households (Machado-Borges 2003: 6; IBGE 2001). Public access to television in shops, restaurants, bars, and even neighbors' homes expands this number, making some exposure to the medium nearly ubiquitous. In fact, by the end of the 1980s, 95 percent of all Brazilians affirmed that they watched television on a regular basis (Lima 1993: 102). By the 1990s, 99 percent of the population was reportedly able to see television on a regular basis (Faria and Potter 1999). For our research site in Gurupá, a relative latecomer to television and a poor place in terms of consumer buying power, our estimates place television possession near 50 percent of homes in town and between 25 percent and 33 percent for the municipal population. Access to viewing the TV sets of others increases this exposure to nearly 100 percent on at least an intermittent level (see Chapter 3).

Beyond television, there are few alternatives available to most Brazilians to obtain information on the national or transnational level. Radio, for example, has never been a national medium of communication — although it is important for 20 to 30 percent of the population with intermittent access to television (Lima 1993: 102; Straubhaar, Olsen, and Nunes 1993: 122). It most commonly has a localizing effect, focusing on local/regional music, talk, and news (Straubhaar 2007: 240). Newspapers and magazines have relatively limited circulation, and their consumption is narrowed further by low levels of literacy for substantial portions of the population (Reis 2000: 201; Lima 1993: 102). In recent years access to the Internet has expanded from 2.9 percent of the population in 2000 to 37.8 percent by 2010 (Internet World Stats 2010). For the remaining 62.2 percent majority, however, Internet use is out of reach and has yet to make its impact. This is clearly the case in our research setting, where only 31.7 percent of the 2009 sample reported using the Internet at least sporadically, and this included 11.9 percent using it only once. For those having Internet service in their homes, access is unfortunately very erratic and unreliable due to technological problems.

Kottak ([1990] 2009: 85, 144) identifies television as the gateway to the global village (à la Marshall McLuhan), despite some inroads from the Internet. He finds that television is often the exclusive conduit for non-local information for many communities. Hoineff (1996: 53) observes that the pervasiveness of television culture is linked directly to the absence of other forms of cultural consumption in Brazil. As a result, he contends, television exerts a tremendous power in Brazilian society.

Network History

Television's unrivaled ability to deliver messages across Brazil is rooted in government policies enacted throughout the last half of the twentieth century, as well as network entrepreneurship. The origins of Brazilian television date to 1950, when the media conglomerate Diários Associados (Associated Dailies), headed by Assis Chateaubriand, launched TV Tupi with regional stations in Rio de Janeiro and São Paulo (Machado-Borges 2003: 28; Mader 1993: 68). At the time there was no expertise in Brazil to run a broadcast station. Chateaubriand was forced to borrow the "know-how" and workers from radio, which was at its peak of popularity. Through this process radio stations, which were privately owned commercial enterprises, became the preferred model, and Brazilian television evolved as a private commercial enterprise instead of a public, nonprofit institution (Vink 1988: 22).

TV Tupi dominated Brazilian television for a decade and a half, although it eventually lost its popularity, became mired in debt, and was closed by the government in 1980 (Vink 1988: 29). In 1953 TV Tupi was joined by the regional network competitors Radio Televisão Paulista (São Paulo) and TV Record Rio. During this time audiences were small in number as TV sets were rare in Brazilian homes. For example, in 1950 there were 200 sets in all of Brazil. By 1952 the number had grown to only 11,000 (Mattos 1990: 10; Tufte 2000: 72, 74), in a nation of nearly 52 million people.

Television viewership began to expand rapidly during the second half of the 1950s as TV sets became more affordable due to domestic production. By 1958 there were an estimated 344,000 sets and by 1960 approximately 598,000, or one for approximately 4.6 percent of Brazilian homes (Mattos 1990: 10; Tufte 2000: 74; Hamburger 2005: 22). The context of this expansion was rapid development and national integration championed by President Juscelino Kubitschek de Oliveira. His famous pledge was to give Brazil fifty years of progress in only five. The most celebrated example of this policy was the building of the new federal capital, Brasília, in only five years. The Kubitschek administration saw television as an essential tool to drive progress and development. The medium provided the means to spread new ideas and values to the populace, particularly those needed for capitalistic expansion and growth of a modern urban society (Mader 1993: 69).

In 1962 the first Telecommunication Code was enacted by Congress; it officially sanctioned the private ownership of television networks, although it left the government the responsibility of installing and operating the telecommunication network, as well as the basic supervision of broadcast licenses (Mattelart and Mattelart 1990: 20). The code, based on policies originating from the military's Superior War School, was anticommunist in format and designed to promote national integration and protect national interests (Mader 1993: 73). The anticommunist obsession led to a preference for near-monopolistic control of all types of media—enabling the government to easily monitor the population's activities (Amaral and Guimarães 1994; Hamburger 2005). The legislation for the code established the National Council for Telecommunications and charged it with oversight responsibilities. Through the council, which in actuality was controlled by the president of Brazil, broadcast concessions and franchises were issued, renewed, and canceled (Vink 1988: 40; also see Kehl 1981: 28–29). Under this arrangement, television licensing and concessions became "*de facto* objects of political bargain" (Mader 1993: 73). By the end of the 1960s Brazil had four competing networks: TV Tupi, TV Escelsior, TV Record, and TV Globo.

The authoritarian military regime that took power in 1964 and ran the country until 1985 greatly affected the development of television. First and foremost, it subsidized television infrastructure, including the creation of a microwave relay system in 1969 and a satellite system in 1985.

In addition, it gave loans to networks, regulated the import of equipment from abroad, and pumped money into networks through government advertising (Vink 1988: 40). The government also encouraged the consumption of television sets by offering generous credit policies (especially installment plans) for low- and moderate-income families (Straubhaar, Olsen, and Nunes 1993: 121; Vink 1988: 42, 67). As a result, household television possession rose to 22.8 percent in 1970 and 56.1 percent in 1980 (Hamburger 2005: 22).

Second, the dictatorship actively intervened in programming content through federal regulations, licensing controls, and censorship, even though network ownership remained in private hands. Using the 1968 Institutional Act No. 5, the military regime gave itself the right to censor any suspicious material in the media. The government published lists containing thousands of themes and words prohibited in program content (Tufte 2000: 78). The main focus of censor oversight was the six to ten o'clock time slots, which aired telenovelas and national news (Kottak 2009: 22).

The government regularly exercised its control over concessions and licensing. For example, in 1970 it revoked TV Escelsior's license and shut it down. This action was supposedly undertaken because of the network's financial insolvency and delays in the payment of service contracts. However, many researchers believe it was more likely a form of belated punishment for the network's condemnation of the coup that brought the military to power (Mader 1993: 72). The heavy hand of the government also led to much self-censorship by networks that were fearful of government retaliation (Tufte 2000: 78; Kottak 2009: 23). In essence, during the dictatorship the government ruled the airwaves (O. Oliveira 1991).

It was in this context that Brazil's foremost television network—Globo—developed and flourished. At its inception in 1965 Globo was a joint venture between the media baron Roberto Marinho (who owned the Rio-based newspaper *O Globo*) and U.S.-based Time-Life. Although this collaboration was not legal according to the Brazilian Constitution (any foreign ownership of any media was prohibited), the military government encouraged the partnership (Tufte 2000: 75; Vink 1988: 41). Through the technical and financial support of Time-Life, Globo rapidly created a sophisticated technological infrastructure (La Pastina 1999: 18; Mader 1993: 71; Straubhaar 2007: 63). Eventually, in 1969, under intense nationalistic pressure, the military regime was forced to require Globo to buy out Time-Life's share in the company, eliminating all foreign influence. But the partnership had given Globo a great advantage over the other networks (Hamburger 2005: 32).

By the early 1970s there were four nationwide networks in operation: Globo, Tupi, Record, and REI (a collection of independent stations). REI closed down in 1976 and was replaced by Bandeirantes, owned by the publishing power João Saad. But the decade belonged to Globo: it became the leading network in Brazil with a near-monopoly on television audiences (Borelli 2005: 188; Vink 1988: 29). The military regime greatly facilitated this process by giving considerable financial incentives and special treatment to Globo (Hamburger 2005: 32; Amaral and Guimarães 1994: 32; Mattos 1984). The network reciprocated with unwavering support for the regime, including active propagation of the regime's ideology (Mattos 1982; Straubhaar 1989; Reis 2000; Vink 1988: 42). Mattos (1982) and Straubhaar (1989) describe Globo's role in support of the military state as only slightly less overt than propaganda but just as effective. By the end of the dictatorship Globo's control of audience share had grown to a daily national average near 70 percent and reached some 100 million viewers (Mader 1993: 67; Necchi 1989). This made it one of the world's most watched commercial networks (Mader 1993: 67). Globo had become the main, and often only, television network available to all Brazilians (La Pastina 1999: 19).

In 1985 the military government relinquished power to a civilian government. With the military leaders gone, censorship of television was greatly relaxed. In 1988, under a new Brazilian constitution, censorship of the media was officially condemned and prohibited (Reis 2000: 194). At this point state interaction with the media shifted from one of authoritarian control to one of granting assistance and favors in order to increase political support. This was particularly prevalent in the granting of broadcast licenses (O. Oliveira 1991: 201). Mader (1993: 68) mentions that by the early 1990s nearly 20 percent of the members of Congress owned shares in at least one television or radio station. Tufte (2000: 85) states that the major media owners have always been closely related to Brazil's elite political circles and to the government. Even more blatant, in 1991 President Fernando Collor de Mello granted himself open-ended licenses for television stations in his home state (Amaral and Guimarães 1994: 35).

Under the new arrangements of the civilian government, Globo lost some of its privileges, just as new networks emerged to challenge its supremacy (Mader 1993: 75). The new networks took advantage of the national satellite communications network established in 1985, which allowed them to reach wider audiences. Among these new networks were Sistema Brasileiro de Televisão (SBT; Brazilian System Television) (created in 1982, it grew to be the second-most-watched network) and Manchete (created in 1983). Both Manchete and SBT divided up the licenses of TV Tupi when it went off the air in 1980. Record and Bandeirantes also continued broadcasting.

By the early 1990s Globo's average audience share had declined to 45 to 50 percent. Selective programs on the other networks periodically overtook Globo's shows—such as Manchete's 1990 telenovela *Pantanal* and its Carnaval coverage, SBT's Sunday variety shows, and Bandeirantes's televised sports (Straubhaar, Olsen, and Nunes 1993: 121; Kottak [1990] 2009: 25). Globo still outpaced its competitors on a day-to-day basis for most programs and continued to receive government favors, but its days of total domination had ended (Borelli 2005: 188; Amaral and Guimarães 1994: 32; Mader 1993: 75; Straubhaar, Olsen, and Nunes 1993: 121).

A diminished but still powerful Globo nonetheless adapted to the new political realities of postdictatorship Brazil. One sign of its continued strength was the influence it exerted on the 1989 presidential elections. Political and media analysts generally agree that Globo slanted its election coverage in favor of the conservative candidate, Collor, whose family just happened to own a Globo affiliate and whose brother had been a regional director of Globo in Recife and São Paulo (Boas 2005: 34; Lima 1993: 103, 106; Straubhaar, Olsen, and Nunes 1993: 123). In addition, Globo aired three telenovelas during the run-up to the elections with intertextual messages sympathetic to Collor's candidacy (see Chapter 6). The basic narrative was that Brazil was a kingdom of political corruption controlled by professional politicians, the solution to which was to elect an "outsider"—much like the young and conservative Collor (Lima 1993: 105–106). Lins da Silva (1993: 142) maintains that the telenovelas did not directly favor a specific candidate; rather, they reflected the mood of the country, captured by the writers and also understood by Collor. This, he states, accounts for the similar discourses in the telenovelas and Collor's speeches—a classic intertextual merger.

Through these actions the network was arguably influential in swaying the close election in Collor's favor (Boas 2005: 45–46; Mader 1993: 81; Lima 1993). Viewers who understood and accepted the preferred message of the telenovelas and news coverage from Globo were likely sympathetic to Collor's candidacy. Other media scholars point out, however, that a sizable portion of the electorate was able to construct oppositional readings of the televised messages and vote for other candidates, including Collor's remaining opponent—Luiz Inácio Lula da Silva of the left-wing Workers' Party—by the end of the election process. Straubhaar and colleagues (1993: 134–135) and Lins da Silva (1993: 144) emphasize that although the television media were powerful in the election process, there were definite limits to that power. Globo's preferred messages were countered by oppositional readings as well as by interpersonal sources of political information from family, friends, colleagues, churches, unions, and neighborhood groups. As Straubhaar and colleagues (1993: 135) quipped, the media "are not a hypodermic needle, capable of injecting opinions, attitudes, and values into the audiences." Clearly Globo's political influence was not insuperable. Collor was impeached for corruption two years after the election, and his opponent, Lula, won the presidential election in 2002.

Since the 1990s Brazilian television has been affected by the increasing availability of pay TV in the form of videocassettes, DVDs, and cable and satellite television. According to Tufte (2000: 84–85), these new forms of media have actually driven Brazilian media in two different directions. The expansion of the videocassette and DVD industry, for example, led to the increasing localization of media production. Small-scale independent producers can afford the technology and produce high-quality shows. To date, most tend to be alternative producers creating tapes, CDs, and DVDs for social and popular movements or for religious, ethnic, and other groups in order to circulate messages outside the constraints of broadcast television (Straubhaar 2007: 119; Tufte 2000: 84). Specialized (often minority) groups typically consume these media, and their distribution is limited. I have seen a few such tapes in Gurupá. All were obtained by the church, the union, or political parties and were used for educational (i.e., consciousness-raising) purposes.

Cable and satellite television, on the other hand, are driving Brazilian media toward globalization. Successful competition with these media requires alliances with large multinational corporations and increased concentration of money, power, and ownership (Tufte 2000: 84–85). Globo, as expected, is a prominent player in this new market, belonging to the Latin American DTH consortia with partners Televisa (Mexico), Fox (USA), and TCI (USA). In Brazil the satellite network is called Sky DTH and carries from 72 to 120 channels, depending on the year and the price one pays. Satellite and cable television are consumed mainly by the middle and upper classes (Tufte 2000: 85). Gurupá, for example, has just four families that can afford Sky satellite television.

By the 2000s there were four main independent commercial networks:

Globo (which still dominates nightly viewership), SBT, Bandeirantes, and Record (Manchete went off the air in 1988 due to bankruptcy). There is one noncommercial/public service network called TV Cultural (with a very low audience share). In addition there are a number of very new networks that broadcast in some parts of the country: MTV, Canal 21, CNT, Gazeta, Rede Brasil, Rede Mulher, Rede TV!, Rede Vida, TV Senado, Nacional, TV Brasília, and TV Apoio. In Gurupá until 2009 only Globo was accessible without an external antenna (see Chapter 4). In 2010 TV Cultural was also received from the town's satellite dish. Only those investing in personal satellite dishes receive other networks such as Bandeirantes, SBT, and Record. None of the most recent networks are available in Gurupá, except for the very few individuals with SKY.

What Is on Television?

Most of the prime-time programs shown and watched on Brazilian television are nationally produced. On its website, for example, Globo (rede globo.globo.com 2011) boasts that nearly 90 percent of its daily broadcasts are produced in its own studios. While foreign imports represented about 35 percent of the total programming for all networks combined in 2001, they only accounted for 25 percent of prime-time slots between 6:00 p.m. and 11:00 p.m. (Straubhaar 2007: 261; also see Mader 1993: 78). In other words, while networks included a lot of foreign imports in their programming (usually movies and documentaries, along with a few serials, all dubbed into Portuguese), Brazilian productions were by far more popular. To find a different pattern in Brazil one must look back to the decade between the late 1950s and the late 1960s when U.S. television serics and films were most popular in Brazil (Tufte 2000: 73). After that period more Brazilian programs became available (especially the telenovela), and audiences switched to domestic productions, which are, as Straubhaar's cultural proximity concept maintains, more culturally relevant, recognizable, understandable, and enjoyable than the imports. This, of course, is a pattern found throughout the world; that is, viewers prefer locally produced shows over foreign imports (Straubhaar 2007: 196).

During six decades of broadcasting the products of Brazilian television and the targeted audiences have varied considerably. The earliest phase of television programming, 1950–1961, was designed for upper-class audiences—the ones who could afford the medium. Principal programs were teletheater, live theater, and music broadcast directly from stages in Rio and São Paulo (Vink 1988: 22–23). During the second phase, 1960–1968, programming was expanded to attract viewers from the middle class and segments of the working class. Mass product advertising was now possible as the number of television sets expanded. Programs of choice were telenovelas, imported films, imported series, and game shows (Staubhaar 1983: 72; Vink 1988: 24). Globo's ascendancy occurred in this phase. According to Vink (1988: 26), the network focused on producing popular programs to build up a mass audience, initially among the working class. Game shows and telenovelas were the keys to Globo's success. Kottak ([1990] 2009: 44) emphasizes that Globo's appeal was linked to its "acceptable consistency" rather than exceptional programming. He maintains that Globo's pattern of quality really meant the network produced a "consistent, reliable, tolerable, culturally appropriate product" that fulfilled the expectations of viewers, regardless of class, ethnicity, or region (44–45).

The third phase, 1968–1982, brought the nightly national news (Globo's *Jornal Nacional*) to its preeminent spot on television. Telenovelas also became standard programming and had a large following. In both cases producers targeted mass audiences. Globo at the time had a near-monopoly on audience share (Vink 1988: 28–29). During the fourth phase (1982–1990s), the various networks defined themselves more precisely by the audience targeted. SBT concentrated on the working class, running game and variety shows as the principal attractions, supplemented by imported telenovelas from Mexico and Venezuela (Kottak [1990] 2009: 27–28). Manchete focused on the elite and the middle class, producing its own telenovelas (Vink 1988: 30).

When Brazilians turn on their television sets today, they can expect a steady diet of telenovelas, news, variety shows, comedy shows, talk shows, and crime shows (Machado-Borges 2003: 34). The content of these programs (with the exception of the news) is overwhelmingly oriented toward entertainment rather than public service or education (with the exception of social merchandising; see below). In terms of classifying the narrative style and repertoire, several researchers have used the phrase "euphoric spectacle" (Machado-Borges 2003: 36). Programming tends to be loud, flashy, nonstop, and carnivalesque. Anything can, and is, packaged as a euphoric, sensuous, visual, and ephemeral spectacle to be consumed, from variety shows, talk shows, and soccer matches to children's programs (Machado-Borges 2003: 36). Mader (1993: 77–78) maintains that Brazilian television is first and foremost an entertainment vehicle, as eight out of every ten hours of broadcasting is pure entertainment, while only one hour is for current affairs or news and one hour is for educational programs. Of course, since Brazilian television is a commercial enterprise, the purpose of entertainment is to create a consuming audience for the selling of products and services (Vink 1988: 242; Kottak [1990] 2009: 23).

In addition to content consistency, the networks tend to follow similar scheduling for programs. On weekends and weekday afternoons the networks run the variety shows and talk shows. News is shown at midday and around 8:30 p.m. Telenovelas run from 6:00 p.m. to 10:00 p.m. Monday through Saturday. Documentaries, serials, and foreign films, which constitute the bulk of imported programs, are shown early in the day, late in the evening, or on weekends (Machado-Borges 2003: 35; Reis 2000: 196).

The telenovela is the most widely watched television genre in Brazil (Straubhaar 2007: 152). Telenovelas are likely the most powerful type of programming disseminating preferred messages. They are particularly potent in providing moral, ethical, and behavioral guidelines to address viewers' personal problems and aspirations (Tufte 1993). According to Costa (2000: 11), due to their immense popularity, the social roles of men and women depicted in the shows often end up dictating real-life behaviors. In other words, the representation becomes the reality.

Telenovelas are melodramatic series produced domestically, distinguishable from their North American counterparts—the soap opera—in that they are broadcast in prime time six nights a week, attract very large audiences, and end after six or seven months of airtime. All age groups watch telenovelas. Despite the stereotype that the shows are primarily for women—and the fact that men often deny watching them—media surveys place males near 40 percent of the audience (Ortiz and Ramos 1989; Hamburger 1999). Whether or not people consistently or directly view telenovelas, most will know the story lines since they are discussed thoroughly in Brazilian society (see La Pastina 2001: 545).

Globo's telenovelas, which are generally the most popular, have audience shares averaging about 40 to 60 percent, with key shows (such as series finales) as high as 100 percent (Mattelart and Mattelart 1990: 79; Vink 1988: 179; Kottak [1990] 2009: 41). Competing networks have also created popular telenovelas from time to time, with Manchete's *Pantanal* being the most successful. Some networks have carved out a niche in the market by importing Mexican, Colombian, and Venezuelan telenovelas and dubbing them into Portuguese.

Globo broadcasts three first-run telenovelas at a time, although there may also be reruns shown during the afternoon. The beginnings and endings of each are staggered so that as one series ends, the others continue. The telenovelas are placed into three time slots, each with a different style and attracting a different audience. For example, the six o'clock telenovela is usually romantic, the seven o'clock is humorous, and the nine o'clock is usually tragic or a mystery but may also contain humor (Vink 1988: 181). The six o'clock telenovela also targets small-town and rural folk, as well as adolescents, maids, and housewives. It frequently has a rural setting. The seven o'clock show expands the target audience to include urbanites and men. The nine o'clock program is for more mature audiences (Kottak [1990] 2009: 40).

As for narrative style, telenovelas have their roots in the oral traditions of storytelling, the circus, the Cordel literature (i.e., a mixture of news and entertainment written in verse, often in the form of a chapbook, and traditionally read out loud or sung in a public setting such as a market), and the *repente* (i.e., verses recited from memory or improvised) (Tufte 2000: 90–93; Straubhaar 2007: 153). Tufte (2000: 94) maintains that the telenovelas borrow comedy and melodrama styles from the circus, especially the music, noisy gestures, and exaggerated expressions that are used to mark important sequences and dramatic climaxes. Telenovelas imitate the Cordel literature and the repente in that they are "open works" that unfold through interaction with the audiences' feelings, interests, and tastes. For most telenovelas the authors write only twenty chapters (nightly shows) ahead of the chapter being broadcast (most telenovelas have 150 to 200 chapters). This gives the writers the opportunity to change elements of the story as it unfolds, all in response to audiences' preferences, which are routinely surveyed (Tufte 2000: 87; Kottak [1990] 2009: 32; Mattelart and Mattelart 1990; Klagsbrunn 1993). In fact, Hamburger (1999) found that telenovela writers receive direct and indirect input from viewers and fans, theatrical productions, commercials, the elite and popular press, institutional networks, audience and marketing research organizations, and other social forces in society such as the Catholic Church, the government, and activist groups.

Telenovelas also mimic oral traditions in that they relate to contemporary events, issues, trends, or fads occurring at all levels of society. Many telenovelas follow the normal calendar for their broadcasts, having its actors celebrate Carnaval when it occurs in real time, taking vacations during real breaks, and so forth (Vink 1988: 171). The shows also weave current events, issues, and recurring social concerns into story lines, such as land reform, political corruption, crime, racial prejudice, women's struggles, neighborhood struggles, and religious conflicts (Mattelart and Mattelart 1990: 79). This practice of reconfiguring traditional melodramatic narratives in terms of current concerns arising from the elite political agenda is labeled social merchandising in Brazil (La Pastina 1999: 12, 34). (See Chapter 6.)

As melodrama, the general story lines (with many variations) center on traditional tensions and conflicts over romantic desires, gender roles, family relationships, and social class (Straubhaar 2007: 156). Narratives deal with conflicts of status reversals (most often upward mobility) and romance (often interclass), normally set in an urban environment and always with a happy ending (Vink 1988: 12, 176; Kottak [1990] 2009: 39; La Pastina 2001: 547; Straubhaar 2007: 156). According to Vink (1988: 181), the best-articulated discourses focus on personal relations as experienced in the context of love, marriage, family, and gender. These relations are presented as private; the telenovela is interested in the problems at home more than those in public life (Vink 1988: 174; Kottak 2009: 91). Lopez (1995: 258) adds that "the telenovela exploits personalization—the individualization of the social world—as an epistemology. It ceaselessly offers the audience dramas of recognition and re-cognition by locating social and political issues in personal and familial terms and thus making sense of an increasingly complex world." Additional discourses in the story line may relate to politics, justice, the role and responsibility of the press, religion, psychoanalysis, artistic life, and, less frequently, race relations (Vink 1988: 181). In telling these stories, telenovelas characteristically reproduce Brazil's urban middle-class worldview (La Pastina 2004: 304; Vink 1988: 193, 195).

What Gurupá Watches

Like all Brazilians, Gurupaenses can expect a steady diet of telenovelas, news, variety shows, comedy shows, talk shows, and crime shows on television (Machado-Borges 2003: 34). According to the surveys we administered in Gurupá, telenovelas are the most popular shows, followed by news (see Table 2.1).[1] This preference parallels the national pattern. Also like most other Brazilians, when Gurupaenses watch television they are likely to tune in to one station, Globo (see Table 2.2). The overwhelming majority of Gurupaenses, however, do not have the option of viewing one of the other twelve or so channels broadcast over the airways as they rely on the municipality's satellite dish, which until 2009 received just Globo.

Table 2.1. Program Preference in Gurupá

	Telenovelas (%)	News (%)	Sports (%)	Films (%)	Variety Shows (%)	Documentaries (%)
1986	40.0	22.9	14.3	5.7	11.4	0.0
1999	44.0	22.0	14.3	13.2	2.2	0.0
2009	49.5	6.9	8.9	29.7	1.0	4.0

Table 2.2. Most Watched Channels

	Globo (%)	Bandeirantes (%)	SBT (%)	Record (%)
1986	100.0	0.0	0.0	0.0
1999	87.9	1.1	8.8	2.2
2009	82.2	1.0	12.9	4.0

Only households with private satellite dishes and the income to pay users' fees have the privilege to watch additional channels.

Preferred Messages

What are the themes hidden or overtly placed in program story lines and advertisements on Brazilian television that interpellate viewers? What stands out in terms of agenda-setting, priming, branding, and framing? What is repeated in different forms over the decades and has the greatest potential to influence viewers? There are a number of Brazilian and Brazilianist scholars who have addressed these questions. Collectively, their work provides a general outline of the preferred messages broadcast on Brazilian television. We extrapolate from their collective findings the principal messages transmitted (in this study we do not consider the content or viewer reception of foreign-produced programs). Since the primary focus of our study is the long-term impact of televisual texts on viewers, we focus on the preferred messages that have been consistently broadcast over the years.

We acknowledge that media scholars may take issue with this approach—as discussed in Chapter 1. They may argue that the preferred messages we identify are too broad and too simplistic, ignoring the potential for polysemic readings. They may wish to see detailed analyses explaining how particular texts are used to frame, brand, and prime preferred messages, as well as to set agendas. Others may find fault with the idea that the messages represent the interests of the powerful or that the messages are hegemonic. Some scholars may emphasize opposite influences, as summarized by Joyce:

> [Telenovelas create spaces] for critical-realist dramas whose narratives and controversial issues, such as women's liberation, political corruption, and homosexuality, have called attention to actual conflicts, and mobilized public opinion for social change. In other words: within certain limits, the telenovela is a vehicle of innovative, provocative, and politically emancipatory popular culture rather than a mere instrument for the reproduction of capitalist ideology and consumer desires. (2010: 20–21)

Without denying the complexity of messages and the potential for polysemic readings by scholars, and of course active audiences, we are interested in the long-term sociocultural impacts of television programming and thus pay critical attention to those messages that have been repeated over and over again for decades. As Chapter 5 shows, viewers are responding to persistent messages collectively, in patterned ways, some of which are empirically measurable. In other words, the viewers we studied do identify preferred messages in many cases. Where they do not, or where they reject or subvert the messages, is the subject of Chapter 6.

We identified four principal televisual messages invoking responses in our research setting, at least some of the time: consumerist texts, national identity texts (including race, class, and gender discourses), developmentalist texts, and political texts. These texts appear in a wide variety of programs but most prominently in the news and telenovelas. A discussion of each follows.

Consumerist Texts

The single most important message conveyed on Brazilian television is consumerism, which, of course, is the principal reason for commercial television. According to Vink (1988: 242), the television industry is foremost interested in selling audience time, to the extent that the content is secondary. The goal is the largest audience possible that possesses the buying power in which advertisers are interested. Kottak (2009: 23) states that the fundamental purpose of commercial television is neither to entertain nor to enlighten but to sell. The goal of programming is to train proper consumers, not proper citizens. La Pastina (2001: 547) adds that telenovelas, in particular, are designed to sell "consumer products and lifestyles that will create a demand for advertised items."

Consumer products and/or services are presented straightforwardly in advertisements during breaks between and during programming or indirectly through product placements. Product placement, or "merchandising" as it is called in Brazil, involves inserting commercials directly into a program's narrative with the intent to increase the visibility and desirability of a product or service (La Pastina 2001: 541; also see Ramos 1987). The commercial insertions do not interrupt the story line; rather they are presented as integral parts of the text. La Pastina (2001: 541) maintains that product placements attempt "to create an organic relationship between the advertised product and the narrative, encouraging viewers to 'read' the product as a quality of the characters using and approving it." Vink (1988: 236), writing in the same vein, states that merchandising is based on the belief that identification with heroes and heroines in the telenovela will increase the sales of all kinds of products. They create an ideal of consumption through their lifestyles and purchasing patterns, which serve as a demonstration effect for viewers (Lopes 2009: 5).

As with all interpellation, the promotion of consumerism has mixed results. For example, in La Pastina's (2001) study of the small rural community of Macambira in Northeast Brazil, he found that most viewers miss product placements in the show, or think they are integral parts of the narrative, meaning that the products are symbols of modernity or the glamour of urban elites, not products for sale. La Pastina (2001: 553) concludes that viewers failed to perceive product placements due to their social, economic, and cultural isolation from urban consumer culture, that is, their lack of cultural capital.

National Identity

Since television's inception in Brazil, the government and intellectual elite have charged the medium with the task of promoting cultural integration and national unity through communication (Machado-Borges 2003: 31;

Mader 1993: 70; Kottak [1990] 2009: 36–37). During the dictatorship, this broadcasting objective became paramount as television networks and the government worked in tandem to spread a new image of the country, one that transformed Brazil from a rural-regional reality to an urban-national one (Kottak [1990] 2009: 36; Straubhaar 1981). The ideal pattern to be diffused to all regions of Brazil was the middle- and upper-class lifestyle of the southeastern states of Rio de Janeiro, São Paulo, Minas Gerais, and Espítiro Santo, with the bourgeois sector of the city of Rio being the most favored setting (Mattelart and Mattelart 1990: 80). Programmers hoped that a core of Brazilian cultural traits might be created through viewer observation of everything from eating habits, leisure activities, dressing styles, decorating styles, greeting customs, and product consumption habits to shared beliefs in the need for economic progress, development, and urbanization taking place in the Southeast (Machado-Borges 2003: 31). The goal was to fashion an imagined community, nationwide, united, and subservient to the central government.

Globo, a loyal ally of the state, openly followed the call of the military and adopted the role of explicitly exhibiting this idealized version of "Brazilianness" while downplaying regionalism (Machado-Borges 2003: 31; Kehl 1981: 24). The network's depiction of Brazil was one of "a populace moving together toward modernity, glamour, and a comfortable, materially enriched, upwardly mobile lifestyle" (Kottak 2009: 37). In sum, "national integration through television has meant an imposition of a Rio/São Paulo culture on the other regions" (Mader 1993: 70).

In the years since the dictatorship, the use of television programming to maintain national unity and construct national identity has continued. A key part of this process is dissemination of idealized representations of race, class, and gender. Each is presented within parameters of what is considered acceptable by producers, writers, advertisers/sponsors, and, to a certain extent, viewers and government censors. There is room for occasional counterhegemonic messages in which the interests of the elite are challenged (see Straubhaar 2007: 157), but in general the elite viewpoint is seen as the norm.

Representations of race on Brazilian television parallel the dominant ideology of the elite. In this view people of European descent are considered the standards of beauty and normalcy—or *branqueamento* (whitening)—in programs and commercials, at the same time insisting that the country is a racial democracy free of prejudice and discrimination (Araújo 2000: 38, 306; Joyce 2010: 37). The preference for branqueamento is demonstrated in a series of studies analyzing the presence of actors of

African descent in a range of programs from telenovelas to commercials (Subervis-Vélez and Oliveira 1991; Lima 1992). The results of these studies clearly indicate that people of color appear on television in numbers far disproportionate to their actual numbers in society. In fact, the first commercial to highlight an African Brazilian family from the middle class did not occur until 1997 and the first prime-time African Brazilian hero-protagonist not in a program about slavery appeared in 2007 (Araújo 2000: 69; Joyce 2010: 68). Of the ninety telenovelas produced by Globo in the 1980s and 1990s, actors of African descent were absent in twenty-eight, while at best comprising barely 10 percent of the cast in another twenty-nine (Araújo 2000: 305). Since the general estimate of people of African descent in Brazil is close to 44 percent of the population, no telenovela has ever come close to realistically representing the ethnic (racial) diversity of the country.

In 2004 the ideal of setting racial quotas for characters on television was discussed as part of the government's attempt to craft affirmative action legislation for government hiring and higher education admission. Although affirmative action policies have been implemented in many Brazilian institutions (Telles 2004: 47), the television landscape, particularly the telenovelas, has not changed much (Joyce 2010: 57). In 2005 another innovation occurred with the creation of the first network dedicated to people of color—TV da Gente (TV of the People). The network was heralded as a significant milestone in Brazil's fight against discrimination and for visibility of minorities. However, the network's distribution was limited, and programming ran for only six hours a day. In 2007 it went off the air.

Despite minor improvements in representing race, television programming continues to reinforce the politics of invisibility for populations of color, which, according to Araújo (2000: 68) attempts to mask inequality and racial discrimination. When people of African descent are shown, they are typically represented according to negative stereotypes. They are depicted as a subaltern class, employed in low-paying jobs (e.g., maids, nannies, manual laborers, drivers, dancers in bars, petty businessmen, low-ranking police) and living in shantytowns. Their roles are tied to poverty, ignorance, drugs, and violence. Their culture is presented as folkloric and limited to Carnaval, samba, and Afro-Brazilian religion (Candomblé and Umbanda) (Araújo 2000: 71–72, 308). Depictions of indigenous populations are arguably worse. They are commonly represented as primitive, savage, ignorant, violent, supranaturalized, and blocking development and progress (Nugent 2007: 13, 24–27, 56–57, 213). Only rarely are they presented in a positive light—for example, as guardians of the rain forest or as unique but disappearing cultures—and this is usually by foreign media interested in rain forest preservation and human rights.

The overall effect of Brazilian programming is to negate racial diversity and present a whitened self-image of the country. There have been some counterhegemonic messages, particularly in the 2000s, with nonwhite actors taking on more important roles and some discussion of racism, as in the 2007 telenovela *Duas caras* (Two Faces). The telenovela is credited with presenting the first black hero in a Brazilian prime-time show that was not about slavery. Still, it did not escape the historic pattern of stereotypical representations (Joyce 2010: 68). Brazilian television continues to rely on programming that disseminates contradictory narratives of branqueamento and racial democracy.

Unlike the negation of racial diversity, social class identity is clearly defined by television. The markers of social class portrayed in telenovelas revolve around wealth and lifestyle. The rich are typically shown as a leisure class that indulges in conspicuous consumption. Their class superiority is indicated not so much by formal discourse as by settings and props (Vink 1988: 176). The rich are shown in opulent mansions, luxury restaurants, or extravagant locales overseas. They are seen swimming in lavish pools, driving expensive cars and high-tech speed boats, or riding horses. The middle class can frequent many of these spaces with the rich, but they do not possess the status items, and, most important, they must work for a living (e.g., as doctors, lawyers, civil servants, businesspeople, reporters, and priests). Members of the working class represented in telenovelas are never really poor. Their homes are comfortable and adequately furnished. Their class position is shown more by bad taste in decorating, the use of slang in place of "proper Portuguese," and the lack of domestic servants (Vink 1988: 177, 190).

The rich are represented as politically and economically powerful but frequently corrupt. Their excesses, in particular, in the treatment of others, often lead to punishment or tragedy. They are rarely depicted as happy (Vink 1988: 189). The working class is given a mixed presentation: sometimes they are shown as sympathetic, sometimes as childish (191). It is only the middle class that escapes with relatively little criticism or moral condemnation (192), which reinforces the middle-class worldview inherent in the programs. In the cases of both the upper class and the middle class wealth is presented as desirable, normal, and natural.

Another pervasive preferred message is the notion of social class mobility (Tufte 2000: 98; Kottak [1990] 2009: 41; Straubhaar 2007: 156).

Although upward mobility is a rare occurrence in Brazil, telenovelas show repeated examples of central characters overcoming the odds to obtain money and prestige, or *subir na vida* (to rise up in life). Kottak ([1990] 2009: 49) suggests these are classic stories of status reversals that dramatize culturally appropriate fantasies of escape. Typical paths to mobility taken by characters include marrying into wealth (interclass romances are ubiquitous themes but rarely happen in real life), rural-to-urban migration (striking it rich in the city), finding a lost wealthy relative, gaining a wealthy benefactor, or discovering children switched at birth between wealthy and poor families (Kottak [1990] 2009: 50–51; Vink 1988: 171). Nearly all paths require personal connections to someone with power, influence, or wealth. Personal traits such as education, intelligence, hard work, or even good looks are not sufficient in and of themselves for mobility. Social mobility resulting from class-based political activism is also negated in programming (Vink 1988: 204).

A number of researchers comment that the connection between interclass romances and upward mobility is deceptive and alienating. Mattelart (1986: 70), for example, states that the scenario negates any real struggle against social inequality. The preferred reading leads to the conclusion that only love can overcome social contradictions and class barriers. But this is accomplished by denying that these exist, a discourse that Mattelart sees as repressive. Vink (1988: 197–199) disagrees. In his reading of telenovelas, the message is that love provides the motivation for the poor lovers to improve their economic situation and cultural capital. Love by itself is not sufficient for mobility. Telenovelas present the topic in this way because their focus is on the personal and intimate rather than the public and political. For Vink (1988: 202), social mobility and change are shown in telenovelas as inevitable, natural processes (i.e., characters opposed to progress end up dying, allowing new ideas to emerge) or as forces of modernization (see below). He does admit that change is never depicted as stemming from working-class self-organization. When change occurs it always comes from initiatives by the upper or middle class (Vink 1988: 204).

As mentioned above, gender roles and relationships are prime foci of telenovelas. Some scholars read the depictions of gender roles as generally conservative. They stereotypically represent women as objects of beauty who are fragile, vain, and inferior to men in the public and professional worlds (Afonso 2005: 136–140, 239–240). At the same time these scholars acknowledge that the shows contain parallel messages that tend not to promulgate the traditional roles found in the *machismo-marianismo* complex (Vink 1988: 175). For example, many of the female characters are given active roles, frequently as active as males (Vink 192). Especially among the middle class, women work and have careers outside the home. They are economically independent and often are equal to men in their professions and can oppose and resist male social control (208). Still, there are limits to female emancipation. For example, Kottak ([1990] 2009: 50, 56) comments that the preferred message on women and social mobility in most telenovelas, at least through the 1980s, focused on success through marriage, not through education or personal achievement. Vink (1988: 212) adds that "[tele]novela discourse on female struggle is ambiguous: women can and shall struggle, but not in an organized way and not as members of the working class."

Developmentalist Texts

Progress through development is another major theme in Brazilian television (Kottak [1990] 2009: 41, 49; Vink 1988: 202). The development model is capitalist and focuses mainly on industrialization. Wage earners in factories are depicted as the ideal. To achieve this ideal the Brazilian political economy must replace the archaic, traditional, and agrarian patterns of the past with a modern, urbanized, and industrial future. Individual and nationwide successes in this endeavor bring Brazil closer to its desired place among the developed, modern first world. At the same time that television programs champion modernization, they also critique it. According to Sodré (1977: 102), in the late 1960s and early 1970s television programs occasionally lamented the loss of popular values, which were being corrupted by rapid modernization. Although the networks presented a patronizing and distorted view of popular values, they successfully identified themselves with the excluded and nonelite sectors of Brazil. Kehl (1980: 63) points out that traditional values, rooted in rural lifestyles or even aristocratic ones, are rarely presented with "total disdain." Change to the modern is seen as inevitable but is sometimes "painted with gloomy colors."

Along the same lines, crime is presented as a lamentable by-product of development and/or of the lack of full-fledged development. This discourse is often tinged with other, either explicit or covert, discourses that focus blame on the poor and people of color (Araújo 2000: 71–72, 308). Brazilian news presents very graphic, detailed narratives and images of crime. Victims of beatings, stabbings, and gunshots, as well as corpses, are shown, and the gory details are discussed (see Chapter 5). Although the televised depictions of crime might seem counterintuitive to the notion of a developing Brazil, they do create a sense of national unity in terms of what to despise (crime), who to blame (poor and people of color), and what to aspire to (modernity).

Political Texts

Political messages are presented in a number of ways on Brazilian television. In the most direct form, political parties are allowed free airtime in the forty-five days leading up to elections — either during hourlong programming in prime time or as shorts (15, 30, or 60 seconds) during commercial advertising breaks (Porto 2005: 133). The amount of time allotted to each party is proportional to the number of seats it holds in the congressional Chamber of Deputies. An additional twenty minutes of airtime is allotted twice a year to political parties to explain policies and ideology. In a less direct way, news broadcasts may support one candidate or party over another. Especially with framing or branding, news may present fairly blatant biases. Globo's thinly veiled support of the Collor candidacy in 1989 is a classic example. Globo has actively intervened on other occasions as well, always in support of the established powers (Porto 2005: 130).

General programming is also used to communicate political messages supportive of those in power. The most explicit example of this occurred during the period of military dictatorship when government regulations and censorship forced networks to produce programming that facilitated the dissemination of pro-government messages, in particular, its views on rapid modernization and national security. At the same time, dissent and protest against the regime were routinely purged from programming. The state was also keen on using the medium as a tool for nation building. Through its influence over program content, for example, the state attempted to forge a pan-Brazilian national identity, integrate the remote regions of the country via communications, create a consumer economy through advertising, and manufacture public support and legitimacy for the military regime, despite its repressive rule (Mattelart and Mattelart 1990: 31; Straubhaar 1982; Tufte 2000: 71; Mader 1993: 71; Mattos 1982).

With regard to the latter, Straubhaar (1989) analyzed the role played by Globo in support of the military government. During the first years of the dictatorship, 1964–1974, a period marked by the severest repression, he notes, Globo produced telenovelas that highlighted the country's progress and development. The programs presented a positive and optimistic view of events unfolding in Brazil (Vink 1988: 42). On the nightly national news, which Globo began broadcasting nationwide in 1969, there was no mention of death squads, disappearances, kidnappings, torture, or unlawful imprisonment (Mader 1993: 78). In fact, in order to avoid any potential conflict with the military regime, Globo hired a professional censor to anticipate any points of contention (Clark 1991: 253).

In the last decade of the dictatorship, 1975–1985, the regime gradually prepared for a transition to civilian rule and slowly lifted some of its censorship (by the 1980s the military had lost nearly all of its political legitimacy due to mismanagement of the economy, recession, inflation, corruption, and continued political repression). Globo's programming, however, changed little to reflect this political shift, and the network's nightly news ignored many of the struggles for democracy against the dictatorship. For example, in 1975 the head of news at the São Paulo Educational TV station was abducted, tortured, and then murdered by military police. The print media reported this event as an important act of resistance to censorship. Globo reported the occurrence much later and insinuated that the death was really a suicide (Mader 1993: 80).

In addition, for months in 1984 Globo ignored a broad-based social movement demanding direct elections for the presidency. When the network weighed in on the matter, it promoted support for indirect elections, through an electoral college, which was the process favored by the government; the military regime was fearful of political adversaries being elected to office by popular vote and then using this as a base to rapidly dismantle the existing system and prosecute human rights abuses. Straubhaar (1989) points out that Globo's news gave much coverage in support of indirect elections while ignoring the massive rallies (attended by as many as 500,000) in support of direct elections in the streets of Brazilian cities.

Preferred Messages: Who Controls Them

According to Straubhaar (2007: 151), there are at least five groups or entities involved in the creation and dissemination of preferred televisual messages: the state, the advertisers (which represent the international and domestic industrial economic elite), the networks, the producers and writers, and the audience. All are able to manifest at least some degree of constraint over the others in terms of programming, although there are significant imbalances. The state has the most power to shape messages through its ability to constrict or facilitate the actions of the networks and producer/writers, as discussed above. This power was especially evident during military rule but continues today, particularly with Globo. The networks also possess degrees of power vis-à-vis the state. As Straubhaar (2007: 151) points out for postdictatorship Brazil, the government, political parties, and political figures need favorable coverage from news and related programs to facilitate governance and reelection. As a result, "a complex dance of mutual constraint extends between media, particularly major television networks, and the government" (151).

Among the networks, Globo enjoys substantial influence to control agendas for program content, given its audience dominance. Yet it often entrusts this influence to writers and producers, as long as they stay within the network's broad parameters for commercial success. Writers and producers can test the cultural, political, and moral boundaries with audiences if a program is still successful—hence the occasional counterhegemonic message. To ensure a program is a commercial success, popular programs like telenovelas are maintained as open works that during production receive input from viewers, fans, commercial interests, the elite and popular press, institutional networks, market research organizations, churches, government censors, and activist groups (Mattelart and Mattelart 1990; Hamburger 1999).

Television's persistent messages about consumerism, national identity, development, and politics have interpellated televiewers in Gurupá for three decades. How Gurupaenses interpret these messages—how they are hybridized, indigenized, or localized—depends on the criteria of cultural capital and cultural proximity, which are principally influenced by the local culture. Therefore, before examining the details of television's impact in Gurupá, we must establish the cultural and historical context of the research setting.

CHAPTER 3

The Setting

Gurupá is the name of a town and its surrounding municipality located on the lower Amazon River in the state of Pará (see Map 3.1 and Figure 3.1). The town and municipality are situated 1° south of the equator, 353 kilometers west of Belém. The municipality of Gurupá encompasses 9,309 square kilometers and has a rural population estimated at close to eighteen thousand (IBGE 2010). The town of Gurupá is located near the center of the municipality on the southern bank of the Amazon River. It has a population estimated to be seven thousand (IBGE 2010).

Gurupá falls within the "island region" of the Amazon drainage system, so named because of the complex maze of islands and channels created as the Amazon River fragments into multiple passages to form the estuary (the physiographic zone is Marajó and Islands). As the Amazon River reaches Gurupá from the west it begins to break up, with channels weaving northward around the Great Island of Gurupá to the city of Macapá and southward around the island of Marajó toward the city of Belém. The southern channel of the river, which passes in front of the town of Gurupá, is five kilometers wide and sufficiently deep to allow the passage of large oceangoing ships.

To reach Gurupá, people typically travel by boat since there are no connecting roads and airplane service is infrequent and expensive. A boat trip from Gurupá to the major port city of Belém (approximately eight hundred nautical kilometers) takes an average of twenty-four hours downstream, with the same trip upstream averaging thirty hours. As of the 2000s, there is boat transportation to and from Gurupá on a near-daily basis (see Figures 3.2 and 3.3). Air travel between Gurupá and Belém takes only 1¾ hours, one way, but there is no regular service. An eighteen-

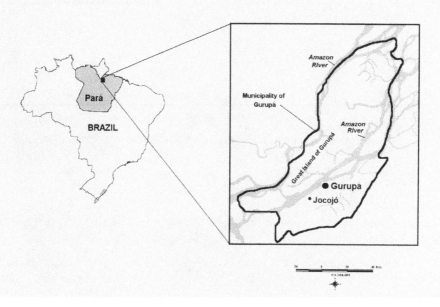

Map 3.1. Town and Municipality of Gurupá. Adapted from FASE 2006.

Figure 3.1. Riverfront view of Gurupá. Photograph by R. Pace, 2010.

Figure 3.2. Boats docking in Gurupá. Photograph by R. Pace, 2010.

kilometer dirt road that runs south of the town ends abruptly as it reaches the Pucuruí River, a small tributary of the Amazon.

About 58 percent of the area of the municipality of Gurupá consists of *várzea*, or floodplain/flooded forest (FASE 2006: 2). This region is inundated by seasonal rains between January and June. Parts of the vár-zea also flood daily due to the rise and fall of the tides—from four to seven meters at the height of the seasonal flooding and from two to three meters during the low season. The várzea forms the eastern extreme of the ecoregion called the Gurupá Várzea, which stretches from the Tapa-jós River to the Great Island of Gurupá. This region is very rich in bio-diversity. According to the World Wildlife Fund (2010) the ecoregion contains 148 mammal species (including deer, armadillos, pacas, agoutis, tapirs, howler monkeys, spider monkeys, tree sloths, giant anteaters, and bats), 558 bird species (including toucans, macaws, parrots, parquets, and hummingbirds), and unknown numbers of fish, crustacean, reptilian, and amphibian species. There are innumerable insect species, ranging from malaria- and dengue-carrying mosquitoes to tarantulas. Although there has been no systematic inventory of plants, the general vegetation classifi-cation for Gurupá is Floresta Pluvial Tropical Rain Forest (World Wildlife Fund 2010; Pires and Prance 1985).

Figure 3.3. West end of town. Photograph by R. Pace, 2010.

The várzea supports approximately 58 percent of Gurupá's rural population (Treccani 2006), although the population density is sparse, about 1.9 people per square kilometer. Homes are typically strung out along the rivers and streams. They are organized into far-flung neighborhoods or communities with a school, a chapel, or a trading post/store serving as the social hub. Transportation throughout the várzea is by twenty-meter diesel-powered cargo boats, smaller boats and canoes with outboard motors, and human-powered canoes. It is common for people living on the várzea to visit the town of Gurupá several times a month to make purchases, receive government pensions and entitlement checks, visit friends and family, and seek entertainment in the form of festivals, concerts, athletic competitions, television, and DVDs and videos. Some families even maintain a second house in town.

The rural inhabitants of the várzea earn a living by the extraction of forest commodities and subsistence fishing. Açaí (*Euterpe oleracea*) is currently the most important extracted commodity by volume and value. The berry of this palm tree is processed into a very popular drink (although eaten with a spoon) that is high in calories and rich in protein, antioxidants, fiber, vitamin E, and various minerals (Rogez 2000: 185). Some of Gurupá's açaí is beginning to enter Brazil's wider domestic market with exports to the city of Belém and to the south of the country. Some may also be entering international markets, where it is powdered or pasteurized and frozen and exported as a health supplement, high-energy food, and fashion food (Brondízio 2008: 185–190).

In addition to açaí, people on the várzea extract heart of palm (from the same tree that produces açaí), timber, *pupunha* (peach palm), oleaginous seeds, cacao, and Brazil nuts. Most of these commodities are for export to southern Brazil or overseas. In the past rubber was the major extracted commodity for the community, but it has been largely abandoned since the 1990s as the prices have fallen sharply. Fishing for subsistence is commonplace. Some várzea residents are employed seasonally in commercial fishing, earning wages from companies based in other cities. In addition, a short growing season for subsistence agriculture is possible in some parts of the várzea. When the waters recede, people plant quick-growing corn and beans. Chickens, ducks, and pigs are also raised. Cattle and water buffalo are sometimes raised in a few select portions of the várzea where there is enough dry land and grasses to support them.

The second ecological zone of Gurupá is the *terra firme* (firm land), the highlands that never flood. The terra firme accounts for 24 percent of the municipality, and about 42 percent of the rural population resides here (the remaining 18 percent of the municipality is water) (Treccani 2006: 82). Homes are often clustered into hamlets with a school, a chapel, or a community building at the center (Figure 3.4). The parts of the terra firme closest to the town of Gurupá are connected by the dirt road. Public transportation in the form of a dump truck—people ride in the large pan—runs the length of the road twice a week, although people traverse the distance daily with motorcycles and bicycles and on foot. To reach the more remote terra firme settlements, however, requires travel by boat.

Livelihood in the terra firme revolves around subsistence agriculture (Figure 3.5). Manioc is the staple crop, supplemented by beans, corn, squash, rice, and a variety of fruit trees. There is also some extraction of timber, açaí, heart of palm, cacao, and Brazil nuts. Chickens, ducks, pigs, and a few head of cattle are raised. Fishing in nearby streams is common. Hunting with rifles for game is done where there is sufficient forest reserve for animals to propagate.

The Town

The town of Gurupá sits upon a rocky bluff rising fifteen meters above the southern shore of the Amazon River near the center of the municipality

Figure 3.4. Fonseca family in front of their home in the community of Bacá in the interior of Gurupá. Photograph by R. Pace, 1986.

Figure 3.5. Slash-and-burn garden (*roça*), community of Jocojó, interior of Gurupá. Photograph by R. Pace, 2002.

Figure 3.6. East end of town. Photograph by R. Pace, 2010.

(Figure 3.6). It serves as the economic, administrative, educational, health service, and entertainment hub of the municipality. The physical dimension of the town is just over one square kilometer. The main part of the town, and the oldest, is situated along the rocky bluff that parallels the river. On the eastern portion of the bluff sits the reconstructed fort that once guarded the lower Amazon River from seventeenth-century colonial intruders (e.g., Dutch, English, Irish, and French) and then served as a control post to oversee river transportation until it was abandoned in the late 1800s. Next to the fort is the small municipal jail. Continuing westward is the church and its associated buildings—among which is a long stucco *barracão* (shelter) with large open arches (covered by bars for security) used for the celebration of the saints' festivals and church meetings.

Between the church and the western end of the bluff—a distance of ¾ kilometer—there is an assortment of residences, shops, and government buildings. The chief government building is the town hall—an infamously extravagant building initiated at the end of the rubber boom (1920s) just as the economic prosperity abated. Successive municipal governments have struggled to maintain the structure, yet it has always stood as source of community pride. Next to the town hall is the hospital, a twenty-six-bed facility that provides basic services and some minor surgery and houses a laboratory. It is staffed by two doctors, a dentist, several nurses, several biochemists, and twenty or so public health assistants or technicians.

Behind the hospital and town hall is the main commercial section of town. It runs along Saint Benedict Avenue and extends west several hundred meters, descending the bluff to the floodplain and the municipal wharf. In the section below the bluff, a fairway built of concrete several meters high helps guard against flooding. Lining the street are many small stores and shops selling clothing, house wares, appliances, school supplies, and groceries. There are also a few pharmacies, restaurants, hotels, and bars. At the end of the street is the municipal wharf (see Figures 3.2 and 3.3), built of concrete and extending seventy meters into the river to allow larger boats to dock.

Beyond the wharf the town stretches to the west over swampy and frequently flooded land. Many of the poor reside here, occupying the less desirable land as the population has grown over the years. Their houses are built upon stilts, although not always elevated sufficiently to prevent flooding by seasonally high waters. This pattern also holds for the easternmost part of town, below the fort. Here, too, people have built their homes over swampy and flooded areas, often because this was the only land available. The local government has endeavored to improve access to these areas by building up the streets to a meter or so above the flood line. People can now reach their houses more easily, although most residences in these sectors are still constructed above standing water.

Back up on the bluff, heading south away from the river, is the main residential section of the town. Rising above the homes is the cellular telephone tower, which has provided service to the town since 2009. Farther south is a cluster of municipal structures: the town council building, one of the town's three schools, the principal soccer field, and a roofed sports complex (for indoor soccer and dance competitions). The town's cemetery is located here as well. Near this complex is the telecommunications center, which consists of a small building adjacent to a large satellite dish, both beneath an eighty-six-meter-high communications tower. The tower is used for radio phone service; the dish receives television signals. Beyond this, to the south and farther to the east, is the town's diesel-powered electrical plant and airstrip. At this point, nearly one kilometer from the river, the town ends and subsistence agricultural plots begin.

The street system of Gurupá is set up on a grid, with streets running parallel and perpendicular to the river. Five of the streets are paved with poured concrete or octagonal concrete cobbles; the rest are dirt (Figures

Figure 3.7. Residential area of Gurupá. Photograph by R. Pace, 2010.

3.7 and 3.8). Along many streets houses are built flush to the sidewalk or road and often adjacent to one another with, at most, only a meter passageway. Behind most houses are long, narrow yards (*quintais*), frequently walled in, with space for washing and drying clothes and raising herbal gardens, fruit trees, and sometimes chickens and ducks. Homes that have satellite dishes may choose to place them in their quintais, but most people like to place them in front of the house for all to see (Figure 3.9).

Construction materials for houses consist of concrete or clay blocks and wood. The most valued houses, nearly all of which are located on the town's bluff, are constructed of stuccoed concrete blocks and brightly painted in a variety of pastel colors. These houses typically have tile roofs and concrete floors. Most are one story, but two-story houses can be found. Only a few have glass windows, and only slightly more possess screens to keep the ever-present mosquitoes out. All homes have shutters to seal off the home from the outside. A few houses have security bars covering windows and doors in the front but rarely in the back. In other words, they seem to be for appearances rather than security.

More common in town, and nearly ubiquitous in the countryside, are wooden houses with wooden floors. Some are two stories, some are painted, and most are raised a meter or so above the ground for cooling

Figure 3.8. Back streets of Gurupá. Photograph by A. Pace, 2011.

Figure 3.9. Placement of satellite dishes. Photograph by R. Pace, 2011.

purposes or flood protection. Roofing materials may be the more expensive ceramic tile or fiber-cement, asbestos-based corrugated roofing (some now made with nonasbestos polyethylene), which is cheap but makes the houses very hot. A few roofs are made of palm thatch, which can protect against downpours for about two years, at which point the thatch begins to rot and must be replaced. The palm thatch is used by only the poorest of the town's residents.

Electricity is available for every home in town that can afford the service. With government subsidies for diesel fuel to run the turbines, nearly three of every four houses have electricity. Water service is more limited due to lack of infrastructure—wells, pipes, and water towers. In most parts of town water is available for an hour or so, twice a day. Many homes have tanks on their roofs that can be filled when water is available. These precautions, however, fail when the municipal wells run dry, especially during the dry season. Wastewater treatment does not exist. Houses in the center of town have septic pits, but their efficiency is limited. Much of the waste drains directly into the river. As a result, periodic outbreaks of waterborne diseases, including diarrhea, dysentery, and hepatitis, are common both in town and in the countryside.

People in town earn their livings in jobs in commerce, government, the service sector, and resource extraction and subsistence farming. Only the government jobs and a few of the more prosperous businesses pay wages sufficient to support a family comfortably. These workers earn approximately two to four minimum salaries (one minimum wage in 2010 is the equivalent of US$1.76 per hour, or US$510 per month). Most other jobs pay poorly, one minimum wage or less (one minimum wage is supposed to cover the food and housing costs for a family of four, but it does not come close). As a result most households require multiple workers to survive, including government pensions of the elderly and sometimes child labor (Hendrickson 2006). In addition, many men travel to other municipalities in the eastern Amazon in search of wage labor, usually in extraction but occasionally in gold mining and forest clearing for cattle ranching (rural inhabitants do this as well). Young girls frequently travel to other urban centers to labor as domestic workers.

Standards of Living

By both Brazilian and international standards, most people in the town and municipality of Gurupá are poor. As rural residents of the state of

Pará, they are among the poorest in all of Brazil. The overall rate of rural poverty in the state is 58.4 percent (compared to 38 percent in the urban areas), while extreme poverty for the rural parts of the state is 44 percent (Verner 2004: 16).[1] The infant mortality rate (IMR) for Gurupá's microregion, which includes its neighboring municipalities, is 56 (calculated as the number of deaths before the first birthday per 1,000 live births) (Verner 2004: 20), although Gurupá's municipality public health records put the IMR closer to 42 (SESPA 2006).

Another indicator of well-being is the Municipal Index of Human Development (IDH-M), which ranks all the municipalities in Brazil according to criteria set by the United Nations Human Development Index. These criteria include life expectancy at birth, education levels, and standard of living (i.e., gross domestic product per capita). Over the past thirty years Gurupá has improved from 0.396 (1981)—which put it at the designation "low level of human development," similar to countries such as Gambia (0.398) and Rwanda (0.395)—to 0.631 (2001), which puts it at the level of "medium human development," similar to countries such as Botswana, Moldova, and Mongolia (the highest score is Norway at 0.938, with the United States at 0.902 and Brazil at 0.699).

Perhaps a more pertinent measurement for purposes of this study is the social-class scale developed by the Instituto Brasileiro de Opinião Pública e Estatística (IBOPE; Brazilian Statistical Public Opinion Research Institute) as a means to measure television audiences' buying power. IBOPE designates six levels of social class based on the amount of disposable household income left after basic expenditures (food, utilities, schooling, clothing, transportation, personal hygiene, medical care, and domestic help). The list of expenditures and assessment of class standing are based on Brazilian cultural standards; for example, middle-class status typically requires the employment of domestic help in the form of a maid or cook, the possession of a car, private schooling, and access to computers and, increasingly, the Internet (see Straubhaar 2007: 207).

Under these criteria, Brazil has a small upper class (A), around 2 percent of the population; a tripartite middle class (B1, B2, B3), approximately 36 percent of the population; an upper working class (C), 36 percent; and a lower working class (D), 26 percent. Both C and D represent households without significant income; D represents households in abject poverty. Using this scale, approximately 95 percent of Gurupá's population falls within the C and D range, with possibly 5 percent reaching the B3 level. In many cases the distinctions between C and B3 in Gurupá are not easily discernible, regardless of whether they are based on income,

Table 3.I. Respondent Self-Designation of Social Class

Self-Designation	1986 (%)	1999 (%)	2009 (%)
Poor	76.1	64.2	79.2
Middle	23.9	35.8	20.8

Note: Because some responses differed from "yes" and "no" categories, percentages did not always total 100 percent.

education, or other forms of cultural capital. In other words, on the whole the population appears fairly homogeneous in social class standing, even though local social hierarchies and power imbalances exist (see Wagley 1976: 105). Relative homogeneity is an important feature to consider when analyzing media impact. If we return to the IBOPE's scale and the notion of consumption, nearly the entirety of Gurupá population lacks significant disposable income to meaningfully participate in the consumer economy promoted by Brazilian commercial television.

In our survey we asked respondents to designate their social class, giving them the options poor (*pobre*), medium (*meio*), or rich (*rico*). Table 3.1 shows the responses. The discrepancy between our estimates of lower-middle-class standing (5 percent) and the answers given by our respondents (20.8–35.9 percent) may be explained by two factors. The first is the concentration of households with limited measures of affluence within the town limits. Since our sample is restricted to town, and does not include the rural interior, we surveyed a greater number of lower-middle-class people than proportionally exists throughout the municipality. The second factor is the tendency of respondents to overestimate their class standing due to a lack of comparative perspective. This is especially evident in the 1999 survey where the surge to 35.8 percent of the sample follows the onset of the açaí economic boom, improvements in local infrastructure (e.g., utilities, transportation), better access to food and health care, and increased access to television. Many people believed these basic improvements indicated a substantial improvement in standards of living, which they interpreted as class mobility (see Chapter 5 for more details).

Development of Cultural Patterns

Although Gurupá is a predominantly poor place in economic terms, the community has a very rich past encompassing millennia of indigenous prehistory and four centuries of Luso-Brazilian history. This past shapes current-day cultural patterns, which in turn profoundly influence the manner in which viewers engage with and interpret television. In order to adequately understand the medium's impact, therefore, we must understand the historical process of cultural construction. By examining the cultural past, we are able to better situate and contextualize the impact of television's introduction into the community.

Prehistory

Although much, if not most, of indigenous culture was destroyed during conquest and colonization, there remains a core of cultural traits—agricultural technology, foodways, language, supernatural beliefs—fundamental to the contemporary culture of Gurupá. There are also traces of genetic heritage perceptible in phenotypes suggesting indigenous descent.

Although to date there have been no archaeological excavations in the municipality of Gurupá, findings from nearby sites, as well as examination of surface finds in the municipality, suggest a very long period of habitation. Since the area probably followed similar patterns of human habitation described in nearby locations (see Roosevelt 1991: 111–115; 1994: 4–11; Silveira, Kern, and Quaresma 2002), it is likely that small bands of foragers began traversing the site sometime after 10,000 years before the present. These bands would have stopped for weeks at a time to collect wild plants and hunt animals (there was no agriculture at this point). By 8,000 to 6,000 years ago populations throughout the Amazon began specializing in fishing, collecting shellfish, gathering fruit, and growing manioc. These groups began to establish semipermanent villages consisting of hundreds of people. Gurupá was possibly the site of such a village. Between 4,500 and 2,000 years ago the indigenous population shifted to greater dependence on agriculture, using slash-and-burn agriculture (*roças*) to grow manioc, corn, rice, beans, sweet potatoes, peanuts, fruits, cotton, and tobacco. It was during this period that many of the subsistence agricultural technologies still used by the farmers of Gurupá were first established. These included multicropping of small plots distanced from one another to protect against the spread of tropical pests, the mixing of species with different growth rates to ensure ground cover and protect against erosion from tropical downpours, use of the ashes of burned vegetation for fertilizer, and long fallow intervals for replenishment of nutrients in the soil. When conducted with low population density, these techniques were sustainable over long periods.

Also developed during this time were technologies to produce hammocks, *tipitis* (woven cylinders for manioc processing), baskets, sieves for food production, palm thatching for housing, and fishing weirs—all of which are still used in Gurupá. Many of the region's foodways were also established at this time (Ribeiro 2000: 62). These include a diet based on manioc (farinha, beiju, and tapioca); fish and fowl prepared with local herbs such as *tacacá no tucupí* (shrimp in a manioc extract sauce) and *pato no tucupí* (roasted duck in tucupí sauce); fruits such as açaí, pineapple, *jambu* (rose apple), and pupunha; and a general lack of vegetables.

By 2,000 years ago the native population grew rapidly, with the establishment of large settlements containing thousands of people. Maize was the staple crop now, supplemented by other native seed crops, manioc, turtles, and fish. By 1,000 years ago, complex political organizations known as chiefdoms developed, also consisting of large settlements containing thousands of people. They had powerful leaders who commanded large armies, and warfare and conquest were common (Meggers 1971). The most recent archaeological finds indicate that it is very likely that these systems existed throughout the Amazon and presumably modified most of the rain forest (Heckenberger, Petersen, and Neves 1999, 2003).

Gurupá appears to have been the site of a smaller chiefdom, as evidenced by ceramic surface finds and the extensive areas of anthropogenic soils in the municipality (known as black earth of the Indians) indicative of intensive human use. The ceramic styles found in Gurupá show influence from the Marajoara culture (from the island of Maraj, a chiefdom complex lasting from 400 to 1300 c.e.) and the Tapajonic culture (originating from the Santarem region and flourishing at the time of European contact).

During the time of the chiefdoms, if not before, certain supernatural beliefs about rain forest fauna, misfortune, and health became widely dispersed throughout the region. In general, the Tupí tribes, which profoundly influenced contemporary Amazon folk culture, explained bad luck, calamity, illness, and other hardships in terms of supernatural interventions by forest spirits and ghosts of the dead (Wagley 1976: 224–

225). Some of these beliefs survive today among the people of Gurupá, although mixed with colonial European and African beliefs to one degree or another.

For example, *bichos visagentos* (magical beasts) are said to take the form of forest animals and cause harm to humans who engage in fauna overkill (Slater 1994; Galvão 1955; Wagley 1976: 233–235). Among the most common bichos visagentos are the *inhambu* (*Crypturellus tataupa*), or in English, tataupa tinamou, and *guariba* (howler monkey). Another rain forest creature is the *curupira*, a small, dark creature whose feet are turned backward. It stalks humans, who upon seeing its footprints try to escape by going the opposite direction, only to run into the awaiting beast. The curupira emits a long, shrill cry but also imitates human voices to lure people into the deep forest (Wagley 1976: 235).

The cobra grande, or giant snake, is another forest spirit that takes the form of a huge anaconda. It is too large to live on land, so it lives in the river where it menaces anyone in or on the water. It is active at night, when its glowing eyes are seen very clearly from afar. Yet another is the boto, or freshwater dolphin. This creature transforms itself into attractive human forms and seduces the unsuspecting. The end result is pregnancy for women and death by drowning for men, although some humans are spared this fate by being taken underwater and transformed into *bichos encantados* (enchanted beings).

In additional to supernatural entities, many of the beliefs and practices of the folk healers found among Tupi are still found in Gurupá. One such healer is the *pajé* (shaman), who can cure illness and protect or heal people harmed by spirits. Although only a few self-proclaimed pajés still live in Gurupá, many of their healing practices—such as messaging, blowing smoke, sucking out foreign objects, and assorted teas and purgatives—are still used by the local traditional folk healers (*benzadores* [blessers] and *curenderios* [curers]).

A final element of the prehistoric adaptation that has survived is the naming of flora, fauna, and geographic locations. Many of the plant and animal names are Tupian in origin, although undoubtedly the phonetics and meanings have shifted somewhat over time as they were influenced by Portuguese and *nheengatu* or *lingua geral* (general language)—a trade language used in the seventeenth and eighteenth centuries that consisted of elements of Tupí mixed with other indigenous languages and Portuguese (Ribeiro 2000: 80). Examples of indigenous language survivals in Gurupá include the name Gurupá, the names of streams and rivers (e.g.,

Pucuruí, Mararú, Baquiá, Jocojó, Itapereira), many of the fauna and flora names, and much of the subsistence agriculture technology.

Contact

Gurupá's historical roots stretch back to the beginning of the seventeenth century. The first Europeans who settled in the municipality were Dutch mariners and traders who built a fort in 1609 (Moraes Rego 1977; Kelly 1984: 25). They traded with the local inhabitants—whom they called the Mariocai—for manatee and turtle meat, animal hides, urucú dye, timber, cacao, oleaginous seeds, and mother-of-pearl (Kelly 1984: 25). The English and the Irish arrived soon after the Dutch, setting up a number of tobacco plantations in the general area between 1611 and 1620. The Portuguese arrived in 1623, attacking and defeating the Dutch, English, and Irish settlements. They built a fort—Saint Anthony of Gurupá—in that same year to guard against future European intrusion (Figure 3.10).

As the Portuguese secured the territory around Gurupá and much of the lower Amazon region from competing European powers and their indigenous allies, they also began developing their colonial economy. Large-scale plantation agriculture proved problematic in the Amazon environment, so the colonists focused on the extraction of a wide variety of forest products, known as *drogas do sertão* (lit., "backland drugs"; cacao, cloves, vanilla, seed oils, and other spices and dyes), which had been used by the indigenous population. The colonists also procured fish, turtles, manatees, and animal skins.

Colonial Amazônia

The colonial system was based on the brutal appropriation of indigenous land, resources, and, most critical for the extractive economy, indigenous labor. The colonists, along with conquered indigenous groups and the offspring of indigenes and the Portuguese, systematically attacked and enslaved or destroyed all indigenous societies within their reach. The historian John Hemming (1978: 217–237) described this process as "anarchy on the Amazon," as any means was used to obtain "red gold" (indigenous labor). The Brazilian sociologist Pasquale Di Paolo (1990: 82) stated that "the Portuguese repression was without precedent, having all the traits of genocide" (my translation).

Gurupá played an infamous role in these raids. By being the forward-most Portuguese settlement with a military garrison in the Amazon until

Figure 3.10. Municipal crest showing the fort and a rubber tree, which also represents a tree cut for timber. Photograph by R. Pace, 2009.

the end of the seventeenth century, it was the staging grounds for slaving raids up and down the river (Kelly 1984: 66). The slaving raids were deadly ventures, often killing many people during capture and transport. The raids quickly depopulated the surrounding areas. A Franciscan missionary, Friar Cristovão de Lisboa, criticized the scandalous nature of the raids and noted that by 1647 there were only "domesticated" Native Americans (individuals working for the Portuguese) for one hundred leagues west of Belém (Kiemen 1954: 56). This area approaches the vicinity of Gurupá. The slavers brought many of the captured people to Gurupá and forced them into extracting forest commodities, paddling canoes for transportation, and food production.

In addition to the violence, Old World diseases devastated the indigenous population. Smallpox, measles, malaria, tuberculosis, and even the common cold (to which the native populations had no resistance) spread rapidly through the region, often arriving ahead of the European contact by decades. Warfare, slavery, and disease—the "three plagues of the white man" (Ribeiro 2000: 59)—created a great dying that left no várzea civilization intact after only 150 years of contact with Europeans (Meggers 1971: 121). Gone was the complex social organization of the chiefdom, as well as much of the ethno-ecological knowledge built up over the millennia to sustain high population levels in the rain forest. This massive dying eliminated an estimated 99 percent of the native population.

The survivors of the New World holocaust (mainly the offspring of Portuguese and indigenes) formed a hybrid culture. They were generically called *tapuios*, those retaining more of their indigenous culture, or *mamelucos*, those forming the hybrid European-indigenous culture. In Gurupá during the seventeenth and eighteenth centuries these two groups worked for the Portuguese as slaves—producing commodities for export, providing labor for transportation, and serving as soldiers for conquest campaigns or as guides and soldiers for slaving raids. Alternatively, they lived in the religious missions run by the Jesuits, where they also produced commodities for export and provided labor for transportation (Kelly 1984: 130; Borromeu 1946: 90). The missioners spoke lingua geral, the trade language, and retained some semblance of their ethnicity under the protection of the Jesuits. Nonetheless, life in the mission, as for the slaves as well, was unvaryingly abysmal.

After a hundred years of existence, during a period known as the Directorate (1759–1799), the mission system throughout Brazil was disbanded. As the missions disappeared the remaining threads of the indigenous cultural integrity for the mission indigenes also disappeared. This occurred as the Portuguese broke up communally owned land, which was the basis of indigenous livelihood, reduced large extended families to small nuclear ones, forbid the use of lingua geral as a way of forcing acculturation, and gave the colonists unfettered access to native labor (Di Paolo 1990: 85–86).

In addition to the European and mixed populations, Gurupá had a sizable African slave population. This was rare in the Amazon since the region was relatively poor—the extractive economy could not generate the revenue that a plantation economy could—and few of the colonists could afford the purchase of slaves. Gurupá, however, was unique, as it was the site of a military garrison, a regional prison, and a tax collection station monitoring river trade. As a result the community supported a number of individuals with the financial resources to import African slaves. Gurupá's African population grew to represent 31 percent of the town's population at the time of the first census, 1783 (Kelly 1984: 141). According to colonial records, the African slaves worked as household servants and in agriculture (143).

By the beginning of the nineteenth century, the colonial economy of the Amazon was in ruins. The indigenous population had been devastated. Overexploitation of natural resources to provide revenue for the colonial economy had impoverished the ecosystem and led to boom-and-bust cycles, which ultimately drove down the meager standards of living for most inhabitants of the region (Bunker 1985: 60–61). In addition, a new type of coerced labor regime emerged in the form of debt peonage, as indigenous slavery and the mission system ended. This system, later known as the *aviamento* system, was organized around the secular trading post and tied in to an export economy (Santos 1980: 156). The system was based on patron-client ties whereby workers (clients) provided extracted commodities to the trading post patron, most of which was sent to Europe, in exchange for certain foods and imported tools, medicines, and industrial goods. The trading post usually maintained a trade monopoly with workers that enabled merchants to manipulate prices (Weinstein 1983: 16, 18, 22, 49; Santos 1980: 170). This combination of price manipulation and credit control often left the workers in perpetual debt and sometimes in conditions of bare survival (Wagley [1953, 1968] 1976: 38).

Adapting to this new economic system, the Amazon populations gradually scattered out along rivers and streams in small family units to conduct the economic activities now directly dictated by the market system and world demand (Ross 1978: 206; Parker 1985: 35). This system required geographic mobility and a loose social organization to function—which is precisely the system that shapes the present-day demographic patterns in Gurupá described above. The remnants of the indigenous and the mixed populations were evolving into an indigenous peasantry.

Cabanagem

Not surprisingly, given the brutality of the conquest and colonial periods in the Amazon, the birth of the indigenous peasantry was marked by violence in the form of the Cabanagem Revolution (ca. 1830–1836). This was a bloody uprising claiming the lives of 20,000 to 30,000 people, or 25 percent of the regional population (Cleary 1998: 111). At the center of the Cabanagem Revolution were the *cabanos*—a political and ethnic cover term for the mameluco and tapuio populations, as well as enslaved and freed Africans. This population made up the majority of the rural population at the time (Moreira-Neto 1992c: 271; Pinheiro 2001: 81). They lived in *cabanas* (huts of adobe or rough wooden planks, covered by palm thatch)—from which their name is derived. The cabanos revolted against the urban elite's colonial domination (involving monopolies on the political system, landownership, commerce, and public administration), the rigidly segregated class system that denied them basic civil and human rights, the persistent lack of food and general misery of the region, and the aviamento system (Di Paolo 1990: 163, Pinheiro 2001: 119).

The cabano forces stormed the city of Belém in 1835 and controlled it until 1836. Gurupá was overrun by cabano forces in 1836 (Hurley 1936). The cabanos' final retreat from Belém came in May 1836, following a siege and bombardment by the Brazilian Imperial Navy, an outbreak of smallpox, and the exhaustion of gunpowder supplies. Over the next four years the Brazilian army pursued all cabanos in a systematic and bloody campaign of repression, causing great loss of life. Gurupá once again served as a staging ground for punitive raids. The scale of repression was so great that some historians have labeled the imperial campaign a virtual war of extermination with undeniable racist intentions (Cleary 1998: 128).

Rubber Boom

Gurupá did not recover from the aftereffects of the Cabanagem Revolution until the 1850s. At this time the rubber boom began. Responding to the demand for raw rubber to produce tires (first for bicycles and then for automobiles), the Amazon region revved up production and eventually provided approximately 50 percent of the rubber on the world market (Coomes and Barham 1994: 241). Profits from rubber production increasingly provided the Amazon with affluence never before experienced. Gurupá was profoundly affected since it had rich concentrations of rubber trees on the várzea. In the early years of the boom Gurupá was one of four municipalities that produced most of the rubber for the entire Amazon region (Weinstein 1983: 52). Gurupá's share of regional rubber production declined as tappers and merchants opened new rubber fields farther west. But the municipality continued to produce significant quantities of rubber throughout the period.

During the "golden years" (1880–1910) of the rubber boom, immigrants from the drought-stricken Northeast swelled the urban and rural population of Gurupá. Landowners and merchants from Gurupá and throughout the Amazon recruited the Northeasterners to tap the rubber trees in an attempt to remedy the shortage of workers, as many from Gurupá had moved to the middle and upper Amazon in search of better-quality rubber trees. In Gurupá's rural interior successful and powerful merchants arose with the rubber trade. They used the existing aviamento system and its reliance on patron-client ties to organize the labor system. Many of these merchants were of Portuguese descent, while at the turn of the century a large population of Moroccan and Spanish Jews came to dominate much of Gurupá's commerce (Kelly 1984: 378; Wagley [1953, 1968] 1976: 48; Barham and Coomes 1994: 49).

During these years the upper class of Gurupá (merchants, large landowners, and some government officials) took on the airs of an aristocracy. People referred to them as *gente de primeira clase* (people of the first class). Socially subservient to the upper class was the working class (*gente de segunda*, or people of the second), which consisted of poor town dwellers, farmers, and extractors. The working class showed deference to the elite by never sitting in their presence and always using the formal term *Senhor* or *Senhora* and *Dona* (Sir or Madam) when addressing or referring to them. At the parties of the elite members of the working class were segregated in a separate room (Wagley [1953, 1968] 1976: 103).

During the rubber boom period several cultural traditions became firmly institutionalized. From the migrants came a love of northeastern music and enthusiastic celebration of Saint John and other June festivals—all of which continue today. From the indigenous peasantry in Gurupá came the two major festivals of Saint Anthony, the town's patron saint, celebrated in June, and Saint Benedict, protector of river travelers and rubber tappers and guardian of the poor, celebrated in December (Borromeu 1946: 105). Saint Benedict was also selected by the community's slave population. By this time the festival of Saint Benedict had developed into the most important celebration in Gurupá, because the festival coincided with the end of the rubber harvest, when a year's profits were at hand.

Religious brotherhoods organized the saints' festivals, and a resident priest (if Gurupá had one at the time) or a visiting priest performed the religious rites (Galvão 1955: 48 ff.; Wagley [1953, 1968] 1976: 188 ff.). The festivals lasted nine days during which there were nightly religious services (*novenas*), culminating with a religious procession on the final day. During the procession the brotherhoods carried a statue of the saint through the streets of town, often accompanied by fireworks and waving banners. For Saint Benedict there was also a boat procession, the *meia lua* (half moon), in front of town.

By the end of the rubber boom in 1910 the peasant lifestyle that first appeared in the late eighteenth century was firmly established (Parker 1985: 37). Even the Northeasterners who came to the region during the boom adopted it. The semi-independent, semi-market-oriented peasants enmeshed in a rigid class system structured around exchange and debt became the dominant actors in the region. The peasantry syncretized indigenous, African, and Iberian knowledge for a unique worldview that became the basis for the evolving Amazônida culture.

Rubber Bust, Mini-Boom, Depression

The collapse of the rubber boom in the Amazon came with the opening of rubber plantations in Malaysia, Ceylon, India, Burma, Borneo, Siam, and the Dutch West Indies, all of which outproduced and undercut the price of rubber from the Amazon (Santos 1980: 230–233, 256). The rubber bust hit Gurupá hard. The community had grown to depend almost exclusively on rubber revenues, and once these revenues disappeared the town quickly deteriorated. The population of the town dwindled to just three hundred by 1920 (Wagley 1976: 51). Many commercial families moved away. A writer for Belém's *Folha do Norte* newspaper who visited Gurupá in 1929 labeled the town an "ex-city" because of its degenerated state (Wagley 1976: 52).

The depression period continued uninterrupted until 1942–1945, when world events briefly created a demand for Amazonian rubber. The Japanese captured the rubber plantations of Malaysia, leaving the Allies in desperate need of an alternative source of rubber. The United States entered into an agreement with the Brazilian government, known as the Washington Accords, to finance the revival of Amazon rubber extraction. Under this program the Brazilian government gave incentives to Northeastern migrants to reopen rubber trails in the Amazon, as well as estab-

Figure 3.11. Second Street, 1948. Photograph by Charles Wagley.

lish a regional health program called Serviço Especial de Saúde Pública (SESP; Public Health Special Service) to oversee the health of workers.

It was in the context of the Washington Accords wartime effort that Charles Wagley first visited Gurupá in 1942 and 1945. Wagley was the director of SESP's educational division and was in charge of improving the working and public health conditions of Northeastern migrants who were once again pouring into the region to tap rubber. He returned to the community in 1948 with colleague Eduardo Galvão and their spouses, Cecília Wagley and Clara Galvão, to conduct anthropological research (Figures 3.11 and 3.12). From this research they published *Amazon Town* (Wagley [1953, 1968] 1976) and *Santos e visagens* (Galvão 1955).

With the end of World War II and the Washington Accords, Gurupá returned to its previous state of economic depression. The economy continued to revolve around the depressed price of rubber. Survival during this period "hung in a delicate balance between starvation and bare subsistence" (Wagley 1976: 300). By the 1960s Gurupá had changed considerably, with an increase in rural-urban migration boosting the town population to over a thousand people (1976: 299). A five-kilometer road was opened into the interior (which later became the eighteen-kilometer

Figure 3.12. Second Street, 2010. Photograph by R. Pace.

road mentioned above), in which rural migrants produced manioc and other crops. Their produce was transported to town for sale by the municipality's truck and jeep. A second major change in Gurupá resulted from triple-digit inflation. Combined with devalued prices for extracted commodities, inflation undermined most merchants' ability to extend credit. Many went out of business, particularly those located in the interior. Only the strongest commercial establishments managed to survive, usually through various combinations of price increases and credit limitations (Wagley 1976: 301).

The highly visible class system once prominent during the rubber boom also changed appreciably. This system had been in a process of decay since the rubber bust. By 1948 the dominant class consisted of only a few impoverished descendants of the old aristocratic rubber merchant families (Wagley 1976: 103). Following the long economic depression of the 1950s and 1960s, these families fell further in their national and local class rankings. The impoverishment of the dominant class led many Gurupaenses to conclude that by the 1960s Gurupá no longer possessed a class system. Everyone was considered a member of the second class, or gente de segunda. Despite the folk view, two classes continued to exist in the municipality: the upper class and the working class. The former consisted of merchants, large landowners, professionals, and civil servants—corresponding to IBOPE's B3 classification. Throughout the period it continued to control the economy and politics, although under reduced circumstances. The latter (IBOPE's C and D) engaged in agro-extractivist activities.

Despite the depressed economic times, there were innovations in the community. Several bars opened, boasting kerosene refrigerators. They sold the traditional *cachaça* alcohol (a type of rum) along with cold beer and soft drinks. People also began playing soccer and volleyball by 1962— which Wagley observed during a revisit. Soccer quickly became the local passion, with two rival teams sporting uniforms and battling each other on Sunday afternoons (Wagley 1976: 302–303).

In addition, entrepreneurs began showing an occasional movie in a large building that served as a dance hall during festival time. This practice continued until the 1980s, finally ending when access to television made the makeshift moving picture shows less desirable. I actually observed the last few showings. The movies were American-made Westerns and Japanese kung-fu. They were subtitled, although given the level of literacy in the community at the time it is doubtful many viewers could read the translations. The audience was dominated by adolescent boys, and the showings proved to be rowdy affairs, with much vocalizing and playacting. After the showing of a kung-fu movie, one was sure to see the playacting continue on the streets for the next week or two. Another important innovation during this period was the introduction of battery-powered radios. The radio began the process of exposing the community to regional and national events in real time.

Dictatorship and Development

By the mid-1960s and continuing for two decades thereafter, a radically different phase in the history of Gurupá and Brazil began. It started with the military regime's overthrow of the civilian government (1964) and the establishment of a repressive, authoritarian dictatorship that lasted until 1985. This regime aggressively pursued a policy of economic modernization (involving industrialization frequently financed with foreign loans and investments). The Amazon fit into the military's plans as a source of raw materials, providing much-needed revenue to help finance industrial development in the Southeast. The regime was also concerned with the need to integrate the region more tightly with the rest of Brazil for geopolitical reasons. Toward this end the dictatorship built roads into the rain forest, constructed new settlements and military posts, and initiated a huge land giveaway (the largest in modern world history) to encourage private and corporate investment in the region. Also critical to the military's plan was the cultural and ideological integration of the country, which led the regime to invest heavily in television as an effective technology for nation building, as discussed in Chapter 2.

The most highly prized development projects, and the most heavily subsidized by the government, were large-scale extractive ones targeting minerals, gold, and timber. The military regime also encouraged and subsidized cattle ranching, despite its mediocre economic returns and its devastating environmental impact. As new roads were built into the Amazon frontier, most areas also experienced a heavy spontaneous migration of subsistence farmers from the Northeast and South, where environmental factors and/or commercialization of export-oriented agriculture and landownership concentration forced them to seek new land (Foweraker 1981: 14; Bunker 1985: 90; Hall 1997: 525; Hecht and Cockburn 1990: 107). They were joined by other small farmers from the Amazon who were likewise looking for land. Once on the frontier, migrants informally appropriated unowned state land for resource extraction or production of subsistence crops and a small marketable surplus.

Conflict between the subsistence farmers and large commercial enterprises quickly followed. The commercial enterprises expropriated land from the migrant farmers, as well as from any other peasant or indigenous group in the area. The use of intimidation and violence was ubiquitous (Martins 1985), with numerous accounts of farmers expelled from their land by hired guns (*pistoleiros*) working in conjunction with the local police. Among the tactics used by hired guns were destruction of property, kidnapping, torture, and assassination. A general atmosphere of lawlessness existed as the state failed to effectively protect small farmers from violence and land expropriation, at least until a cycle of private accumulation of land by a few politically powerful and large-scale landowners and business enterprises was complete (Foweraker 1981: 124).

The Amazon development process had a great impact on Gurupá, although violence was not as prevalent as on the frontier. Large domestic and international commercial enterprises entered the municipality in the 1970s and began expropriating land, mainly on the várzea for timber extraction. Since land titling was chaotic in the municipality (as was the case in most of the Amazon), with overlapping claims, counterfeit titles, usufruct or de facto ownership claims by occupants based on decades of land use, and imprecise demarcation of property, it was easy for firms with only modest legal and financial resources to manipulate the local legal system to obtain titles (Trecanni 2006). Once a title was obtained legally or illegally, the new owners could count on local henchmen, supported by the local government and police force at the time, to use intimidation and destruction of property to expel resident families (Pace 1998; P. Oliveira 1991).

Activism

At first there was only fragmented resistance in Gurupá, mostly in the form of isolated struggles by small landowners and occupants against the commercial enterprises and owners of large landholdings. By the mid-1970s, however, organized resistance emerged under the tutelage of the Catholic Church. The church, led by the Italian priest Giúlio Luppi, has been strongly influenced by liberation theology, which in Brazil is an interpretation of Christian faith from the point of view of the disenfranchised sectors of society (Berryman 1987: 4). This focus on the poor and oppressed led church activists and social progressives to intertwine the traditional goals of spiritual salvation with alleviation of material suffering. According to Bruneau (1982: 50), the rationale for this view is that religious influence makes sense only when people have the appropriate living conditions to "feel fully human"—that is, when they have the basic necessities to survive and are free of oppression and exploitation. Proponents of liberation theology therefore focus on the causes of disenfranchisement, which leads them to criticize the Brazilian and global political economy—in particular, the structural sins of capitalism. They call for social and political enfranchisement of the excluded sectors of society through social reform or revolution (Follmann 1985: 79).

In Gurupá Padre Giúlio steadfastly preached liberation theology. During weekly mass and a variety of yearly meetings (e.g., Catechism Week, agricultural workers' meetings, and Women's Week), he and the church laity openly criticized local inequalities (Figure 3.13). For example, they decried the unfair exchange rates for commodities—a fraction of the market value—that the trading post merchants gave their customers. They encouraged farmers and extractors to form independent cooperatives in order to bypass trading posts for the sale and purchase of produce and basic necessities and detailed land rights abuses by members of the dominant class (see Wesche and Bruneau 1990: 38). The church brought in experts from the Pastoral Land Commission to explain occupants' rights to land. They implored families threatened with expulsion to demand their

Figure 3.13. Outdoor mass for Saint Benedict Festival. Photograph by R. Pace, 2011.

usufruct rights to the land or at least their indemnification rights for improvements made to the land. They attacked local political corruption and suppression of human rights, which twice resulted in the priest's arrest for stirring up class conflict. They also urged participation in rural union and political elections.

In addition to articulating liberation theology's ideological message, the progressive sector of the Catholic Church promoted social activism through the formation of lay religious–political groups known as comunidades eclesiais de base (CEBs; Christian base communities). Sixty-six CEBs, or *comunidades* as they are more commonly called, have been established throughout the municipality of Gurupá, frequently building on the traditional *irmandades*, or religious brotherhoods, that were organized to conduct the festivals in honor of neighborhood patron saints. They continued these functions at the same time that they organized labor exchanges for mutual aid and established cooperatives for the sale of extracted and agricultural products and the purchase of medicine.

Some of the comunidades engaged in more drastic behavior. They joined together to boycott merchants' trading posts as they formed their own cooperatives. They physically blocked the evictions of their fellows from land through *empates* (lit., "tying up"), in which women, men, and children formed a human barrier to protect those who were threatened by henchmen and even the police. They also used empates to thwart extraction of timber and heart of palm from property contested by occupants of land who lacked land titles. As the comunidades grew in number and strength, they began to focus on reorganization of the Rural Workers' Union (Sindicato dos Trabalhadores Rurais [STR]), which was a key institution needed to establish legal rights to land for the agro-extractivists. When union elections were near, members of the communidades uncovered voter registration fraud designed to stop the progressive unionists from winning.

What followed in 1986 was an intense confrontation between conservative members of Gurupá who supported the military regime and progressives who supported the church. The progressives staged mass rallies to protest the fraud and even orchestrated a fifty-four-day occupation of union headquarters as a way to demand an investigation. In the end they were successful and took over the union. With this base, they also began organizing a political party—the Workers' Party (Partido dos Trabalhadores [PT])—which eventually achieved success in local elections (see Pace 1998: 177–182).

By the 1990s Gurupá's progressive movement attracted the attention of several social activist groups and NGOs. In 1992 the European Union sponsored a small program to improve manioc production in the municipality. Later a town in Belgium adopted Gurupá as its sister city and has made donations of computers and medical supplies ever since. This was followed by a much larger project initiated by FASE in 1997 that sought to regularize land titles in Gurupá, assist in the formation of extractive reserves and quilombos, and conduct a number of demonstration projects in sustainable agriculture. By the end of the project in the late 2000s, most of the municipal lands were legally titled and under strict sustainable use plans.

Television arrived at the end of the tumultuous dictatorship and the beginning of the activist phase of Gurupá's history. In the following chapter we examine how the local community engaged this novelty.

CHAPTER 4

The Arrival of Television

In June 1982 three families in Gurupá had twenty-inch black-and-white television sets in their living rooms. The families purchased the TV sets in the port city of Belém, had them shipped by riverboat to Gurupá, and then connected them to antennas set atop ten-meter towers, complete with reception boosters. For this costly endeavor the families were rewarded with fuzzy but discernible images. They considered the effort a great success, timed as it was to coincide with the opening of the World Cup soccer finals in Spain. For the first time in Gurupá these three families along with their kin, friends, and neighbors, and even strangers who could catch a glimpse of the TV through an open window, watched an important event with the rest of the country in real time. The momentous occasion also marked the first time that the townsfolk of Gurupá were in direct audio and visual contact not only with the rest of Brazil but with the global community as well.

By the following year there were five more TV sets in Gurupá, for a total of eight—or one TV set for every 375 people in town. In 1986, after the installation of a municipal satellite dish negated the need for expensive individual antenna towers, I counted eighty-six functioning TVs in town (approximately one for every 46 people) and dozens in the interior. By 1990 there were 158 sets in town (one for every 28 people) and probably half as many in the interior. In 1999, following the stabilization of the Brazilian currency and the end of three- and four-digit inflation, television consumption boomed. I estimated that there were 700 sets in town (one for every 9 people) and an untold number in the interior.[1] Satellite dishes likewise became affordable at this time, with 163 in the town of Gurupá alone (see La Pastina 2001: 546 for similar observations). By 2005 I estimated 900 TV sets in town (one for every 7 people) and counted 300-plus satellite dishes. Vendors of satellite dishes in town told me they had sold hundreds to people in the interior. Finally, in 2009, television and satellite ownership in town was commonplace. We estimated close to 1,200 sets in town, or one for every 6 people. We asked numerous residents for an estimate of the number in the interior. Their estimates ranged from 25 percent to 33 percent of homes possessing one. Altogether, we estimate that at least 50 percent of homes in town and as high as 33 percent of homes in the interior of Gurupá possess televisions.

This burst in television consumption over a twenty-eight-year period has led to an intriguing array of changes in Gurupá. In this chapter we focus on the changes generated by the introduction of television as a new technology, in particular the social interactions with and around television. Following Peterson (2003: 128–137), among the features and processes we analyze are the constraints of the technology on viewing, the intersection of TV ownership with local class structure, the signification of TV as a material object and communication modality, the displacement of public activities by TV viewing, and the habits of spectatorship such as viewing participation, viewing etiquette, and patterns of visitation.

To place these features and processes into proper context, we divide the arrival of television in Gurupá into two stages. These stages are based on Kottak's work (2009: 139), which suggests a five-stage framework for interpreting TV's impact in Brazil, as discussed in Chapter 1. Gurupá has experienced the first two stages of Kottak's framework but has not entered the last stages. Stage I is the initial contact with television. Lasting about ten years in the case of Gurupá, Stage I is marked by the strangeness and novelty of the new technology. Paraphrasing Marshall McLuhan's aphorism, at this point the medium rather than the message is the mesmerizer. In Stage II people become more familiar with and accustomed to TV. Over a period of ten to twenty years viewers begin a process of selective acceptance, rejection, interpretation, and reworking of TV messages. Television saturation (i.e., long-term, medium-to-heavy daily viewing) is only partial for the population at this stage.

Stage III, which Gurupá had not entered at the time of this research, is the saturation point. It occurs as nearly all homes in a locale have TV. Negative attitudes toward the medium begin to develop. At the same time television has a powerful, yet subtle, influence in shaping worldview. Stage IV involves lifelong exposure to televiewing for adults. The more profound and long-term sociocultural effects of television become discernible at this point. Stage V entails the proliferation and diversification of media technology. Various recording devices and the Internet give viewers greater control over the timing of viewing as well as greater access to a wide variety of entertainment and news outlets. This capability transforms television and associated media from agents of mass enculturation into technologies of segmental appeal.

Stage I: 1982–1992

I arrived in Gurupá one year after the introduction of television there and well before it became accessible to large numbers of people. During this early period it was not unusual for me to converse with individuals who had never seen TV, especially people living in the interior. From this vantage point I was able to witness the initial reaction to the strange and novel medium. I saw the intense excitement it generated and its grip on the community as more TV sets arrived in town.

Technological Constraints on Viewing

The first hurdle to watching television, however, was obtaining the correct technology. From 1982 to 1986 it required traveling twenty-four hours downstream by riverboat to Belém to purchase a black-and-white set (usually a Phillips or Telefunken), an antenna, antenna wire, and a reception booster. These materials were then shipped to Gurupá, a thirty-six-hour boat trip upstream. Back in Gurupá the new TV owner had to construct a ten-meter wooden antenna tower, install and align the antenna, connect the antenna wire and reception booster to the TV set, and plug in the TV set and reception booster. For TV owners in the interior and for those in town wanting to watch when the town's electricity was turned off, the TV and reception booster had to be connected to a diesel-powered generator. The cost of the equipment and transportation, minus the cost of labor and the diesel generator, could range from US$170 to US$700, depending on the type of TV set. Even the lower price was a hefty sum of money at the time for a typical family in Gurupá.

The second hurdle was reception. Before 1986 Gurupá received its best transmission signals from Belém, 353 kilometers to the east; Monte Dourado, 112 kilometers to the northwest; and Macapá, 173 kilometers to the northeast (there were also occasional, faint images coming from Venezuela, but the broadcast was in Spanish). Quality of reception over these distances depended greatly on weather conditions. Many people commented to me, and I also observed directly, that after a rainstorm the reception was extremely clear. Usually reception tended to be fuzzy and lasted from fifteen to thirty minutes before fading away. Reception might return after fifteen minutes or so, or the image might return without sound, or the sound might return without the image. If weather conditions remained poor, neither an image nor sound was received. Watching television at this time demanded great patience.

Changing channels was an additional chore. Globo, relayed from a transmission tower in Monte Dourado, provided the best reception. If, however, viewers wished to watch Bandeirantes, relayed from Macapá, a realignment of the antenna was necessary. This task required scaling the tower and manually rotating the antenna. There were interesting innovations to reduce the inherent risks involved in channel changing. The most practical was the attachment of an eight-meter metal rod to the antenna, which then extended down through the middle of the tower to two meters above the ground. A second metal rod, one-half meter in length, was inserted horizontally through the vertical rod and used to turn the antenna.

I observed several channel-changing episodes. The process usually began when reception failed and there were hopes that the other station might be viewable or when there was a conflict over watching a telenovela on one station and a soccer match on the other. After some discussion on the merits of switching a channel, one of the men was sent to rotate the antenna. Once outside, you could hear the individual grunting as he wrestled the antenna into position. Next came the question, "Pegou, já pegou?"—"Did it catch?" After hearing the okay from inside, the individual returned and resumed viewing. Because of the trouble, most TV owners simply left their sets on one channel, usually Globo, and made do with its programming.

Another constraint to televiewing was electricity rationing. At that time Gurupá, like most towns in the region, used large-capacity diesel-powered generators to produce electricity. The cost of producing electricity was very high, particularly for a population with such meager incomes. Yet the state and federal governments were committed to their belief in the social, economic, and political benefits of electrifying small towns in the countryside. To accomplish its goal, the federal government heavily subsidized electricity production. A drawback to this system, however, was that there were not enough resources to provide all the towns in the region with electricity twenty-four hours a day. What budget constraints did permit was six hours of electricity daily. In Gurupá electricity was available from six o'clock in the evening to midnight.

The daily six o'clock energy surge was typically greeted with joyful outcries as refrigerators began buzzing (with the promise of a cool drink and ice), açaí presses began to grind loudly (creating the cherished drink), radios and stereos boomed out the latest songs, and, of course, TVs blared out the first evening telenovela (if there was reception). *Movimento*—"movement," but here denoting the hustle and bustle of town life, or modernity—arrived, at least for a while. The midnight power outage, of course, returned the town to its former state, with only candles and oil lamps to light the way.

Although the six daily hours of electricity limited the amount of televiewing possible, it coincided with the broadcast of telenovelas and national news, two of the most highly valued shows throughout Brazil. There were also exceptions made to the timing of electricity rationing when an important national event occurred outside of the six-to-midnight time slot. For these occasions, the mayor could ask permission from the state government to turn on the diesel generators so people could watch television sets. I observed this for the funeral of President-elect Tancredo Neves (1985), the Olympics, and important soccer matches such as World Cup games. To compensate for the extra fuel consumed, electricity was turned off earlier over the following days until the town was back on its fuel usage schedule. This was the same rationing system developed to allow electricity usage after midnight during the festivals of Saints Benedict and Anthony.

A final constraint to televiewing during this period was the risk of lightning strikes. The antenna towers rose above all structures in town and often extended above the trees. The towers were perfect targets for lightning. Poor grounding ensured that once lightning struck, anything connected to the tower or the electrical grid in the house would be damaged or destroyed. In my walk-throughs of the town I never failed to find two or three abandoned towers with antennas and all wiring removed, casualties of a lightning strike.

One of my neighbors and key consultants, Zeca (a retired prosecutor in his seventies), described his encounter with lightning. He told me that the year before he had scraped together funds for a TV set, sent for one in Belém, and had it delivered and installed. For the next four months he greatly enjoyed watching his set. Then one afternoon a storm came and lightning struck his tower. Even though the TV set was not turned on, lightning traveled through the wires and blew out the set. Zeca saw it explode before his eyes. As disturbing as the TV's destruction was, what traumatized him was the memory of his *filho de criação* (adopted son) struck and killed by lightning in the same house two decades earlier. Zeca shuddered as he retold the story of the poor man's screams and his burned body. Without hesitation, Zeca had the antenna and wiring removed and swore he would never again have a television set, and to my knowledge he never did.

Early in 1986 the technological constraints of televiewing changed radically. The town installed a satellite dish that received transmissions directly from Rio de Janeiro and relayed them to the surrounding area. With the dish the quality of reception improved greatly, and there was no longer a need to use individual antenna towers. A TV set with an attachable antenna (rabbit ears) was all that was needed. The drawback was that viewers received only one channel. If an additional channel was desired, the old individual antenna tower system was required. Few people in town, however, chose this option.

The politics of the dish's installation indicate the value placed on the medium by the local population as well as politicians. I first heard rumors about the state government's plans to improve the town's television reception in 1983. At this point the proposed technology involved a relay antenna (Port. *repetidora*) that would receive signals from Belém and then retransmit them locally. There was much debate in town over the likelihood of a small, poor place such as Gurupá being able to persuade the state government to provide funds for such a luxury. "É dificil"—"It's tough"—for a place such as Gurupá to merit such a device was a common sentiment. By 1984 excitement grew as more rumors circulated that the state had set aside funds for a relay antenna for Gurupá. Skepticism also remained high, and I heard other rumors circulating that politicians in Belém were meddling in the process and that they might abscond with the funds. By 1985 people were no longer talking about a relay antenna but a satellite dish that was slated for installation. For some reason, unknown to the people in Gurupá, its installation was being delayed. Finally, in early 1986, the dish arrived and was installed amid much fanfare. At that point I obtained the complete story of the delay from one of Gurupá's *delegados* (municipal council members).

The delegado told me that the original request for a relay antenna was delayed because of repeated funding shortfalls, as well as concerns over quality of reception (relay antennas were notorious for poor reception; see Reis 2000: 206). However, as satellite technology became available in Brazil the federal government pushed to use the technology in the most distant parts of the country, such as the Amazon region. By 1985 the state had acquired the needed funding, purchased the satellite dish, and was ready to send it to Gurupá. At this point a *deputado* (state senator) held up the process. It seems he was scheduled to be at the inauguration of Gurupá's first and only bank earlier that year but became sick, so a deputado from an opposing political party presided over the event. Afraid of losing more political capital, the first deputado decided that he had to preside over and receive credit for the dish installation. The dish had to wait until he could make the trip, which occurred in early 1986.

With the satellite dish in place, television consumption expanded rapidly. The old antennas, wires, and reception boosters were sold off to people living in the interior who, now possessing this technology, could receive sharp images rebroadcast from Gurupá. These TV owners, however, still faced the risk of lightning strikes.

TV Ownership and Local Class Structure: Who Gets TV

Throughout Stage I, the cost of owning a television set and its accoutrements was prohibitive for most Gurupaenses. Ownership paralleled class distinctions—with a few exceptions. Only members of social class B3, such as local business and political leaders, large landowners, civil servants, and a few lesser merchants, were able to afford the medium. In addition, a few full-time store clerks with higher than usual salaries were able to buy sets. By contrast, the bulk of the population—forest resource extractors, subsistence farmers, fishers, and menial wage earners—were all but priced out of the market.

For example, a TV set and required equipment cost a typical household engaged in forest resource extraction and/or subsistence agriculture (approximately 80 percent of the population) about six months of earnings. For a family living in the interior, that amount was tripled due to the need for a diesel-powered generator. Funds in this quantity, at least for television without the generator, might be available after an especially good rubber harvest or after working many months cutting timber. Even with money in hand, before a family could consider buying a television it had to expend funds on clothing, housewares, tools, food, medicines, religious obligations, and so forth. Rarely were there surplus funds sufficient for such a large purchase. In addition, because of rampant inflation, no trading post merchant or store owner would agree to finance a TV set over time without charging exorbitant interest rates. Therefore members of the working class had few ways to obtain the needed capital to buy a TV.

For the local middle-class the cost of television was substantial but not insurmountable, particularly after the town's satellite dish was installed. In order to purchase a set individuals in this group might sell off some land or timber or redirect profits from commerce. A civil servant with a steady wage might negotiate credit with a store or pay the extremely high interest rates to finance the purchase. The few store clerks with TV sets made special arrangements with the store owner to deduct the costs from their salaries.

As a result of ownership distribution, working-class individuals could gain access to televiewing only through the more affluent members of the community. Televiewing during Stage I was shaped by social stratification. For example, I observed that proximity to the TV set during televiewing was used by some TV owners as a reward for desired behavior, reinforcing hierarchical relationships between individuals, particularly patron-client ties. For working-class individuals, the closer one got to the TV, the more likely one was a good client and in the good graces of the owner. The most privileged position for viewing was in the room with the set, on a chair or a sofa. This was typically reserved for the owner's family and friends, in other words, social equals. The second-best viewing area was on the floor, or to the side of the room, or along the back wall facing the television; this area was typically reserved for trusted and well-liked workers who nonetheless had lower social status. Outside viewing through open windows was the least favored option, available to anyone passing by in the street.

I participated in this proximity hierarchy. On many occasions at night I would stand in the street amid a gathering to watch television through a window. People in the street immediately recognized me and, out of politeness, respect, or class obligation, ushered me to a better vantage point closer to the window. Once there, I was often recognized by people inside the house and urged to come in—separating me from the outside gathering and placing me among social peers. Once inside I was typically offered a chair (denoting high status), bumping someone from it who descended to the floor, who then displaced someone to the side of the room, and so forth, until someone likely stepped outside the house to make more room.

Beyond a reward and reinforcement of social class hierarchies, access to televiewing was used by some TV owners as a means to economic and political ends. For example, all the first TV owners in Gurupá were merchants and politicians. During these early years they opened their homes to large numbers of televiewers. They did this every night, despite the inconvenience. I asked one of these merchants how he put up with the nightly gatherings. He responded frankly that the crowds watching TV in and outside his house were simply good for business (later, in the mid-

1990s, this same merchant was one of the first in Gurupá to put a TV in his store for public viewing). The mayor at the time was particularly vigilant about public access to her TV set. Her house was open every night, even when she and her family were out working, attending an event, traveling, or visiting a neighbor. The apparent assumption was, give people access to television and possibly secure their votes.

Signification of TV as a Material Object and Communication Modality

The manner in which television is integrated into the social space of the home can indicate much about the value attached to the new technology (Peterson 2003: 129). Through this assimilation process television as a material object, as well as a communication modality, becomes part of a sociotechnical system that produces new meanings (Pfaffenberger 1992). In Gurupá we collected data on the values and meanings attached to the medium in two ways: observing the physical placement of the apparatus in the home and noting surrounding items; and recording TV-talk about the significance of television.

During Stage I making observations about TV placement in homes was a simple undertaking. Because of the custom of leaving shutters wide open during the day to allow circulation of air,[2] anyone passing by a house could easily look inside without violating privacy rules. The most visible rooms, and the most public living spaces, were the front rooms with doors and windows opening onto the street, pathway, or plaza. Here families gathered to relax and interact, especially in the evenings. The front room was also where families received visitors. Many times people sat by the window in these rooms, gazing out at the passersby and talking to neighbors. By the same token, it was accepted, if not expected, for passersby to look into the front rooms. Since theft was not a major problem in Gurupá, with nowhere to hide stolen goods and no easy way to transport such goods out of the community, a family's most prized possessions worthy of public display were located here, strategically positioned for viewing from the outside.

TV sets were always located in the front rooms (Figure 4.1). Typically they were placed on tables or wall shelves facing a window and were clearly visible to passersby (also see Reis 2000: 111). Around the TV sets were decorations and status items, including religious icons, porcelain figurines, books, radios, and stereos. On the walls above were family portraits, many of which were hand-painted photographs, religious calendars, or sometimes crucifixes. The TV sets often served as the centerpiece

Figure 4.1. Television placement for viewing. Photograph by O. Pace, 2011.

of this eclectic assemblage (Figure 4.2). The prominent position of the TV sets clearly indicated that no social stigma was attached to their display (unlike in the United States, where considerable propaganda and decorative carapace were required before TV sets were accepted as mainstays in home furnishings; see Tichi 1991: 18–23).

In fact, in a couple of houses where an additional set was owned but not being used it was displayed in the same room as the working TV. I even saw broken TVs, incapable of functioning, left as centerpieces.

Public display of television as a symbol of prestige was the rule during Stage I. When the electricity came on at 6:00 p.m., TVs were immediately turned on and the volume turned up for all to hear (the same was done with radios and stereos in other houses). The TVs remained on until 10:00 p.m. or so, regardless of programming or quality of reception. Many times I observed television sets broadcasting to the street when weather conditions reduced images to pure static or simply left on while the owners sat in their doorways, their backs to the set, watching people pass by on the street. In part this behavior reflected the value given to movimento, of which TV pictures (even when reduced to static) and noise had become an integral part.

During Stage I talk about the value of television as a communication

Figure 4.2. Television as centerpiece. Photograph by R. Pace, 2011.

modality was overwhelmingly positive (see table 4.2). People spoke of their amazement, as well as puzzlement, at the array of novel images and messages coming from the medium. The immediate impact is hard to overstate. For a population with restricted access to information about the world, even the rest of Brazil, television was an eye-opening experience of incalculable value. One show in particular stood out as a prime source of novel information about the world for people in Gurupá. This show, *Fantástico* (Fantastic), a two-hour variety show/newsmagazine popular in small towns and rural zones throughout Brazil (Kottak 2009: 27), aired on Sunday evenings. *Fantástico* drew crowds in Gurupá that occasionally surpassed the audiences for the news and telenovelas. On Mondays, after the show, townspeople discussed the the program's stories and commented on the images shown. Since many of the stories involved footage from the United States, I was often drawn into conversations to give my opinions.

Exposure to TV shows like *Fantástico*, as well as the news, telenovelas, films, documentaries, and so forth, quickly created a greater awareness of the world beyond Gurupá. Before the spread of television, conversations commonly heard among Gurupaenses focused on local events; gossip; prices of commodities such as food, rubber, and timber; soccer; or regional or national politics. I was asked questions about what kind of jungle grows in the United States, whether all Americans are rich, and what cowboys are like. As TV spread the conversations became more diverse and more cosmopolitan. Gurupaenses discussed events in North America, Europe, and the Middle East in great detail and scrutinized national politics. I found myself discussing the ambitions of the American space program, the foreign policy strategies of then-President Reagan, income distribution in the United States, and the geophysical causes of earthquakes.

Beyond the value of expanding general knowledge about the world, another frequently cited advantage of television in Gurupá was the ability to experience national or international events, both visually and audibly, simultaneously with their occurrence. People were fascinated by inaugurations, funerals, soccer games, and other important events in real time. Participation in these events, even if only vicariously, gave people a sense of commonality with the rest of Brazil that was otherwise rare (Gurupá celebrated Independence Day and Carnaval, but these were perfunctory and clearly secondary to local celebrations such as the saints' festivals).

The most public displays of "belonging" through televiewing that I personally observed were the World Cup soccer games of 1986 and 2000. Preceding the games, streets and walls were painted with Brazilian flags or simply Brazil's colors (yellow, green, and blue). During the games people set off fireworks, danced, and sang patriotic songs. After victories, gleeful shouts of "Brasil" could be heard for hours. After defeats, cries of "Que vergonha Brasil"—"What shame Brazil"—were mournfully uttered, sometimes for days. According to my consultants, nothing like this outpouring of nationalistic pride and pain ever occurred in Gurupá before the arrival of television. Local politicians and of course leaders in the state and federal governments were well aware of television's ability to stir nationalistic emotions and create feelings of unity and belonging. Accordingly, they worked very hard to provide electricity to the town so that people could watch important events when they occurred outside the normal time slot.

Gurupaenses also told me that they valued television because of the speed with which they could learn the news. People reported that news reached them much more quickly than what they were accustomed to with radio. They also noted the national and international scope of the TV news versus the regional focus of radio. Many mentioned that television was more explanatory than radio, likely due to the visual stimulus offered by the medium. For example, on March 10, 1985, when the leader of the Soviet Union, Konstantin Chernenko, died, I went next door to report this to my neighbor, Zeca. As he mulled over the global ramifications of the unexpected death, he nodded his head pensively, very pleased with the speed the news had traveled to Gurupá. He looked at me and commented, "This is why television is good."

A final view on the value of television as a communication modality involved the medium's "babysitting" capabilities. Parents of young and adolescent children were impressed with the ability of TV to hold the attention of their offspring, who would watch for hours if allowed, even though the programming was not child oriented. The parents were happy to see their children in the house where they could keep an eye on them and not outside where they could get into trouble (particularly in the streets of town). Interestingly, the comments I heard were always about managing children's time. During Stage I, I did not come across anyone praising TV for its educational value for children. And only rarely did I hear criticisms about television's harmful effects on the young, such as exposure to violent and sexual programming.

Displacement of Public Activities

One of the most noticeable changes for an outsider visiting Gurupá during Stage I was the displacement of public activities by televiewing. The most obvious example was the curtailing of the nightly promenade through the streets of town, which took place between seven and ten o'clock as the cool night air replaced the oppressive heat of the day. The town came alive with movimento. The electricity was turned on, one or more dance halls blasted its music, and people gathered at their doorsteps to relax and watch other people pass by in the streets. Young people dressed in their finest jeans, which were too hot to wear during the day, and wandered the streets in search of friends, gossip, and flirtation. Older adults also strolled the streets, chaperoning the young and visiting friends and relatives.

As access to televiewing expanded, far fewer people strolled through the streets at night, and the nightly promenade all but ended. During the week at the nine o'clock telenovela time, the streets were practically deserted. Except for a stray drunk or one of Gurupá's few Pentecostals (who were discouraged from watching television) returning from religious services, the only people on the streets were the small crowds huddled in front of windows opened to blaring television sets. During the weekends there were more people in the streets between seven and ten o'clock. Many of them had come from the rural interior to visit friends and relatives, who were often glued to their sets. After the final telenovela or Sunday's *Fantástico* finished, people did pursue nighttime activities and the streets livened up but never to the level of the promenade event.

Another noticeable change was the near-complete alteration of night-life to accommodate the viewing of the nine o'clock telenovela. It pre-empted parties, festivals, and even night school. No public activity was planned to start until after the telenovela. For example, the popular auction (*leilão*) held during the festivals of Saints Benedict and Anthony did not begin until after the telenovela ended. The church personnel commented that it was useless to begin earlier since few people would attend, which meant bidding for food and other goods would not be competitive and revenue earned for the church would be low.

Festivities for the dry season celebrations of Saints John and Peter, such as *quadrilhas* (square dances) and *festas de caboclo* (rustic festivals), were also delayed until the telenovela ended. Even the night classes at the school ended earlier so that students and teachers could get home in time for the show. The nine o'clock telenovela hour dominated most people's evening activities so thoroughly that time began to be conceptualized in terms of nightly programming (also see Reis 2000: 232). A common time reference for the evening hours was "na hora da telenovela" (telenovela time).

Habits of Spectatorship

When television was introduced into Gurupá there were few rules governing social interaction while viewing. Televiewers had to make many adjustments as new rules of spectatorship were established and other rules of social interaction discarded. By the end of this stage I was able to identify emerging patterns of televiewing. These patterns, or habits of spectatorship (see Armbrust 1998: 413), covered an array of behaviors, from who watches to how one watches, as well as social etiquette and visitation rules.

As discussed earlier, a key determinant to television access was one's social class. The greater one's affluence, the greater the likelihood of frequent televiewing. A corollary to this rule was that close social or economic ties to a member of the middle class (such as patron-client ties) often led to greater TV access. Town residence was another important factor determining who watched television. Because of the custom of leaving shutters open and TV sets facing out to be viewed by the public, living in town assured one the opportunity to view TV, if only at a distance. People living in the interior, by contrast, rarely had access to TV. Only when visiting town were they able to partake in televiewing. In terms of age, the young and old watched television together. A typical household scene during

Stage I included a core of adults seated in front of the TV on chairs or on the floor surrounded by children of all ages, many wedged between the adults. Outside, children were interspersed among the adults, with the smallest congregating in front of the window for the best view.

Inside the home women and men, both young and old, watched together. I could discern no spatial segregation by gender, but programming choice did play a role in the relative numbers of men and women in the audience. A preponderance of men would watch sports, a mixed audience viewed the news, and more women than men typically watched the telenovelas. Outside, groups of five to twenty people watched from the street. Male participation in this street activity was the expected norm for Brazilian society, where males dominate the public sphere and females are traditionally relegated to the domestic sphere (DaMatta 1987: 167). What was interesting, however, was that the lure of television was so strong that women viewed alongside the men. Such indiscriminate mixing of the sexes in public, and at night, was unparalleled in Gurupá. It is clear from local responses, however, that televiewing from the street was not considered a breach of the local male/female and street/house dichotomies but constituted a special case in which domestic space is symbolically extended through the window to the televiewing area.

Several groups refused to watch television. The largest among these was the seventy members of the Pentecostal church. They found viewing TV too worldly and disliked exposure to sinful temptations. Much smaller in number was a group of devout Catholics who also eschewed TV because of its worldliness and temptations. A third group, also small in number, was composed of highly politicized individuals associated with the progressive movement in the Catholic Church and the Rural Workers' Union. This group rejected TV because of its hegemonic discourses justifying, or obfuscating, inequality and exploitation in Brazilian society. In other words, this group of political dissenters criticized Brazilian commercial television in the larger context of criticizing social stratification and capitalism.

How to watch television in a social setting was another facet of spectatorship that required behavioral modification. There was no other activity quite like it. Neither storytelling nor listening to the radio in a group had the same restrictions that television seemed to demand. The cultural requirements for televiewing that I observed during Stage I called for silence, gazes fixed on the TV set, and highly restricted bodily movement. The rule of silence during televiewing, in particular, was close to absolute. When programs or commercials were on, conversation was absent. Only during breaks when a blank screen or test pattern with no sound appeared would some conversation start up (this occurred after the installation of the satellite dish; the breaks were for local commercials, but since the programming came directly from Rio with no local retransmission, the screen was blank). In many cases I observed that even during these breaks people would remain silent, although they might stretch or stand up and walk around. Once programming resumed, everyone returned to their places and ongoing conversations ended. Any breach of this rule led to immediate reprimand, ranging from hostile stares and hisses to an occasional "*Fecha boca*" ("Shut up"). Noisy or rambunctious children were not tolerated. Mothers or older siblings quickly removed misbehaving children from the TV viewing area.

There were, of course, exceptions to this rule. Most commonly people of higher social status could speak during programming if they desired. But the interesting fact that I repeatedly observed in Gurupá was that no one wanted to talk. Everyone was more interested in absorbing the information and images emanating from the TV set. I once observed a clash of spectatorship rules when the manager of Gurupá's now-defunct bank and his wife, both outsiders from the state of São Paulo, visited the mayor during news time on a weekday evening. To the Paulistas (people from São Paulo), who had had television for several decades (Stage III), television etiquette required no strict rules on silence, gaze, or physical movement, and they proceeded to converse throughout the program. The people from Gurupá, by contrast, were caught in an uncomfortable bind. Etiquette required them to entertain the Paulistas, who were of a higher social status. This necessitated paying careful attention to their conversation, maintaining eye contact, serving them cafezinhos, and so forth. At the same time the Gurupaenses wanted to stare uninterrupted at the television program. The result was an awkward encounter. The people from Gurupá responded by constantly fidgeting in their seats, unable to watch or listen to television or to properly entertain their visitors.

During Stage I in Gurupá I did not observe people engaging in other activities during televiewing. I saw no one doing domestic chores or homework, or eating, sewing, or knitting. If these activities occurred during TV time they took place in separate rooms with no line of vision to the TV set. It is possible that people engaged in other activities in other locations in the house and simply listened to the television. Probable reasons for the lack of alternative activities during televiewing are the strict rules for spectatorship, which forced people to remain quiet and still while watching TV, and the public nature of televiewing (usually with visitors present as well as bypassers watching through the front windows), which meant people should not engage in private activities out of politeness.

This pattern of the mesmerized viewer—sitting quietly, engaging in no other activity, the gaze fixed on the TV set—challenges statements by some U.S. researchers that televiewing has never involved the total absorption of the viewer (Williams 1986: 10). The stage of television exposure and the dictates of the culture will largely determine the amount of secondary or nonviewing activity that accompanies televiewing. This observation is supported by the research of Szalai and collaborators (1972) in twelve nations across Europe, North America, and Latin America. Their data demonstrate that in varying cultural settings secondary activity such as eating, talking, or working occurred during as much as 40 percent of the televiewing period to as little as zero percent.

An additional rule of spectatorship that developed during Stage I required public access to privately owned TV sets. The rule stipulated that televiewing should be accessible from the outside of the house for everyone. If this public service was not granted, social pressure was applied to those who did not conform. I discovered this rule after a few months in Gurupá. As part of the research project, I had purchased and transported a television set and antenna to my house. For a month I turned on the set and displayed it in front of our window. I invited friends in, while many passersby watched through the window. However, the reception was poor, with the picture fading every five minutes or so (part of the problem was that the reception booster I had was too weak). Growing tired of this nuisance, I disconnected the television and packed it away and, for privacy and to keep out mosquitoes, closed the shutters at night. A few weeks later, during a religious festival, a young man I did not know, who had a few drinks to bolster his courage, approached me on the street and sarcastically commented, "It is real nice to close your shutters at night and watch television all by yourself, isn't it?" On realizing that I was being chastised for hoarding a scarce public form of information and entertainment, I tried to explain that the television did not work properly and was not being used. To prove my point, I left the shutters open for the next few evenings, clearly demonstrating that the television was not in use.

Due to the public access rule, as well as the general excitement of viewing television, possession of a TV during Stage I increased one's social contact with family, neighbors, friends, and even strangers. To quantify this observation, we asked several questions on the interview schedules to ascertain the level of social contact as related to the average number of hours of daily televiewing. Among the questions were the following: How many of your neighbors visited you in the last eight days? When was the last time you were visited by someone from (a) the interior or the town of Gurupá, (b) another city of Pará, (c) a city outside of Pará, and (d) from another country? Multiple regression analysis of the data revealed a significant correlation between the rate of visitation and viewing hours (Kottak 2009: 146, 221–222). In other words, in Gurupá during Stage I the more television one watched, the more visitors one had.

The increased rate of visitation required the suspension of certain traditions of hospitality, most noticeably, the serving of cafezinho. Before television was introduced a visitor in one's house, particularly a formal visit by someone of equal or higher social status, was served a demitasse of thick coffee (espresso) with a lot of sugar added. This occurred in households of all income levels. Even poor families that had great difficulty purchasing coffee and sugar would make the sacrifice to serve cafezinhos. With the arrival of television and increased visitation, serving coffee was suspended for television viewers as it simply became too expensive to do on a nightly basis (for a similar discussion of early televiewing hospitality rules in the United States, see Tichi 1991: 24).

Stage II: 1993–2010

From approximately 300 sets in 1992, there were well over a thousand sets in town and countryside by 2005 and probably several thousand by 2010. As familiarity with the medium grew, a process of selective acceptance and rejection of television and its messages occurred. The initial excitement I witnessed in Stage I was now replaced by more temperate attitudes, although, as shown below, positive attitudes toward television still outweighed negative ones.

Technological Constraints to Viewing

Several events occurred during this period to significantly increase people's access to television. The first and most important to the average consumer was the greatly reduced rate of inflation achieved during the Cardoso presidency. Through a number of fiscal policies, the inflation rate for Brazil as a whole fell from a high of 2,948 percent per year in 1990 to a low of 7 percent per year in 2000 (Singh et al. 2005). For consumers in places like Gurupá the value of wages remained relatively constant, giving individuals the opportunity to save for costly purchases like television sets. Reduced inflation rates also enabled merchants to sell expensive items like TVs on installment plans without the interest charges tripling or quadrupling the base price. In addition, Gurupá's extraction boom, first timber and then açaí, added much-needed revenue to the municipality, some of which was used to buy televisions.

Not only did the increased buying power allow more households to buy TV sets; it also enabled many to upgrade their television systems. For example, by my visit in 1999 color TVs had become a common sight in homes and public places like stores and restaurants. I estimated that one-fourth of all TV sets in Gurupá were color by 2005. By 2009 there were no black-and-white TV sets in use. Other noticeable upgrades included individually owned satellite dishes, with some three hundred in town and hundreds more in the interior by 2005. With a satellite dish there are fifteen channels available. If a person could afford it, SKY satellite television offered a package deal with 90 to 120 channels. This programming included shows in a number of languages, but the cost of the system was high. As a result only four families in town had SKY.

Reception with satellite dishes was fairly constant, with sharp images. However, I did observe episodes, some lasting several days, when reception was blurred and sound muddled. Neither the picture nor the sound was so poor that viewing was impossible, but the defects were noticeable. These defects occurred with the municipal satellite dish as well. People in Gurupá told me these were common problems that occurred from time to time, and most blamed problems on equipment malfunctions at the site of transmission.

In 1998 the state government secured funds to provide (and subsidize) electricity twenty-four hours a day year-round. The end of rationing meant that people were no longer limited to the six hours of daily televiewing but could watch as much as desired or practical. When I asked people to recall the first year of round-the-clock TV access for those owning sets, respondents reported that most people maintained a schedule of watching telenovelas, news, and sports on week nights. On weekends there was additional viewing throughout the day and into the night of movies, sports, and variety shows. There were tales of some individuals who developed an addiction to televiewing, spending practically every waking hour in front of the set. I observed one such case in 2004 involving a teenage boy who would lie in his hammock and watch TV, stopping only to eat and make trips to the outhouse. The mother of the boy explained that he was unemployed (very common for that age group) and

Table 4.I. Amount of Daily Televiewing per Category and Daily Mean

Year	Nonviewers (%)	Light Viewers (%)	Medium Viewers (%)	Heavy Viewers (%)	Mean Hours (%)
1986	60.9	27.5	7.2	4.2	0.86
1999	1.2	26.5	42.2	30.0	4.17
2009	0.0	49.5	45.6	5.0	2.58

Note: Nonviewers reported never watching TV; light viewers watched 1–2 hours daily; medium viewers watched more than 2 and up to 4 hours daily; heavy viewers watched more than 4 hours per day.

simply preferred TV to being outside the house. The boy's behavior was considered unusual but was tolerated by the family (at least during my contact with them).

As with the 1986 interview schedule, in the 1999 and 2009 surveys we asked how many hours a day people watched television. Table 4.1 indicates the changes in patterns of televiewing among the sample population. The peak occurred in the 1999 sample but leveled off by 2009, apparently as the novelty began to end.

Except in a few cases, Gurupá's energy grid did not extend beyond the town limits. Communities in the interior remained without electricity, unless someone had a diesel generator. Consumers' increased buying power and improved technology for signal reception, therefore, did not help most people living in the interior. Daily televiewing hours for this population remained near zero. Nonetheless, I observed people making considerable effort to watch television under challenging circumstances.

One such case occurred in the hamlet of Jocojó, half a day's canoe trip upriver from town (see Map 3.1). Jocojó is a subsistence farming and extraction community, with a population of sixty, many of them descendants of Gurupá's slave population (Jocojó is officially listed as a slave refuge, or quilombo). In the 1980s many Jocojoenses migrated to Monte Dourado and the Jarí tree plantation in search of wage labor. One of these families returned in the late 1990s, bringing a TV set and a satellite dish. Around that time the hamlet made a communal purchase of a diesel generator to provide electricity. At first the combination of the communal generator and the family's TV proved to be a popular mix, providing nightly news and one or two telenovelas. Most of the hamlet's residents crowded into the house to enjoy the luxury. However, problems soon emerged over funding for fuel. The original plan was for community members to rotate fuel purchases, but several families found this arrangement impractical, often not having funds available or wishing to spend what they had on other things. The end result was intermittent fuel purchase, inconsistent electricity generation, and, as a result, sporadic televiewing. But when there was fuel and television, there was excitement and movimento in the hamlet.

Who Gets TV?

During Stage II the increased buying power of the population meant that many more people, especially those in town, acquired television. With inflation significantly reduced, the extraction boom economy in full swing, and the opportunity to migrate to other places for wages, more people from the working class could gather the needed capital for a TV set. As a result about one-half of the homes in town possessed a TV set by 2009 (in our sample, 49.5 percent reporting owning a set).

In the interior that number was significantly lower. In the late 1990s I estimated only 10 percent of homes had television. In part this lower ownership rate was due to a higher percentage of families engaging in subsistence agriculture, which did not generate the higher returns of extraction. In addition, families indebted to merchants and large landowners through debt peonage were not able to accumulate enough capital to purchase a set. But the most common reason for a lack of television was the absence of publicly subsidized electricity. Expensive energy from diesel generators was the principal option, and most could not afford it. Some people ran TVs off of car batteries, but they had to have access to electricity for recharging. This meant they had to have access to a diesel generator or electricity while in town. By the 2000s the number of TV sets rose in the interior. The açaí boom was principally responsible for this shift because it generated significantly more cash income for families. The increased funds were often used to buy televisions, satellite dishes, and diesel generators. As mentioned earlier, the estimated number of homes with TV in the interior rose to approximately 33 percent.

TV ownership in town cut across class lines. The old Stage I patterns of proximity rules reinforcing social hierarchy were gone. Rules for public access to privately owned TV sets were also modified (see below). Merchants still used TV to attract business to their stores and restaurants, although they were rarely able to draw much of an audience (the excep-

Figure 4.3. Public viewing of soccer games. Photograph by A. Pace, 2011.

tion was important soccer matches; see Figure 4.3). Typically it was the clerks, waiters, or cooks who watched television. At least one politician, the former mayor, Cecília, continued to allow public viewing of TV in her home, but there was rarely a crowd. In the interior things were different because limited access to televiewing meant there continued to be many occasions to use proximity rules as a reward for subservience. The ability to view TV still functioned to reinforce social hierarchy.

Signification of TV as a Material Object and Communication Modality

Throughout Stage II television remained a highly prized commodity and communication modality. Most families continued to place their TV sets in front rooms so that they could be viewed from outside. These sets still served as the centerpiece of an eclectic assemblage of status items and decorations. But there were some modifications. Increased buying power among consumers meant that some families now owned more than one TV set. These sets were not on display as status items and were typically placed in the private parts of the house, most frequently the bedroom. In these more secluded quarters few status items surrounded the sets.

Television pictures and sound continued to be markers of movimento,

Table 4.2. Attitudes toward Television

	Positive Attitude (%)	Neutral Attitude (%)	Negative Attitude (%)
1986	66.3	33.3	0.0
1999	92.3	0.0	7.6
2009	99.0	1.0	0.0

but with the increased number of sets in town and electricity twenty-four hours a day, there was no longer the need to announce ownership by blasting the sound just as electricity was turned on. Instead, many people left their TV sets on at moderate volume and without much fanfare. In the 1999 and 2009 interview schedules we asked people to estimate how many hours a day they had their TV sets on. Among our sample 86.4 percent in 1999 and 84.0 percent in 2009 reported leaving their TV sets on for four or more hours a day, with 38.3 percent of the 1999 sample leaving their sets on for ten or more hours a day, which fell to only 5.5 percent in 2009.

By Stage II, I did not observe the pattern of leaving sets on when reception was poor (of course, these episodes were rare with satellite dishes). I continued to observe the pattern of people turning their backs to the screen while watching passersby. I also observed a new pattern for Gurupá: the TV set was left on, with good reception, but no one was watching, and sometimes no one was in the room. This nonviewing pattern occurred most often in the mornings and afternoons, less frequently in the evenings when the news and telenovelas were on. According to consultants, leaving a television on and not watching it provided background noise and companionship (in many cases replacing the role of the radio). Nonetheless, this nonviewing pattern signaled a shift in spectator habits and indicated slippage in the Stage I pattern of total absorption by the medium, regardless of the programming.

Talk about the value of television as a communication modality changed only slightly during Stage II. As indicated in Table 4.2 there was only a negligible rise in negative views in 1999, then a return to zero. Overwhelmingly, people saw television as a good thing for the community. Positive features of television listed by our sample include the following: it educates, informs, provides culture and civilization, offers consumer information on prices of goods, and, in the case of religious programming, affords religious benefits. The few negative comments we were able to collect about television as a communication modality focused on children's exposure to violence.

Viewers also considered television an important force for social and economic development. In 2009 we asked respondents if they considered Gurupá more developed after the arrival of television. More than 90 percent of respondents answered in the affirmative. Among the reported benefits of development that arrived with TV include the following: people are now more educated, there is more incentive for education, there is more information available to people, there are better ways of communicating, there is better technology in town, there is more movimento and more entertainment, people are happier, and there is more religious solidarity.

People still regarded the medium as a valuable asset in the struggle to keep children at home and safe. Despite some concern with violence in TV programming, most families I talked to wanted their children to watch television instead of roaming the streets. This positive attitude toward TV's baby-sitting properties is highlighted by responses to queries concerning who in the family watches the most television. About 86 percent of the 2009 respondents reported that it was their children (household members sixteen years of age or younger).

Displacement of Public Activities

By 1999, well into Stage II, an obvious reversal of television's role in the displacement of public activities in town had occurred. In short, the town's very public nightlife, played out in the streets, the dance halls, and the churches, returned. Except for a few TV sets in bars and restaurants and the occasional flash of color visible through a window where someone left a set on, television's impact on nightly public activities was clearly reduced. Since very few people owned VCRs to record programs and lack of Internet access prohibited viewing missed programs, people were simply not watching as much nighttime programming.

I regularly observed scores of people during the weekday evenings and hundreds during the weekends congregating in the praças, by the dance halls, in front of doorsteps, near the soccer fields, around bars and luncheonettes, and on well-lit street corners. As in the 1980s, young people dressed in their finest attire and went in search of friends, gossip, and flirtation, while older adults chaperoned and visited friends and relatives. Unlike the 1980s, people did not stroll in a loop through the first two streets. The loss of the promenade route was likely due to the town's growth (it had added six streets and more than doubled in population by Stage II) and the dispersal of gathering places across a much wider area. The best places to interact with others remained the streets nearest the river, but walking from one location to another did not result in a loop pattern. Regardless of this detail, the main point was that many people were out socializing, not watching TV.

But not everything had returned to the pre-televiewing days. Big public events like dance contests (quadrilhas), concerts, and community-wide festivals started after the last telenovela ended (around 10:00 p.m.). Yet there were many exceptions. Neighborhood saints' festivals, church auctions, church services (Catholic and Protestant), small-scale religious processions, political meetings, rehearsals for the quadrilhas, and so forth were well attended without interference from televiewing. Night classes at the school continued regardless of nighttime programming. I also noticed that time references were no longer linked to telenovela programming. During research visits from 1999 to 2009 I did not hear anyone tell time by referring to "na hora da telenovela."

In my 2002 field notes I recorded the following nightly street activity and televiewing patterns as I walked through town during a two-week period. Beginning at 5:00 p.m., as the day cooled off, many people were in the streets, buying açaí for supper, playing soccer and volleyball. Some TV sets were on but with a minimal audience. Between 6:00 and 7:00 p.m., at sunset, many people were still in the streets. TV sets were on, with most tuned to Globo's first telenovela but with few people watching. Often the television was on with only a child watching. Sometimes the TV was on and no one was watching. From 7:00 to 7:20 p.m., when regional news was shown on TV, more people watched but not as many as in the 1980s. By 7:30 p.m. the second telenovela was on. There were more people in the houses watching but even more people still in the street paying no attention to the telenovela. At 8:30 the national news was on. This drew many adults off the streets and into the homes to watch. Teens and younger children were still in the streets, playing, talking, and flirting. From 9:00 to 10:00 p.m. Globo's third telenovela was on, attracting the largest audience. The weekday nightlife began to wind down, and there were few people in the streets. On weekends, however, the streets began to fill up by 9:30—before the end of Saturday's telenovela—especially if there was a big dance or festival.

Habits of Spectatorship

As with the changes in television's displacement of public activities, I witnessed prominent changes in the rules governing spectatorship during Stage II. These changes were likely the result of the increased number of TV sets and the long-term, around-the-clock access to television for many Gurupaenses. The novelty and strangeness of the medium was replaced by familiarity, and habits of spectatorship reflected this shift. In town, social class became much less of a determinant of televiewing. Numerous sets, even in the poorest parts of town, ensured ready access to everyone. As a consequence, the need to mix audiences of different social classes to allow widespread access to televiewing evaporated. Spectatorship patterns began to resemble other patterns of social class segregation for public and private events. The poor watched the TV sets of the poor (mostly located in the portions of town farthest from the river or in the swampy area), while the more affluent watched together. I observed only three exceptions. In bars, restaurants, and stores with publicly accessible TV sets there were occasional gatherings of mixed audiences for special events, most often soccer games. In the private homes of the middle class, cooks and nannies sometimes watched TV with their employers in the evenings. Finally, in the interior, where television sets were still limited, I continued to observe the Stage I patterns of class mixing.

Age and gender mixing in private viewing spaces persisted. There was no apparent segregation, although audience composition varied by programming. In terms of age and gender mixing in public spaces, the increased number of TV sets largely negated the need to watch television from the streets. By Stage II gone were the crowds peering into the homes of television owners to catch a glimpse of the nightly programming. Also gone was the gender mixing in the street at night.

Stage II also marked an end to the strict rules of spectatorship governing silence, gaze, and bodily movement. In town I did not observe the same mesmerized audiences, silently engrossed in televiewing, eyes fixated on the screen, bodies nearly frozen in place. Silence, for example, was no longer required for televiewing. Although people did not talk freely throughout a television program, we observed frequent comments made to others about the program content and story line. This was a rare occurrence in Stage I. On occasion I heard people discussing matters unrelated to television content but always so as to not completely obstruct the television audio.

Relaxation of the rules governing gazes meant that people were far more likely to watch one another while televiewing. I both observed and experienced this behavior. When something exciting, controversial, or humorous occurred on the screen, it was common for someone in the audience to turn and look at someone to gauge his or her reaction. While I was unable to discern if the gazes among the Gurupaenses were for reassurance, confirmation of belief, solidarity, or curiosity, I was told that people liked to observe me to see how I reacted, especially during stories about the United States. Often I would receive an analytic gaze, followed by a question as to the veracity of a story. People would also study my face during comedy shows and telenovelas to see if I understood a particular joke.

Bodily movements were also much less restrained in Stage II. Fidgeting in place, changing locations in a room, walking to an open window or door to greet a passerby, and even leaving the room and returning were now common occurrences. Stage II also marked the beginning of people viewing television while engaging in other activities. I observed people paying varying degrees of attention to television while cooking, eating, sweeping, sewing, conducting business (usually sales in the home or store), doing schoolwork, and so forth.

Viewing saturation among TV-owning families was likely responsible for these changes, as televiewing overlapped with the need to complete other activities. The compromise was combining televiewing with other reasonably compatible tasks. In addition, the increase in TV access throughout town meant that private activities in the home around the TV were much less likely to be viewed by a public audience stationed in front of an open door or window. A certain degree of privacy while watching television was now expected. A strong indicator of this change that I observed was the widespread use of hammocks to view television—a behavior absent in Stage I. In Gurupá hammocks serve as both beds and chairs, yet it is considered bad manners to hang them in public view, unless it is nighttime and someone is sleeping in them. Otherwise hammocks are carefully rolled up and tied to a hook or completely removed from the room. During Stage II, I constantly visited homes where someone was lying in a hammock while watching TV, both during the day and at night. Once I was invited in, of course, the hammock was quickly removed and a bench or chair provided for me.

Due to the widespread presence of television in town during Stage II, rules requiring public access to privately owned TV sets waned. Easy access to televiewing in a relative's, friend's, or neighbor's house meant standing in the street and watching a stranger's television was neither necessary nor desirable. I did observe cases of streetside televiewing in 2003 and 2005, but in each case it was a single individual, usually a child. In 1999 we asked respondents if they allowed people to watch from the street. From the sample, 47.4 percent said they did, and 52.6 percent said they did not. We next asked whether the family typically watched television with friends or neighbors. Only 32.2 percent said they did so; 67.8 percent said they did not.

These data, along with our observations, suggest that the rule of public access to privately owned TV sets was being phased out in the town. With this change, the high rates of visitation noted in Stage I declined for TV-owning families. Televiewing was becoming less of a public undertaking and much more of a private event. Yet the private viewing of television did not impede the very public evening and nighttime interactions of town. Even though television was a highly valued communication modality, for many there were other attractions, or demands, that drew them away from televiewing. Exactly what attracted or repelled an audience and what impact this had on worldview, social identity, and behavior are the subjects of the next two chapters.

CHAPTER 5

Heeding Interpellation

Since the 1980s the television viewers of Gurupá have been exposed to a steady stream of messages interpellating them to accept and submit to sets of social identities and worldviews presented in programming. As discussed in Chapter 2, the messages call upon viewers to join in national unity, adopt a pan-Brazilian lifestyle and worldview, and consume products advertised on television. They show viewers the virtues of modernization and progress, warn of the corresponding problems of crime and violence, tell of the possibility of class mobility, depict women as active and as the equal of men as well as sexualized objects, and inform of both the corruption and the valor of politicians. They provide glimpses into other social worlds, tell stories about how to deal with both the mundane and the extraordinary problems of life, and provide bits of narrative to allow viewers to imagine different lives. The questions we want to address are, How do Gurupaenses respond to this deluge of information, and how do all the messages, representations, narratives of the possible, and warnings of the improper alter or reinforce viewers' social identities, worldviews, and behaviors?

In this chapter we focus on how Gurupaenses respond positively to televisual messages (Figures 5.1 and 5.2). We are interested in the process of heeding interpellation, beginning with the most easily identifiable types of changes, namely, those found in observable behavior such as TV-talk, consumption, and display of material items. We also discuss changes that are more difficult to detect, such as those found in shifts in social identities and worldviews. Even when the audience accepts a preferred message or social identity, a certain amount of interpretation, reworking, negotiating, or hybridization to fit preexisting cultural patterns must take place. In addition, parts of messages may be heeded, or heeded

Figure 5.1. Rosi and Meire's family watching television. Photograph by R. Pace, 2011.

Figure 5.2. TV viewing in the Dias household. Photograph by R. Pace, 2011.

sometimes, but also missed, ignored, or resisted. Further complicating matters, the messages broadcast on television may be polysemic; that is, they may have contradictory messages. Despite these difficulties, we have found consistent and identifiable patterns in how people heed television's interpellation.

Perhaps surprisingly, we do not find strong statistical relationships between viewer reception and the demographic factors of social class, age, and gender. Even though Kottak's television reception model predicts well-marked statistical correlations between viewing and other factors in the early phases of television acculturation, in the Gurupá sample social class, age, and gender are not among them. The key to understanding this pattern, we suggest, lies in the relatively homogeneous class structure of the community. From a comparative perspective (which differs somewhat from respondents' self-reported class standings), approximately 95 percent of Gurupá's population falls within the C and D range on the IBOPE social class scale (i.e., working class) and only about 5 percent at the B3 level (i.e., the lowest stratum of the middle class). In addition, the differences between C and B3 households in terms of wealth, income, occupational prestige, education, and consumer purchasing power are incremental, making it difficult to clearly delineate social class hierarchies, which is an observation also supported by local perceptions.

Given the relatively small variation in socioeconomic terms, it is less surprising that our findings show little or no statistically significant relationships between responses and social class standing. Explaining the lack of strong statistical variations in terms of age and gender is more problematic. We suspect the recent and rapid spread of the medium negates strong age-related variations. The variations we find in gendered responses, which exist but are not statistically significant, may indicate that at least in this stage of television exposure perceptions stemming from social class homogeneity are more critical and powerful than gendered perceptions.

TV-Talk

"TV-talk" refers to the manner in which viewers discuss new ideas, concepts, and beliefs presented on television. These discussions are essential to creating meaning and relevance through interpretive discourse (Wilk 2002a; Lull 1988; Katz and Liebes 1984). When viewers do this collectively in their community or region or nationally, they participate in a discourse community. In Gurupá we find that viewers' participation in television discourse communities provides them with novel information to rethink all kinds of social identities, worldviews, and behaviors. It provides them with additional layers of awareness about national tastes and habits, international events, and ideas about race and gender, all of which can change locally held definitions and stereotypes (Straubhaar 2007: 240). TV-talk, therefore, is a fundamental part of change (also see Lopes 2009).

Repeating new terms and phrases introduced in television programming in day-to-day conversation is one of the most noticeable forms of TV-talk we have observed over the years. As television exposure expands, we find corresponding growth in new word, phrase, and cliché usage easily traceable to the medium. If a phrase or term catches on in the community, it is used repeatedly, if not incessantly, in creative discourse, or linguistic play, until its popularity wanes. When we asked our consultants why people choose to use such phrases and terms, we received the following responses: it is something new, exciting, and fun to do; it is what the rest of Brazil is doing, so why not follow along; it shows that the speaker knows what is happening in the world; or it just slips out since so many other people are using it.

By analyzing and classifying these types of responses, we find that TV-talk in Gurupá tends to fall into two categories: identity-talk and awareness-talk. Identity-talk is performed as a way to establish links to the national culture and notions of modernity in real time. It is also used as a way to establish social boundaries—such as between insiders and outsiders. Awareness-talk is discourse used to understand new ideas, issues, or events. It often involves interpretive discourse to place the idea, issue, or event in a localized context. Examples of each follow.

Identity-Talk

By observing this form of TV-talk, we discover that its performance links the speaker to the greater Brazilian culture in real time. It is a marker of identity with much that is considered contemporary and modern by the speaker. This appears to be an important speech act, given the relative isolation of Gurupá, both geographically and culturally, from the rest of Brazil. At the same time, we noted that people in Gurupá are very apt at applying the new vocabulary to situations very different from the original context presented on television. The vocabulary is appropriated into local discourse to show identity with Brazilian culture while at the same time being altered or transformed to fit the local imagination.

One of the first examples of vocabulary diffusion that I recorded was the introduction of the word *cambalacho*, a slang expression meaning "a mess" or "complicated troubles." This term surfaced in 1986 during the running of the telenovela by the same name. While the telenovela was on the air I was accustomed to hearing someone describe a difficult situation as cambalacho several times a day. Before the telenovela I had never heard the word used in Gurupá. When the telenovela ended the word gradually disappeared from usage. By 2010, when we asked people to define the word, only a few were able to do so.

Among the usages of cambalacho I recorded were the following: fights between boyfriends and girlfriends, problems with a trading post patron, paying for and then not receiving goods, providing goods or services and then not receiving compensation, the tangling of fishing nets, and the untidiness of a house. The latter two usages are novel applications, far removed from the story line and usage of the term in the telenovela.

Another example occurred during the 2009 broadcast of the telenovela *Caminho das Índias* (Passage to India), which depicted a highly stereotypical view of life in India. A commonly uttered phrase from the telenovela was *arre baba*, a Hindi exclamation similar to "Hey buddy" and spoken when something is amiss. In the telenovela the phrase was glossed with the Portuguese expressions *meu Deus* (my God) and *nosso Senhora* (Our Lady) and interspersed in dialogue as one would use these phrases in Brazil (Kottak 2009:xxix). The saying caught on in Gurupá, as in much of the rest of Brazil, and was used creatively in countless ways, far beyond its application in the program. We recorded the phrase being used to express surprise, disbelief, pain, satisfaction, excitement, and even pleasure. We overheard children exclaiming "ali baba" (their linguistic version of *arre baba*) during play, but adults were prone to use it frequently as well. When the telenovela ended the term quickly disappeared from local usage. During my visit in 2011, I heard no one use the term.

An example of politico-TV-talk as identity-talk occurred with the introduction of the word *grampo*, literally "staple" but also slang for a criminal sting operation. In early 1990s when President Collor was caught in the corruption scandal that eventually led to his impeachment and resignation from office, the nightly news was replete with references to grampo—as were telenovelas and comedy shows. During this time in Gurupá, I heard the word used repeatedly for a wide array of circumstances, ranging from being caught in marital infidelity to wrangling over credit with merchants. As news coverage of Collor's scandal faded, so did the word's usage in Gurupá. When new sting operations exposing corruption occurred and were reported on the news, the term periodically reemerged in the community's discourse.

Another, slightly different example of lexicon diffusion was the appropriation of names from telenovelas. For example, a local entrepreneur built a portable bar cart to sell mixed drinks wherever a crowd gathered. Across the front of the cart he draped an elaborately hand-painted banner with the name of the popular telenovela airing at the time, *Kubacanan* (2003). He carefully copied the stylized logo that appeared when the show was announced. The proprietor of the cart said he planned to keep the banner for a year or two and then create a new one if a more popular telenovela aired (for similar patterns throughout Brazil of name borrowing for bars, dance halls, and even personal names, see Vink 1988: 227; Lopes 2009: 9).

In each of these cases the utterance or display of the term links the speaker to the telenovela and the nationwide discourse community. Unity and identification with the Brazilian world beyond Gurupá is the great attraction, or, as in the last case, a way to sell products. Most of these diffused terms are not particularly useful over the long term and fade from use after the telenovela ends. This suggests that usage primarily links the speaker to real-time Brazilian identity. Identity-talk is for the moment, and its linguistic value is in its connection to the greater nation-state.

Yet another example of identity-talk that I observed came from the introduction of the Internet in the 1995 telenovela *Explode Coração* (Exploding Heart). At this time in Gurupá there was no access to the Internet. In fact, it was only in 2002 that government offices gained access, in 2005 when the NGO FASE offered free community access but with only two computers and exceedingly slow service, and in 2008 when two Internet cafés opened with four computers each offering pay-by-the-hour service but likewise with very slow and erratic service. By 2010 public access to the Internet ended as the cyber cafés closed due to poor service and dwindling demand. Even before this, Internet usage had been limited. In our 2009 survey we found only 31.7 percent of the sample population had used the Internet, which included 11.9 percent using it only once.

Despite limited access, people eagerly absorbed the basic technology-based vocabulary to talk about the Internet. We found this beginning with the running of *Explode Coração* and the related talk on news and other programs. Key terms that diffused into the community and formed the core of Internet-speak are *pesquisa* (research), as in the context of search, and the cognates *site* for website, *cyber* for cyber café, and *email*. Usage of these terms, we observed, became important markers of identity for individuals desiring to be associated with the world beyond Gurupá. Some of these individuals went to great lengths to set up Internet accounts, even though they could not afford to use the service but once a month or less.

One of our key consultants, Milton, is one such example. Milton is a middle school teacher in his thirties who first observed the Internet depicted on television and then tried it once when a government ship docked for two days at the town's wharf and offered free access. As public access became available, initially through FASE and then the cyber cafés, Milton would wait in long lines to use the service. The Pace family was among his contacts, with whom he would correspond every few weeks. He would laboriously type a few lines (he, like most Gurupaenses, had no typing skills), the content of which was basically the same: "My family is well, how is yours?" Occasionally Milton would report a problem of poor health in his family or mention that an important local celebration was occurring. During my 2009 visit to Gurupá, I asked Milton about all the time and effort he put into using the Internet. He replied that it was worth it because he was keeping in touch with us even though we were far away. He went on to display his mastery of Internet-speak. He said he liked email best because it was cheaper than a telephone. He commented that he did not spend too much time *pesquisando* (searching) because of the expense and bad service. But when he did, he liked to visit "sites" that told of international news and travel. He also reported he preferred FASE (for Internet service) over the "cybers" because it was free.

Another version of identity-talk is discourse to set boundaries. In this category people appropriate phrases and terms from programming and then use them to create codes to classify insiders and outsiders (e.g., people from Gurupá, from Pará, from the South). One example of this type of boundary-talk was the diffusion of the term *gringo*. Before the 1990s I had never heard the term used in Gurupá. Foreigners were typically labeled by nationality, such as American, Italian, French, Dutch, Portuguese, or Japanese. By the 1990s a number of telenovelas and comedy, news, and variety shows had used the term. When I returned to Gurupá in 1999 people referred to me for the first time as a gringo. They also tended to lump all Europeans together as gringos, which is a common practice throughout Brazil (Ribeiro 2000: 310). This same group was also called *americano*: it seems that for many people in Gurupá gringo and americano are the same, regardless of national origin.

Surprisingly, Brazilians of European descent from the South—as well as Brazilians of Asian descent—were also called gringos. One example is the geographer and founder of FASE, Paulo Oliveira, who is from the southern state of São Paulo. Paulo worked in Gurupá from the mid-1980s until 2002. In 2000 he commented to me, "People here keep calling me a gringo. I am Brazilian. I was born in Brazil, and my parents were born in Brazil. I do not have a foreign accent when I speak, but people insist I am a gringo." In this case it is apparent that people in Gurupá have appropriated the term from television and applied it to an "us" versus "them" dichotomy. In this view the gringo is anyone not from the North, especially if she or he has what Gurupaenses consider European or Asian features. Gurupaenses respond to television's interpellation for a national discourse community but rework the message to also signify regional identity.

Another example of boundary-talk is the use of the title of the 1995 telenovela, *Explode Coração*, as the name for one of Gurupá's June Festival quadrilhas. When I asked group members why they chose the telenovela title, they reported that it was a favorite show of the organizers and they liked being identified with the actors and themes of the program. Among the themes of the telenovela are fighting against tradition and exploring the Internet, both of which signify modernity.

Being somewhat puzzled by this choice, since June Festivals are typically associated with tradition and not modernity and certainly not fighting against tradition, I asked if the name was really appropriate. The response from the group was a passionate yes. The team members explained that what they danced in the June Festivals was considered the modern style (*estilo moderno*), with a much faster pace and flashier steps. They explained that the dance routines and costumes were not traditional but creatively incorporated ideas and fashions from all kinds of places.

From our observations of the dances, it is clear that each of Gurupá's four quadrilhas regularly adds eclectic themes, dance steps, and costumes to the traditional dance routines. Particularly for the Mises (literally "Miss," as in "Miss Universe"), the lead female dancer who solos at the beginning of the routine, there is a great deal of flexibility. In most cases the Mises dresses and dances in ways very similar to samba dancers typical of Carnaval. In 2009 we also observed the incorporation of music, dance, and costumes from India into one quadrilha's dance routine—all copied from the popular telenovela *Caminho das Índias*.

These patterns tie the performers into a version of modernity and rebellion against the old and traditional, even though the context of their performance is very much a traditional event. The modern and traditional are intertwined, negotiated, and altered, which in and of itself is a very Brazilian pattern (Ribeiro 2000; Lopes 2009: 5). Boundaries are drawn between the local and national but not in predictable ways. All the while, television programming serves as the principal resource for information.

Figure 5.3. June Festival dancers. Photograph by Pedro Alves, 2010.

Awareness-Talk

We noted a large amount of TV-talk associated with attempts to interpret and integrate new concepts and terms into community discourse. Some of these caught on in local usage and became new points of reference—as in the example of Internet-speak above. Tichi (1991: 36–37) noted similar changes in the United States and likened the newly expanded television lexicon to "a parent language, furnishing the governing terms by which non-TV phenomena can be expressed and grasped." One such concept diffused through television was *trabalho infantil* (child labor), discussed in the 1997 telenovela *A Indomada* (The Untamed) and also touched on in the 1996 telenovela *Explode Coração*. The phrase has also been widely discussed on the news in terms of the government's *bolsa familiar* (family allowance) program designed to pay poor families to keep their children in school. Through this media coverage television viewers are told that an estimated four and a half million children, ages five to fifteen, work in Brazil. Most of the working children are involved in agriculture—although urban labor includes shining shoes, selling newspapers, and hauling garbage—and one of every two girls works for her family on an unpaid basis (Hecht 1998; Salazar and Glasinovich 1998).

Before the telenovela and news coverage, the concept of child labor as a social problem was nonexistent in Gurupá. In fact, according to research conducted by Monte Hendrickson (2006: 45), nearly all adults interviewed in Gurupá acknowledge working hard as children and consider it normal. When she asked if it is appropriate for children to work today (2005), eight years after the telenovela discussed the problem and two years after the bolsa familiar program began, nearly all respondents said that they should not and that they should be in school.

Juma, a thirty-eight-year-old mother of three, who was employed washing clothes and cleaning rooms at a small hotel, commented to Hendrickson:

> My children don't work. I won't allow it. Right now, she [her daughter, age thirteen] needs to go to school and study so that she can do more than wash people's clothes and cook for someone. I tell her there are many things that she can do in life. . . . I want her to have more opportunities than what I have . . . but without it [education] there is only cleaning and cooking and washing clothes. (2006: 48)

These views directly reflect the messages from the telenovela, news, and local government proclamations. It appears the messages made an impact.

However, with greater ethnographic scrutiny, Hendrickson found that definitions of what actually constitutes child labor in Gurupá differ sharply from the government standards. According to Article 227 of the 1988 Brazilian Constitution, child labor is any work, paid or unpaid, that a person under the age of fourteen does for one or more hours per week (Gustafsson-Wright and Pyne 2002). Hendrickson found that in Gurupá people described child labor as occurring only if money is earned and the time spent "working" takes away from school time. For most girls in Gurupá from the age of five onward, she continued,

> life revolves around cooking, cleaning, washing, and caring for children. If the girl happens to earn a wage for her work, then it is called child labor. If the girl works within her home and does not earn a wage, it is called training and responsibility. If a boy sells things in the street or collects things in the rain forest to sell, it is called child labor. However, if the boy is collecting food from the rain forest, especially açaí, then it is considered helping the family. . . . Child labor is defined most often by the Gurupaenses when there is a wage attached to the work. (Hendrickson 2006: 93–94)

Table 5.1. Influence of Television Advertisements

	1999 (%)	2009 (%)
No or not much	39.9	50.5
Yes or a little	60.1	49.5

The introduction of the term *trabalho infintil* and discussion of its meaning had an impact in Gurupá. Following the airing of the telenovela and other media discussions, people in Gurupá talked about child labor and considered it neither good nor healthy. However, people frequently do not accept the media and government definition. They view children working in the home or in food procurement but not being paid and still going to school as acceptable and often essential for a family's well-being. In the example of Juma, even though her thirteen-year-old daughter was in school, she was responsible for maintaining the household (e.g., cleaning, cooking, watching her siblings), which freed her mother to work for a wage (Hendrickson 2006: 87). As in Juma's case and that of most Gurupaenses, people heed the social message but interpret it according to their own social reality.

Consumption

Another easily identifiable category of positive response to interpellation is the consumption of products advertised on television. These products are either presented straightforwardly in advertisements or indirectly in product placements. These advertisements—and television programming in general—attempt to structure the nature of consumerist desire and offer possibilities to satisfy it. In Gurupá, however, the weak purchasing power of consumers limits this influence. Among the more common products advertised on television that we observed Gurupaenses consuming were shampoos, laundry detergent, cheap watches, and canned beer. Only occasionally did someone possess an iPod or a pair of expensive shoes and jeans shown on television.

Table 5.1 lists the response to our question about the influence of television advertisements. Although there is a drop in acknowledgment of influence between 1999 and 2009, about one-half of respondents said that there is at least some influence. Among those acknowledging influence, the effect is seen as positive, such as showing prices or new brand names, which enables consumers to choose products more wisely. No one in our sample expressed any cynicism about the veracity of advertising or concern about its persuasive power. Only one person I met during my years of fieldwork articulated a critique of advertising by pointing out the potential for consumer exploitation through deceptive marketing.

Another way we attempted to ascertain the impact of advertising on consumption was to ask Gurupá merchants if they noticed a correspondence between particular television advertising campaigns and increases in demand for products. Many merchants pointed to what they deem the most obvious example, a spike in demand for name-brand beers during important televised sports programs. The 2002 World Cup is a prime example. During this competition, Brahma Beer, a major sponsor, ran its advertisements repeatedly throughout the event. As a result, according to merchants, bar owners, and restaurant owners, consumption of Brahma Beer increased significantly to the point that additional orders were placed and specially shipped in by riverboat. Several clerks and waiters reported that people (usually men) who typically drank other beers switched to Brahma (at least temporarily) and that others who were accustomed to hard liquor, especially the sugarcane-based *cachaça* and *pinga*, also switched during the advertising barrage.

In addition to the straightforward heeding of the call for product consumption, we also identified a relationship between consumption and national identity. Foster (1999: 250, 270) makes such a connection in his study of Papua New Guinea, noting that consumption of advertised goods is a powerful way to "materialize nationality"—in a sense forming an imagined community of consumption. In the same fashion, Machado-Borges (2003: 203–204) found in a study of televiewers in the Brazilian city of Belo Horizonte that consumption produces "a feeling of belonging, a feeling of collective participation in national rituals and national passions." In Gurupá the Brahma Beer advertisements during the 2002 World Cup created such a scenario, as consumption surged sharply. When I asked my consultants the reason behind the surge, all pointed to the television advertisements, adding that drinking the beer during the competition made them feel more Brazilian. One individual declared, "I drink Brahma because I am a Brazilian. This is Brazil's beer."

Another positive response to television advertisement is the consumption of the sugar substitute Zero-cal. The product is in liquid form and comes in a squeeze bottle. In Gurupá Zero-cal is used primarily to sweeten coffee, particularly the strong cafezinho served in a demitasse, and on occasion to sweeten fruit drinks. A few drops are placed in the coffee or glass of juice, which is then stirred and consumed. I found Zero-cal used in many of the restaurants and in some homes. Ironically, the product is designed for weight reduction, which has not been a problem for most Gurupaenses, who until quite recently often struggled to get enough to eat.

Zero-cal is shown in television advertisements as a convenient, healthy, and classy or chic way to sweeten drinks while dieting (see Machado-Borges 2003: 102). In Gurupá people comment that the product is convenient, in the sense that you do not have to contend with sugar spilling and attracting ants. But to most people, the cost of the product outweighs its convenience value. According to many respondents, the product's most important quality is its association with social class. Having Zero-cal on one's table is a show of status, taste, and refinement. The purported weight loss properties are largely irrelevant and ignored. Machado-Borges (2003: 102) made a similar point: "In a country such as Brazil, where millions of people daily struggle to eat in order to survive, the preoccupation to avoid calories [by consuming Zero-cal] is definitely class specific."

Material Displays

Television provides substance for social identity and worldview formation through the presentation of material objects. When people in Gurupá obtain these objects and display them in public and private spaces, they are engaged in the process of identity construction using elements that extend far beyond the local community. One prominent example, mentioned in Chapter 3, is the decoration of the community for World Cup competitions. During these times, every four years, Gurupaenses hang banners and streamers and paint their streets, sidewalks, light posts, and walls with Brazilian colors and sports slogans—replicating images they see on television as well as in magazines. This is an important sign of national unity as countless other Brazilians decorate their communities in much the same way. The decorations define the community and individuals as Brazilian as they collectively join in the thrill (and agony) of competition.

Christmas decorations are another example of television's influence. In the early 1980s I only occasionally encountered symbols of the season—most of which were international in origin. They included a picture or two of Santa Claus, reindeer, or Christmas trees that residents displayed in homes or in public buildings. But little else was visible, including religious imagery. Historically, Christmas is not an important celebration in

Gurupá. The festival of Saint Benedict overshadows it, dating back to at least the rubber boom period (see Chapter 3). Following the introduction of television, however, with its extensive coverage of Christmas celebrations and traditions from the South of Brazil, as well as internationally, the popularity of Christmas in Gurupá began to grow. When we asked people to rank local celebrations on the interview schedule, 27.9 percent in 1986 and 25.8 percent in 1999 said Christmas was the most important festival. In 2009 the response rate for Christmas rose sharply to 48.5 percent.

Commensurate with this rise in popularity was a growing interest in decorating the home for Christmas. By the 1990s a tremendous increase in the display of international Christmas symbols was evident. There were many images of Santa Claus, reindeer, and even snowmen/women. Christmas trees (small and medium-size artificial ones) and colored, flashing electric lights were also commonplace. In the 1999 survey sample 72.9 percent of respondents reported decorating their homes for Christmas, with 67.2 percent stating they put up some type of Christmas tree. In 2009 respondents displaying decorations rose to 88.1 percent, with Christmas lights replacing the trees as the decoration of choice for 70.3 percent of the sample. When queried, our key consultants report that the idea to use Christmas decorations in the home comes from watching television, particularly the telenovelas that show families using the decorations in real time. The marketing and availability of inexpensive decorations has also contributed to these changes.

Another class of noticeable changes, and positive responses to television's interpellation, are alterations in personal adornment. Clothing and hairstyles in Gurupá frequently reflect the latest trends of popular telenovela stars. People comment that the length of girls' skirts, the types of shoes or watches, or the streaks in boys' hair reflect what is shown on television. As early as the telenovela *Roque Santeiro* (1985–1986) I observed women using ribbons in their hair in the fashion of the telenovela character Porcina (for similar observations, see Machado-Borges 2003: 7). In 2009 the trend of imitating dress and adornments extended to fashions from India. During the airing of *Caminho das Índias* we observed women in Gurupá wearing headscarves imported from India. As noted earlier, we also saw Indian dress and dance styles in the very local but eclectic June Festival competitive dances. Efficient marketing and ready supplies greatly facilitated these trends—all part of a well-established telenovela flow.

People respond to calls for nationalistic pride during sports events through dress as well. Fans don the soccer jerseys of the national, regional, or local teams on game days. For important international competitions, such as the World Cup, people wear hats and hair ribbons and paint their faces with national colors. None of these behaviors are particular to Gurupá. On the contrary; they unite the community with the rest of Brazil (Vink 1988: 227–228). None of the behaviors, however, were common in Gurupá before the spread of television.

Heeding Interpellation for New Social Identities

The acceptance and appropriation of social identities portrayed in programming are essential parts of heeding television's interpellation. Social identities may be defined in a number of ways. They can be ways of thinking about oneself in the context of one's personal background, allowing individuals to answer basic questions such as, "What should I do, how should I act, or who should I be?" (Giddens 1991: 53). Identities may be tied to ideology in that they explain and justify social relations—like one's place in society and access to or limitations on aspirations for socioeconomic mobility—in ways that legitimize the interests of the powerful (Althusser 1971).

Identities may also be discursive constructions, or socially shared and regulated ways of speaking (Barker 1999: 31). As discourse they are signified, given meaning, and shaped through relations to other discursive constructions. This means they are not essential constructs, as they do not consist of a fixed list of traits or attributes. By contrast, they are understood as portrayals of the self in language that are in constant flux (as is all language), always in the process of becoming or being produced—always shifting, proliferating, overlapping, fragmenting, and becoming more hybrid—but never finished. In this view, one can still talk of social identities but only in a context that recognizes shifts, flows, and layers.

Whether identity is a reflexive understanding of self, an ideological positioning of the social self within stratified society, or an ever-changing discursive construct, in today's world much of the material used to construct identities comes from television's representations of reality (Canclini 1995; Barker 1999; Straubhaar 2007; Lopes 2009). Television accomplishes this by offering a bricolage of representations denoting appropriate ranges of behaviors, norms, and attitudes that attempt to define social and cultural roles relating to nationality, class, gender, race/ethnicity, age, sexuality, religion, morality, and so forth. Identities can be spatial—local, regional, national, supranational—or cultural—linguistic, religious, and

Table 5.2. Are Telenovelas Realistic?

	1986 (%)	1999 (%)	2009 (%)
No	53.3	47.7	16.8
Some	23.3	10.5	30.7
Yes	23.3	41.9	52.5

Table 5.3. Are Telenovelas Realistic? (by Gender)

	1986		1999		2009	
	Men (%)	Women (%)	Men (%)	Women (%)	Men (%)	Women (%)
No	75.0	45.5	51.2	44.2	26.8	10.0
Some	0.0	31.8	11.6	9.3	34.1	28.3
Yes	25.0	22.7	37.2	46.5	39.0	61.7

ethnic (Straubhaar 2007: 197–198). Television does not construct identities for the audience but serves as a principal resource offering material to be accepted, transformed, or otherwise worked out in the formation of identity (Hall 1992: 277; Barker 1999: 3, 7, 23; Lopes 2009).

Assessing changes in social identity influenced by television programming is a complicated endeavor. The responses to several questions asked in our survey exemplify this complexity. In order to gauge viewers' ability to identify with messages and personalities in television programming—which we assume play a role in changing or maintaining one's social identity, worldview, and behavior—we asked, Are telenovelas realistic and are TV personages like you? See Tables 5.2 through 5.6 for results.

The responses exhibit a clear pattern of Gurupaeneses finding the program content of telenovelas more realistic and TV personages more like themselves as the community passes from Stage I to Stage II viewing. The greatest changes can be seen in the opinions about telenovelas. Between 1986 and 2009 respondents answering that some or all telenovelas are realistic rose from 46.6 percent to 83.2 percent. Women show the greatest change over this period, with a 39.0 percent increase in reporting telenovelas as realistic—compared to changes in men's positive re-

**Table 5.4. Telenovelas Are Not Realistic
(by Viewing Levels)**

	1986 (%)	1999 (%)	2009 (%)
Light	56.3	12.2	52.9
Medium	37.5	43.9	41.2
Heavy	6.3	43.9	5.9
All	53.3	47.7	16.8

**Table 5.5. Are Television Personages
Like You?**

	1986 (%)	1999 (%)	2009 (%)
No	93.5	90.7	60.4
Yes	4.8	8.2	39.6

Table 5.6. Are Television Personages Like You? (by Gender)

	1986		1999		2009	
	Men (%)	Women (%)	Men (%)	Women (%)	Men (%)	Women (%)
No	90.0	97.6	90.5	93.0	56.1	63.3
Yes	10.0	2.4	9.5	7.0	43.9	36.7

sponse, which increased by only 14.0 percent. The changes for identification with personages are a more modest 34.8 percent. Interestingly, more men identify with television personages in each survey, with the greatest gap in 2009 as 43.9 percent of men and only 36.7 percent of women report identifying with characters.

How can we interpret these findings in terms of the relationship between television representations of social identity and viewers' identity construction? If there is a link between seeing programming as realistic and identity formation, then there is support for the idea that at least for telenovelas Gurupaenses are increasingly trusting the medium as a source of information for identity referencing. Of course, people can use fiction—myths, fantasy, science fiction—to do the same thing, so seeing the source of information as real may be only one factor contributing to identity formation. More problematic is the high number of people who do not identify with television personages (60.4 percent by 2009). If the people observed on TV are not considered similar to viewers, will lifestyle representations and worldviews still influence the audience? Will issues of cultural proximity and cultural capital block identification and adaptation of attitudes and behaviors? Or, on the other hand, might viewers still use the program representations and narratives to add to, or reassess, their lives? Although our research cannot offer a definitive answer to these questions, our evidence suggests a link between program content and social identity and worldview formation in certain instances. The strongest examples come from the formation of nationalistic identity, particularly when juxtaposed to other nationalities, and gender identities.

National Identity

Of the many topics circulating in Gurupá's TV-talk, we found that texts with international foci make the most obvious impact on social identity formation. Viewers are also most likely to accept messages in an uncritical fashion, since most have few alternative sources of information to assess or challenge them (see Lins da Silva 1985). Whether it is Brazil's opposition to the U.S. war in Iraq or outrage at racial slurs directed at the Brazilian national soccer team by Argentines, opinions vary little from the preferred nationalistic position expressed in the media. These televisual messages function well to create feelings of national unity—especially when contrasted with an objectified international "other" whose foreignness accentuates Brazilian "sameness" (for similar observations, see Wilk 2002b: 295 for Belize; Hamilton 2002: 166 for Thailand).

I observed several examples of these processes during the 2005 airing of *América*, a popular telenovela that followed the experience of a Brazilian woman who travels to the United States as an undocumented worker. As part of the story line the actors discussed cultural differences between the United States and Brazil. In one episode, which I watched with a small group of Gurupaenses, the telenovela explored the contrast in public displays of affection. Two Brazilian "cowboys" were in Miami making a purchase in a store. One began to flirt with a female clerk, taking her hand and kissing it. The clerk angrily responded, "Are you sexually harassing me?"

To avoid any conflict, the flirting Brazilian was rushed out of the store by a bilingual companion, who said to the clerk, "He's just Brazilian."

The play on Brazilian "passion" and American "reserve," as well as the meaning of harassment, became the immediate topic of discussion among my informal focus group. I was asked about American strangeness regarding female-male interactions and why Americans seemed so stand-offish and distant. As the discussion continued, my fellow viewers talked of *jeitos brasileiros* (Brazilian ways) and their naturalness and normalcy with gender interactions versus American awkwardness. What surprised me about this exchange was the degree of identification my fellow viewers had with the Brazilian characters and their experiences in a foreign setting. This was especially vexing because the depiction of flirtation in the episode, if played out in Gurupá, would have likewise created an uncomfortable situation since such public displays of affection, particularly with strangers, are atypical. Yet the viewers suspended this localized interpretation and associated with the generic "Brazilian" position.[1] By the end of this gender-interaction discussion, our TV-talk highlighted and accentuated the awareness of foreign, national, and local identities.

In another example from *América*, I observed a germinating awareness of citizenship and nationhood through the discussion of passports and visas. In the story the main character, Sol, is passionate about living in the United States. Unable to enter the country legally, she resorts to crossing the Mexico-U.S. border illegally. As the border crossing events unfolded on television, there was much discussion in Gurupá about the need for legal documents to move between countries. TV-talk centered on passports and visas and the complexities of immigration policies. During this time I was asked repeatedly by Gurupaenses whether I had a passport, how they could obtain one, and how easy it was to cross the border into the United States in real life. Many of these questions came from teenagers who stopped me in the street to ask their questions. In nearly three decades of fieldwork in Gurupá I had never before experienced such assertive behavior from individuals I did not know.

The telenovela created interest in life in the United States but at the same time helped define Brazilian citizenship from a bureaucratic-legalistic perspective. The idea that travel between countries requires documentation that identifies individuals as Brazilian was an interesting new concept. Few people in Gurupá have traveled outside the region, and only four (to my knowledge) had traveled internationally by 2010. People have experience with national identity cards (*carteira de identidade*) required for government benefits, but these cards do not lead to the same type of awareness of nationality that passports do. As people in Gurupá watched the telenovela, the knowledge that these documents exist and that they establish a Brazilian identity while at the same time allowing freedom to visit and explore all other types of national identities was an eye-opening experience.

Many other examples of accepting a "Brazilian view" vis-à-vis international events came from watching the *Jornal Nacional* on Globo. In Gurupá practically all information about current global events was obtained from Globo's news. One series of events that I followed closely when I was in Gurupá were the local viewpoints about the various U.S. wars in the Middle East. I quickly found that opinions on the wars deviated very little from the perspective presented on the news. Gurupaenses, in line with Globo news coverage, were indecisive about the war in Kuwait, initially supportive of the war in Afghanistan but then against it, and always against the war in Iraq. Strengthening the dislike of the war in Iraq, in particular, were graphic depictions of the violence on the news. Bloody and mangled bodies, people screaming in agony, and even children's corpses were common fare on television. In other words, all the scenes censored by U.S. television networks (such as those filmed for Al Jazeera) were televised in Brazil.

When I engaged people in conversation about the wars, many were polite with me personally but clearly condescending about the behavior of the United States. President George W. Bush was roundly and harshly criticized, and many repeatedly asked why the U.S. populace allowed the war to continue. For example, in one exchange with José, a fifty-two-year-old small business owner, just after we watched images of children allegedly shot in a U.S. raid ("collateral damage"), he turned to me and said, "How can the American people stand by and watch this? Aren't you sickened? Doesn't it make your people want to stop it?" I explained that many people in the United States oppose the war, but others see it in a different context, such as making the world better by eliminating a troublesome dictator. José, however, reiterated, "But what about all these dead children? How can your country do that?" I responded that we do not see those images in our media. He was astounded and quipped, "And America is the land of the free?"

Of all the conversations I had about the Iraq war, only on a few occasions did individuals support the United States but always with caveats. Oseas, a fifty-five-year-old former policeman and now owner of an outdoor bar behind the courthouse, is one such example. One evening in 2001 he commented to me, "I agree with the war in Iraq. I think it is justified. But I don't like the way the U.S. is conducting the war. There are far too many innocent people killed. With all that technology, can't you do better?"

Gender Roles

Since the 1980s there have been significant changes in traditional patterns of gendered occupations that set the community of Gurupá apart from neighboring municipalities (Pace 1995). The most apparent changes are the large number of women employed in the political, legal, and medical fields. Over the past three decades women have held the positions of mayor, vice-mayor, council members, judge, prosecutor, doctor, and dentist and are also very active in the Rural Workers' Union and the Fishers' Union.

There are various underlying reasons for this occurrence. They include a national trend wherein greater numbers of women than men are entering the legal and medical professions. Related to this is a regional trend placing women professionals(e.g., judges, prosecutors, doctors, dentists) from Belém in Gurupá because of its relative safety (as compared to municipalities on the Transamazon Highway) and its proximity, which allows them to remain near their families. There are also local trends wherein increasing numbers of women are active in the Rural Workers' Union and the Fishers' Union, including leadership positions, as part of the empowerment campaign of the Catholic Church, which extends to the unions and Workers' Party (Pace 1995). As for women politicians, in some cases their success is due to their political abilities and in others it is due to the support of a spouse or male politician who aids in their election with the goal of manipulating them—referred to as the "puppet syndrome" (Blay 1981; Pace 1995).

At the same time that these changes are taking place, many people in the community continue to express traditional viewpoints on gender roles. They assign male responsibilities to the public realm and female responsibilities to the domestic realm—the so-called machismo-marianismo divide. Folk views and actual behavior, therefore, appear to be very much in flux and frequently at odds.

To assess what impact televiewing might have on these changes, we asked a series of questions on appropriate gender roles. In one series we requested that respondents rate a list of occupations, stating whether the jobs are best suited for men, women, or both (see Table 5.7). We found that over the years responses relating to jobs locally performed remained fairly consistent. For example, jobs considered appropriate for men only,

Table 5.7. Job Appropriateness Ranking for Men and Both Women and Men and Response Change Percentage between 1986 and 2009

Occupation Ranking for "Appropriate for Men" in 2009	Percentage for "Men" Appropriate	Percentage Change 1986–2009	Occupation Ranking for "Appropriate for Both" in 2009	Percentage for "Both" Appropriate	Percentage Change 1986–2009
Mason	69.3	−24.8	Teacher	100.0	+14.7
Heavy machine operator	71.3	−6.6	Doctor	99.0	+6.2
Bookie	51.5	−16.1	Artist	99.0	+35.8
Fisher	50.5	−40.7	Nurse	97.0	+5.8
Farmer	44.6	+3.4	Lawyer	96.0	+17.7
Driver	41.6	−38.7	Mayor	93.1	+39.7
Small business owner	13.9	−28.7	Big business owner	90.1	+54.8
Engineer	12.9	−56.2	Engineer	87.1	+56.2
Big business owner	9.9	−54.8	Small business owner	86.1	+28.7
Mayor	6.9	−38.7	Driver	58.4	+39.3
Lawyer	4.0	−16.3	Farmer	55.4	−3.4
Artist	1.1	−34.3	Fisher	50.5	−43.1
Nurse	0.0	−5.9	Bookie	48.5	+16.1
Doctor	0.0	−2.9	Mason	30.7	+24.8
Teacher	0.0	−4.4	Heavy machine operator	28.7	+6.6

such as masons and operators of heavy machinery, received response rates above 69 percent. Jobs considered appropriate for both sexes (in the local context), such as teachers, doctors, and nurses, remained above 80 percent. Farming also remained steady, with over 40 percent finding it appropriate for men only and over 50 percent finding it appropriate for both.

The biggest changes we recorded were in the perceptions of gender appropriateness of jobs that are not found locally. In each case, our results indicated a shift away from appropriateness for men toward appropriateness for both women and men. Occupations showing this shift are engineering, big business owners, drivers, and artists. Anomalies occur for fishers and small business owners, which are common local jobs but have undergone significant response changes nonetheless.[2] But how might these changes relate to televiewing?

As discussed in Chapter 2, gender roles are prime foci of telenovelas. The shows, however, tend not to promulgate the traditional roles found in the machismo-marianismo complex, especially in depicting middle-class women who work and have careers outside the home (Vink 1988: 175). Many of these female characters are given roles as active as men, are shown to be economically independent, and are often depicted as equal to men in their professions (Vink 1988: 192, 208). They can oppose and resist male social control, although there are usually limitations and caveats to female emancipation inserted into the story lines. For Gurupaenses, watching women in telenovelas run large businesses, work as engineers, drive cars, and be artists makes an impression, unchallenged by local realities for there are no large business owners in town, no engineers or artists, and hardly any cars to drive. Exposure to these possibilities for gender roles appears to correlate with shifting opinions, sometimes very dramatically. In addition, lawyers and doctors portrayed by both female and male actors undoubtedly reinforce the local viewpoint (and practice) that these occupations are appropriate for both sexes.

In a 2010 discussion with Gurupá's first female mayor, Cecília, she explained her views on the impact of television on gender roles for women: "It [television] lit the fire [*ascendeu o fogo*] of what is possible. A girl watching TV and seeing all that the other women can do thinks, why not me? Once they think that way, there is no holding them back."

Of course, not all changes in job appropriateness have links to the media. The category of fisher and its 40.7 percent drop in male-only appropriateness does not correspond to any widespread depiction of women as fishers on television or in any other media available in Gurupá. It does, however, mirror a shift that occurred within the local Fishers' Union. Women have become active as union president and rank-and-file members, in large part due to enfranchisement efforts promoted by the Catholic Church. The rise in the "both male/female appropriateness" response reflects this change.

The changes seen in the categories of mason and heavy machine operator are more complicated. Like fishers, there are no regular depictions of women doing these jobs on television. Likewise, women are not working in these occupations locally. Despite this, around 30 percent of the respondents said the jobs are appropriate for both women and men. To ascertain why, we revisited our data and concluded that people reporting these jobs as appropriate for "both" answered that way for all occupations listed. Also, most are women and self-reported as middle class. In other words, as these individuals responded to our questions, they took the strict "liberal" view that Kottak (2009) referred to and stated that all jobs are interchangeable, regardless of local realities or media depictions.

At the same time that some gender roles for women have expanded to traditionally male jobs in the public sector, there have been limitations and drawbacks. Cecília summed up the difficulties in terms of politics.

> Women have not participated [in politics] as much in Gurupá. I was the first woman mayor, followed by Esmeralda. But there have been no more. There is currently only one *vereadora* [councilwoman]. In the past, most have served one term and then gave up [she named three]. Even in my case it was not easy. I was gone all the time and couldn't do the traditional things at home. My husband, Chico, at first complained about me being gone from the house. But I reminded him that when he asked for my hand in marriage, my father told him I am a person who will always be working and be outside the home. Each time Chico complained, I reminded him of that conversation with my father. Still, after our daughter was born, I was gone so much as mayor that Chico would joke and tell people he was the real mother [smiling].

In another example of women entering the traditional male sphere and experiencing difficulties, Maria, a forty-seven-year-old from the interior community of Gurupá-Mirim made the following comment as my wife, Olga, and I were visiting at her home in 2010. We were looking at Charles Wagley's 1948 pictures of the Saint Benedict procession. She gazed at all the men in the pictures and said to us, "Doesn't that seem wrong? Doesn't that seem unfair that there were no women in the *folia* [procession group]?"

Maria continued, commenting that ten years ago she began questioning why there were no women in the folia.

> A friend of mine and I thought it was time to open up the all-men's group. So we became part of the folia. That was the easy part. When the Saint Benedict festival came up, we found out how much work it was to be in the folia. You have to get up early, around 5:00 in the morning, to accompany the saint, then do all the necessary rituals in the day, get your clothes washed and eat, stay up late at night, then get up early the next day. It was extra hard for a woman since there was no one washing

clothes for you or making food. From the twenty-fifth to the twenty-eighth of December [the main days of the celebration] I really do not sleep. I do the folia and then take care of my family. It must be easier for a man. At least he gets his laundry done and food prepared. I have done the folia since 1999. I plan on continuing, but it is very hard to do.

Cecília's and Maria's narratives emphasize the point that women active in the public sphere in Gurupá still have strong expectations about duties in the domestic sphere. Traditional gender role duties often overwhelm them. Unlike many of the women represented as active and engaged in the public sphere on television, most Gurupaensas are unable to afford domestic help to relieve them of household tasks.

To ascertain the gap between the gender behavior as shown with middle-class women on television and the reality experienced in Gurupá, we asked a series of questions about gendered behavior (see Table 5.8). For the first few questions we asked opinions on social behavior (smoking, frequenting bars, flirting). In each wave of data respondents

Table 5.8. Positive Responses to Gender Role Questions by Year

	1986 Yes (%)	1999 Yes (%)	2009 Yes (%)
Ugly for a woman to smoke?	58.0	81.1	52.5
Ugly for a man to smoke?	10.1	47.4	39.6
Ugly for a woman to frequent a bar?	85.5	73.7	37.6
Ugly for a man to frequent a bar?	—	24.2	20.8
Ugly for a woman to flirt?	75.0	54.7	41.6
Ugly for a man to flirt?	—	27.4	1.0
Woman should work when pregnant?	11.6	9.5	13.9
Is it good for girls to play sports?	—	77.9	74.3
Is it good for boys to play sports?	—	95.8	87.1
Should girls play soccer?	—	64.2	76.2
Should men wash clothes?	42.0	53.7	88.1
Should men cook?	71.0	75.8	83.2
Should men raise children?	—	76.6	72.3
Woman should work if husband earns poorly?	94.2	87.4	92.1
Woman should work if husband earns well?	13.0	25.3	31.7
Should a man stay home and let the wife work if she earns better?	—	71.3	30.7

reported that it is more appropriate for men to engage in these behaviors than women. The largest gap is between the appropriateness of men flirting versus women flirting. At the same time there are major opinion shifts by 2009 toward greater acceptance of women in bars and women flirting. We asked our key consultants what was creating these opinion shifts and if there was any relationship to television programming. All of them acknowledged that there have been many telenovelas showing women of all socioeconomic backgrounds and ages in bars without any mention of inappropriateness or scandal. They also mentioned that women's flirtation is an invariable story line element in telenovelas. Seeing such behavior on television, our consultants reasoned, makes it easier to accept it locally.

Divina, a sixty-two-year-old housewife who has raised all her children in Gurupá, commented on women flirting and changes she has witnessed over the years. She stated that she is not happy with the changes and that she is glad she does not have to raise her daughters now. She continued:

> Before you turn around they are with their boyfriends and pregnant. They are *na mata sem cachorro* [lost in the forest without a dog to guide them]. Everyone says it is normal, though. My *comadre* [co-mother] even said to me the other day, look at all the girls on television who flirt and are fine. She doesn't see a problem with it.

In terms of frequenting bars, others add that the reality in Gurupá has changed in the past three decades. The seedy establishments down by the dock, known for prostitution, now have competition from higher-quality dance halls with bars and even a nightclub (Gurupá's first) in the nicer parts of town. Patronizing these establishments does not carry the stigma for women that bars once did.

The next set of questions deal with involvement in physical activity. On the conservative end, respondents expressed overwhelmingly negative opinions about women working while pregnant. At the same time evaluations of girls' sports participation received fairly high positive responses, even though the responses trail the value attached to boys' participation. Our observations match these survey results. We have observed girls playing volleyball and soccer (especially indoor soccer) on teams in increasing numbers over the years. However, they do not have organized leagues like the boys. In 2010 girls' sports were still largely novelties without structure, but their popularity is growing. When we asked our consultants about depictions of women playing sports on television and the growing acceptance of girls' sports locally, all of them responded it is likely or prob-

**Table 5.9. Positive Response to the Question,
Should a Woman Work and the Man Stay Home
with the Children If She Earns More?**

1999		2009	
Women's Response (%)	Men's Response (%)	Women's Response (%)	Men's Response (%)
76.1	66.6	51.7	0.0

able, and none negated the possibility. No one, however, expressed a view of direct cause and effect; they only reasoned that it is logical.

The last questions probe opinions on household tasks and economics. Significant changes in opinions about men's domestic responsibilities over the years appear to suggest an increased acceptance of domestic gender role equity. For example, the idea that men should wash clothes (which has risen very sharply), cook, and raise children receives high response rates of 70 percent to 80 percent or more by 2009. The idea that women should work outside the home if the husband does not earn a good income remains very high in all three surveys. The last two questions, however, diverge sharply from this pattern. The appropriateness of a woman working outside the home when the man earns well has increased slightly but is still seen as undesirable by over 70 percent of respondents. The view that a man should stay home and raise children to let the woman work if she earns more initially had a high agreement rate but fell precipitously by 2009, especially among men. In both cases in the 2009 data, women provided all positive responses to questions about working outside the home. When we asked our key consultants about this drop, the most frequent response pointed to several well-known cases in town where the woman worked and the man stayed home. The outcome was disastrous, with one of the couples divorcing.

When asked about connections between these shifting attitudes and television programming, our consultants could see no link. Most pointed out that telenovelas do not show men washing clothes, nor is there much emphasis on men cooking (beyond professional chefs) or staying home with the children while the wife works. Our ethnographic data indicate that it is probable that these attitude changes are more closely linked to the enfranchisement and egalitarian messages emanating from the Catholic Church and repeated in the Rural Workers' Union and Workers' Party. They are also "ideal" notions that are not always replicated in actual behavior. In fact, over twenty-seven years of research, I have seen men washing clothes and cooking only when they were traveling in the interior without any women present. Men caring for young children in Gurupá is common, however, especially among grandfathers.

One hypothesis to explain the varying responses between more egalitarian views on domestic gendered tasks and largely nonegalitarian attitudes toward household economics relates to the intransience or permanence of such gender roles. Washing clothes, cooking, and caring for children is understood as ancillary behavior for men, not primary tasks. Staying home so that a wife can earn a better income, however, places the full domestic responsibility on the man, which is viewed as unacceptable by men and many women. In other words, at the most basic level the machismo-marianismo pattern persists, despite the liberal messages to the contrary coming from television and the successes of some women in the public sphere.

Another hypothesis follows Afonso's (2005: 136–140, 239–240) view that telenovelas contain parallel or polysemic messages that promulgate as well as challenge the traditional roles found in the machismo-marianismo pattern. Viewers actually may be heeding the conservative message at times and the liberal message at other times, depending on the circumstances—like the notions of intransience and permanence suggested above.

Worldview

Overlapping and intertwined with changes in social identity are changes in worldview. We define *worldview* as the conceptions or framework of ideas and beliefs of a society or individual used to interpret the workings of the world and one's place in it. In our research data we found three cases in which worldview closely mirrors the viewpoints shown on television. Each is discussed below.

Development

What development is and how to achieve it are much discussed topics in Gurupá. We found that the notions of development are greatly influenced by national and regional media discourses while also interwoven with per-

Table 5.10. Shifts in Definitions of Development

Development Criteria	1986 (%)	1999 (%)	2009 (%)
Industry and jobs	50.9	6.3	2.0
Education	8.8	8.3	—
Infrastructure	11.3	6.3	—
Social development	—	31.3	8.0
Better technology, novelties	1.8	25.0	21.0
Growth	—	—	44.0

Table 5.11. Responses to Question, What Is Gurupá's Biggest Problem?

Problem Area	1986 (%)	1999 (%)	2009 (%)
Jobs/industry	50.0	60.2	39.6
Cost of living	19.2	—	—
Hunger/health	7.6	12.5	7.9
Social problems	7.7	10.1	18.8
Transportation	3.8	—	—
Government administration	3.8	—	8.9
Poverty	—	—	26.8

spectives from the Rural Workers' Union, political parties, NGOs, and the Catholic Church. Over the years we have asked respondents to define development, as well as list what they consider the biggest problems facing Gurupá. As Tables 5.10 and 5.11 indicate, perceptions shift over time.

In the 1986 survey respondents reported that the idea of development centers on improvement in the local economy through the establishment of industry that produces wage-labor jobs. In general, Gurupaenses have undervalued jobs in subsistence agriculture and extraction of forest commodities; these jobs pay poorly, are physically strenuous, and are prone to cause physical injury. They also require a patron-client tie with a local trading post or other merchant for security. Through these ties goods are bought and sold on credit, but a tradition of unequal exchange typically leaves the client in debt. This is the old aviamento system based on debt peonage (see Chapter 3). In 1986 people in Gurupá felt that earning wages and bypassing the trading post would break the aviamento system and improve their standard of living. Further complicating matters was the high inflation rates, up to 3,000 percent per year, that spiraled debts beyond the workers' ability to repay. In fact, cost of living, cited as the biggest local problem by nearly 20 percent of respondents (Table 5.11), is directly related to inflation rates.

By 1999 the component elements and terminology of development have shifted. The notion of social development—strengthening democratic institutions, combating political corruption, reducing social ills, and managing the environment better—has become widespread. Economic development is part of this idea but is not seen as a simple cure-all as previously. Still, the most frequent response to Gurupá's biggest problem continues to be a lack of jobs (see Table 5.11). In the second highest response, people identified the acquisition of technology as the prime marker of development. The types of technology people reported include communications (e.g., more television stations, better telephone service, and Internet access), technology for mapping property, and medical technology, for surgery in particular.

By 2009 the concept of development has been redefined again as "growth" (*cresimento*). This idea now measures development by job creation, infrastructure improvement, and an increase in the size of the town. The second most stated characteristic is the need for entertainment and the hustle-and-bustle of city life (movimento). In terms of biggest problems, poverty nearly equals the lack of jobs as the primary concern.

How do these shifts in development-talk reflect local changes vis-à-vis messages from the media? In the 1986 results those who defined development as the process of wage labor job creation through industrial growth parallel the view that has been promoted through the national media since the 1960s. The framing of development as industrialization, repeated countless times over the decades, undoubtedly shapes the parameters of the local discussion. However, when we asked for specifics, the idea of development is localized. What Gurupá needs to develop are wage labor jobs secured in a sawmill or heart of palm processing plant—both part of the extractive economy and both actual development initiatives taken in neighboring municipalities. Once wage-earning jobs are established, our respondents reasoned, prosperity (primarily in terms of increased consumption) will naturally follow.

The shift by 1999 to "social development" by more than 30 percent of respondents reflects a different set of influences. Locally, Gurupaenses were beginning to establish extractive reserves and sustainable development plans for large parts of the municipality (Pace 2004; FASE 2006). As part of this process, the Catholic Church, the Rural Workers' Union, the Workers' Party, and FASE successfully cultivated discourses on social justice combined with incipient environmental and sustainable development discourses. Preservation of the rain forest through sustainable economic activities became the focus of this view.

At the same time, the new policies created by the Lula government to eradicate hunger and improve education for the poor (e.g., Zero Fome [Zero Hunger] and Bolsa Escolar [School Grants]) were labeled as social development. There was even a new government ministry established, the Ministry of Social Development and Eradication of Hunger, that highlights the term. "Social development" was clearly part of TV-talk. As a result, the notion of social development in Gurupá reflects parts of the national discourse but is strongly localized by events occurring in the municipality. The shift between the national and local discourses also explains the response by 60 percent of those interviewed that the biggest problem for Gurupá continues to be the lack of industry and jobs. This is clearly part of the economic development discourse common in the community for decades and not the main focus of the newly emerging social development discourse.

The second highest response to defining development in 1999 was improvement in technology. This response is closely tied to television's messages. From documentaries to telenovelas, people in Gurupá were shown the value and importance of new technologies ranging from computers to GPS units. Few of these devices were available locally, but they nonetheless became standards by which to judge development. Television is clearly the medium through which they learned of such things.

In 2009 the reframing of development-talk was also tied to television programming. Growth, both economically and socially, is an often-discussed term on the news and telenovelas. It is used to explain Brazil's resilient and expanding economy, even during a global recession, and improvement in the standards of living for millions. There is also the Lula administration's flagship program, the Growth Acceleration Program (Programa de Aceleração do Crescimento [PAC]), a cover term for thousands of infrastructure projects in construction, sanitation, energy, and transportation. Many of these projects are designed to improve the plight of disadvantaged members of Brazilian society. The expansion of Gurupá's airport under way in 2010, for example, is one such application of PAC funds. The term is appropriated by Gurupaenses and used to explain local needs.

Following closely behind the idea of growth is the need for better technology as a marker of development. Unlike in 1999, consumption of technology in Gurupá has increased. People have improved access to computers and the Internet (until the cyber cafés closed), iPods, digital cameras, DVD players, and by late 2009, cell phones. Finally, the idea that poverty is a major problem for Gurupá parallels widespread television discussions of President Lula's programs to alleviate hunger and raise substantial numbers of Brazilians out of abject poverty—both fairly successful endeavors by 2009.

The shifts in definitions of development, from jobs and industry, social development, and technology, to growth and technology reflect changes in national discourses and the reality of local circumstances. As indicated earlier, when the national is localized, changes are necessary. Sometimes, however, the changes lead to inconsistencies and contradictions. A case in point is the Gurupaense perspective on the proposed Belo Monte Dam, planned for construction upstream on the Xingu River. Once completed, the dam will be the third largest hydroelectric dam complex on the planet. It will generate 11,000 megawatts of electricity and increase Brazil's electric power capacity by nearly 20 percent. It will temporarily employ over eighty thousand workers and substantially expand roads, housing, electrical grids, and other associated infrastructure. The dam will also flood an estimated 668 square kilometers of rain forest, disrupt water flow with unforeseen consequences for aquatic and adjacent ecosystems, displace a minimum of twenty thousand people as it also attracts temporary workers, and alter economic livelihoods far beyond the immediate confines of the dam project (Nascimento 2011: 16–18; www.xinguvivo.org .br/2010/10/14/perguntaas-frequentes).

Gurupá falls within the government's designated area of indirect influence from the dam and will experience some of these socioeconomic and environmental impacts, although no one is certain which ones or how severely. People in Gurupá have begun to discuss the evolving viewpoints favoring and opposing the dam—which receive considerable attention in the media. In favor are factions emphasizing the economic benefits of the project, particularly in terms of generating employment and energy for industry in the region. They champion the traditional industrial growth model of development pushed by the Brazilian government since the 1960s. Opposed are a number of groups dedicated to environmental and social justice (including the Catholic Church) that emphasize the regional and global environmental damage that will occur, as well as the massive displacement of indigenous peoples, traditional peasants, and city dwellers.

Table 5.12. Environmental Questions

Question	Positive Response (%)
Deforestation will hurt global climate?	97.0
Deforestation threatens regional development?	71.3
Deforestation threatens Gurupá's development?	69.3
Should the rain forest be conserved to ensure future biodiversity?	99.0
Does the Amazon offer solutions to global problems like overcoming incurable diseases?	90.1
Does the life of traditional agro-extractivists conserve nature?	97.0

People in Gurupá are caught up in the middle of these debates. When we surveyed attitudes toward the dam as the debate was just being initiated (2007–2009), 63.4 percent of the sample said they are in favor. When we asked why, they responded that it will create jobs, boost the economy, and improve standards of living. Curiously, many who responded with a pro-development view also responded to other questions on the survey that could be construed as pro-environment (see Table 5.12). Large majorities of respondents agreed that deforestation will result in environmental and development problems, including an adverse impact on global warming. They also agreed on the value of conserving the rain forest's biodiversity. Ironically, once the dam is constructed, by nearly all estimates it will destroy a large portion of a very diverse segment of rain forest and aquatic ecosystems and release large quantities of methane gas as submerged vegetation decomposes.

When we asked about sources of information on these environmental concerns, beyond their own personal experiences, the respondents reported school, television, and books, as well as the church and Rural Workers' Union. These environmental concerns, of course, are part of a global concern and are widely circulated in the media and academia and among activists. They are also part of the reconceptualization of indigenous and traditional peoples as rain forest stewards or guardians since, according to researchers, their traditional lifestyles maintain or increase biodiversity (Sponsel 1995: 23; Smith and Wishnie 2000: 495–496, 514; Schwartzman, Nepstad, and Moreira 2000: 1371). The question in Table 5.12 about agro-extractivists conserving nature is part of that discourse and appears to have been adopted by Gurupaenses. Despite this seemingly progressive view on environmental issues, when we asked whether the Belo Monte Dam will be bad for Gurupá, only 36.6 percent answered that it would. The reasons this group gave for the dam's harmful effects relate principally to concerns about crime as people immigrate to work at the dam (24.8 percent), with only 13 percent mentioning environmental problems (e.g., destroying the forest, diminishing fish stocks, impacting climate change, causing pollution, and destroying the river).

From our statistical results and ethnographic observations, it appears Gurupaenses are in fact heeding two preferred messages, developmentalist and environmentalist. Both are found in television programming, with additional emphasis on the environment and social justice coming from the church, the union, and NGOs. The two messages are often at odds in the media, as in politics, and therefore when heeding these messages Gurupaenses must negotiate the inherent contradictions. As the national is localized, in terms of the dam's development potential and environmental impact, the contradictions will be dealt with, ignored, and/or rationalized. It will be an interesting process as national ideologies are indigenized while people experience firsthand the socioeconomic and environmental effects of the dam.

Fear of Crime

Gurupaenses express considerable fear of crime, both in faraway places and at home. When we queried individuals about generic examples of crime (i.e., cases not personally experienced), most told detailed stories of violent assaults, beatings, muggings, robberies, and murders they had heard about from acquaintances or from the media. When we asked if they have ever been violently assaulted (*assaltado*), none answered affirmatively. When asked if they have been nonviolently assaulted, for example, by pickpockets or thieves, the numbers rose from 8.7 percent to 18.8 percent over the years. When we asked if they knew someone who was a victim of crime, the numbers were more substantial, rising to over 85 percent by 2009. Nearly all of these crimes are nonviolent as well.

How do these experiences correspond to attitudes and fears about crime? In the 1999 and 2009 surveys we asked if people are afraid of being assaulted (in all its forms) in different places. In all three surveys we asked whether different locations are dangerous and whether respondents are afraid to walk the streets of Gurupá at night (see Tables 5.12–5.18). The responses to these questions are complex, but in general there is a movement in attitudes to see all places (Gurupá, Belém, Rio, and the world)

Table 5.13. Percentage of People Who Have Been Assaulted

1986 (%)	1999 (%)	2009 (%)
8.7	18.5	18.8

Table 5.14. Where Assaulted?

	Gurupá (%)	Belém (%)	Santarém (%)	Breves (%)
1986	—	50.0	50.0	—
1999	50.0	50.0	—	—
2009	52.6	42.1	—	5.3

Table 5.15. Do You Know Someone Who Has Been Assaulted?

1986 (%)	1999 (%)	2009 (%)
21.7	61.4	85.1

Table 5.16. Where Were They Assaulted?

	Gurupá (%)	Belém (%)	Santarém (%)	Breves (%)	Macapá (%)	Santana (%)	Other (%)
1986	15.4	84.6	—	—	—	—	—
1999	26.4	43.4	9.4	5.7	5.7	5.7	3.8
2009	2.8	27.6	—	4.8	20.0	22.8	22.0

**Table 5.17. Are You Afraid of Assault?
(by City)**

	Gurupá (%)	Belém (%)	Rio de Janeiro (%)
1999	31.2	94.6	95.8
2009	22.8	85.1	92.1

Table 5.18. Dangerous Place by Location

	Very Dangerous			More or Less Dangerous			Not at All Dangerous		
	1986 (%)	1999 (%)	2009 (%)	1986 (%)	1999 (%)	2009 (%)	1986 (%)	1999 (%)	2009 (%)
Gurupá	8.7	8.4	2.0	14.5	49.5	80.2	76.8	42.1	17.8
Belém	92.8	46.3	30.7	4.3	49.5	69.3	2.9	4.2	0.0
World	79.1	44.2	20.8	10.4	46.3	79.2	10.4	9.5	0.0

**Table 5.19. Afraid to Walk
Streets at Night in Gurupá**

1986 (%)	1999 (%)	2009 (%)
65.2	36.8	22.8

as "more or less dangerous." Gurupá's danger rating has increased substantially from "not dangerous at all" to "more or less dangerous" over the years. At the same time, fear of walking the streets in Gurupá shows a significant decline and fear of being assaulted in Gurupá declines as well. Belém and the world, on the other hand, have moved from "very dangerous" to "more or less dangerous." Despite this shift, fear of being assaulted in Belém and Rio remain very high.

Table 5.20. Source of Information on Rio de Janeiro and São Paulo

	1986 (%)	1999 (%)	2009 (%)
Television	19.7	88.9	78.0
Radio	56.1	0.0	15.0
Newspaper	6.1	2.5	1.0
Internet	0.0	0.0	4.0

Note: Some answers included a combination of media sources and are not listed here. Therefore responses do not add up to 100 percent.

How can these shifts be explained, and is there a connection to the media? In terms of fear of crime in distant places (e.g., the world, Rio de Janeiro, or São Paulo) where only a very few people in Gurupá have visited, the information on which these anxieties are based came overwhelmingly from television. Respondents verified this connection, reporting that they get their information about events in Rio and São Paulo from television (Table 5.20). Even reports of crime in Belém, a city many in Gurupá have visited, came principally from media. When we asked key consultants about news of crime in Belém, they mentioned television, supplemented by regional newspapers and radio reports.

One only needs to watch Brazilian TV news to understand the reason for the elevated level of fear. On a daily basis Gurupaenses are exposed to crime stories from Belém, Rio de Janeiro, and São Paulo that are replete with detailed and graphic depictions of violence. Wounds from beatings, stabbings, and gunshots are commonly shown, as are corpses. In addition, radio programs such as the *Patrulha da Cidide* (City Patrol) and the crime report sections of regional newspapers from Belém describe explicit, gory details of crimes. The long-term exposure to these images and narratives appears to have created a heightened fear of crime, especially in the distant urban spaces that receive most media attention.

Fear of crime in Gurupá, however, requires a more nuanced explanation. In Gurupá there has been a modest increase in petty crime over the years, while serious crimes (e.g., rape, attempted murder, murder) remain very rare. In our samples about 10 percent of respondents in 1999 and 2009 reported being the victim of petty theft in Gurupá. For individuals reporting knowing someone assaulted, Gurupá accounted for 15.4 percent of the total in 1986, 26.4 percent in 1999, and then a significant drop to 5.8 percent in 2009. In conversations with local police and various judges we learned that the increase in petty crime is not serious and is to be expected as the population increases (from approximately 3,000 in town in the 1980s to nearly 7,000 by 2010). In their view Gurupá is a safe place.

Pedro, a forty-year-old who has worked for FASE, told us a story of the type of thief that is common in Gurupá. By the mid-2000s, as a perk of his work, he owned a laptop computer, which was a rarity in Gurupá. One evening he came home early from a festival and encountered a thief in his house. Pedro related the story to me.

> I opened the door, which was locked, and turned on the light. I heard a noise inside the house. I saw a figure in the kitchen run by. The person hid his face and then climbed up through a hole in the ceiling he had made by removing the roofing tiles. I didn't chase the person because I found it so strange that someone was in the house, and I didn't even think at the moment that someone might be trying to rob us. As I walked around the house I noticed drawers in the bedroom were open and things thrown about. It was only then I realized the person was looking for my laptop. The more I thought about it, I realized it had to be a neighbor or an acquaintance of my children who knew we were out of the house, that I had a laptop, and that you could get in the house through the roof in the kitchen. I am sure this is why he hid his face from me.

If by these standards crime is relatively low and nonviolent in Gurupá, why do people find the community increasingly dangerous? The key we identify is the media, which increases fears beyond lived experiences. In a reversal of other examples whereby the national is indigenized, in the case of crime anxiety it appears that the local is nationalized. The following narrative offers an example of this process. Meire, a middle school teacher in her thirties, told a story about a "shootout" by her house a few years earlier. The exchange of gunfire was the first and only occurrence of this type in Gurupá, and nothing like it has happened since.

> We heard the gunshots in the late afternoon. We were at home at the time. The boys were playing video games, and I was with the baby. We heard the shots and ran outside to see what was going on. Someone yelled it was a bunch of *muleques* [street kids] with guns and they had run

away. We ran back inside and hid. I kept thinking this sounds like Rio. I begin thinking it must be a *quadrilho* [drug gang], like the ones I had seen on television. Later in the evening a neighbor came by and said the police had caught the youths, and no one was hurt. The neighbor laughed, saying there is nowhere to hide in Gurupá and everyone knew who they were. They were bad kids, not from Gurupá, and they will be sent to Belém for punishment.

After that, I try and keep my doors and windows locked and ask my boys not to stray too far from home, but they don't listen. They don't think things are dangerous here, but I have seen too many stories on television, so I know there is danger here. It is not as bad as Rio or Belém, but I am still afraid.

Despite common viewpoints like Meire's, other responses to survey questions point in the opposite direction. The decrease in being afraid to walk the streets at night is one such case. Another can be seen in the set of questions asking people to list the best places to live (see Table 5.22 below). For those who listed Gurupá as the top choice, the common justification was its tranquility—in part meaning a lack of crime and violence.

Why this vacillation? We speculate that while general questions about crime tend to be framed within the national TV discourse, with considerable violence and danger as the main focal points, questions about the best place to live and actual behavior like walking the streets at night call for local views and actual experiences. The framework is local, not national. In other words the responses to our inquiries indicate that most people realize Gurupá is a relatively safe place to live from their own experiences, but when crime is discussed the template for discussion is the national discourse, with its focus on danger and violence.[3] Once again, people heed the national interpellation on crime—but not always—and in unpredictable ways.

Best Place to Live

Viewers' opinions on the best place to live indicate changes in worldview linked to television messages. We queried respondents on two sets of comparisons. In the first we asked them to rate where life is better, Gurupá or Belém, and then explain why. As indicated in Table 5.21, Gurupá is favored by three to one in the 1986 and 1999 surveys and then surges to a 97 percent favorability rating by 2009. This is an interesting reversal from the statements I had gathered previously. In 1983 and again in 1984 my key consultants insisted that Gurupá was in fact the least desirable place to live among all surrounding municipalities. It was considered a *povoada atrasada* (backward community) because of lack of food, jobs, health care, and educational facilities (Pace 1998: 30). When I asked my consultants to list the local communities in terms of the best place to live, Belém topped the list, followed by Santarém, Macapá, Breves, Óbidos, Almeirim, and Porto de Moz. Gurupá always came in last.

What accounts for the increase in Gurupá's valuation as a better place to live and Belém's decline? Two factors are likely behind these opinion shifts. The first involves significant improvements in the local infrastructure and economy between the 1980s and 2000s. Among these are twenty-four-hour electricity, greater access to radio and television, daily boat service to other towns, daily availability of meat and fish, better access to health care, improvements in the educational system, and a boom in the extraction of palm-berry açaí, which raised per capita income (FASE 2006). There was also a fundamental shift in political power with the Workers' Party's rise to power, which has increased levels of local political participation. These changes have generated the feeling that the municipality is rapidly progressing. Gurupá seems to be a good place to live. The second factor is a significant rise in fear of crime in the world beyond Gurupá, as discussed above. When we asked respondents why they overwhelmingly preferred Gurupá, 82.8 percent in 1999 and 75.2 percent in 2009 said it was due to concerns about crime. As discussed above, the fear of crime in Belém among Gurupaenses has ties to media representations that elevate fears beyond any personal experience.

The second set of questions asked respondents in 1999 and 2009 to rank Gurupá, Belém, Rio de Janeiro, and the United States on the basis of quality of life. The results are shown in Table 5.22.

The reason for the extremely negative responses to living in Rio de Janeiro parallels the reasons given for Belém. People have a firm belief that the cities are extremely crime-ridden and violent. This viewpoint is highlighted by Table 5.23, which presents respondents' perceptions of problems in both Rio de Janeiro and São Paulo. As stated above, these impressions are determined primarily by television representations.

The rise of the United States as a preferred place to live, and the corresponding reduction in Gurupá's favorability rating in the 2009 survey, is one of the strongest indicators of the influence of telenovelas on opinion formation that we encountered. The shift in opinion followed the broadcast of the telenovela *América*. Because the messages were transmitted in Portuguese and in culturally relevant terms, Gurupaenses understood for

Table 5.21. Life Is Better:
Gurupá versus Belém

Year	Gurupá (%)	Belém (%)
1986	76.9	21.5
1999	74.5	25.5
2009	97.0	3.0

Table 5.22. Life Is Better, by Location

Year	U.S. (%)	Rio (%)	Belém (%)	Gurupá (%)
1999	20.2	3.2	3.2	73.4
2009	50.5	0.0	1.0	48.5

Table 5.23. Problems in Rio de Janeiro and São Paulo

	1986 (%)	1999 (%)	2009 (%)
Crime related	50.0	88.3	84.0
Pollution	4.5	2.6	—
Auto accidents	13.6	—	—
Cold climate	9.1	—	—
Unemployment/inequality	4.5	3.9	4.0
Everything	13.6	—	8.0

the first time the quality of life that exists in the United States. They witnessed depictions of material affluence and economic opportunity that contrasted sharply with television's depiction of life in Brazil, as well as their own experiences in Gurupá. As for the 48.5 percent of respondents who still prefer Gurupá over all other locales, safety and tranquillity continue to be the critical factors.[4]

There are many more examples of people heeding the call of television's messages and changing their behavior. Suffice it to say that many Gurupaenses respond to what they see on television and try to imitate behavior, consume goods, or adopt depicted social identities as best they can. But there are limitations. Variants of cultural capital, problems with cultural proximity, geographic isolation, lack of access to consumer goods, and poverty block full participation in these forms of Brazilianness as defined by television programming. For some, this creates frustration, sometimes remedied by leaving Gurupá for a larger city where they hope fuller participation in "Brazilian" life is possible. Other people ignore or resist television's messages; still others simply miss the intended messages because they are not applicable to their lives. These cases of missing, ignoring, and resisting interpellation are examined in the next chapter.

CHAPTER 6

Missing, Ignoring, and Resisting Interpellation

As shown in the previous chapter, even the most straightforward heeding of television's messages can leave room for viewer interpretation. In Gurupá we found that people are apt to indigenize the national and, on occasion, nationalize the local as they accept and integrate televisual messages into their lives. Beyond the category of heeding, where the positive correspondence between intended and received message is the highest, we identified three other categories in which television messages regularly miss their mark. In these cases the messages may go unnoticed, awry, or backfire as people miss, ignore, or resist them. Here we focus on how intended program messages and the ensuing interpretations fail to match. We do not find statistically significant variations in terms of social class, age, and gender. As in Chapter 5 we speculate this is due to a relatively homogeneous class structure, the recent arrival and rapid spread of the medium, and the primacy of class views over gender variations.

Missing Interpellation

Missing interpellation means that viewers lack the necessary background and familiarity with program content—or cultural capital and cultural proximity—to recognize and understand what writers and producers may wish to communicate. In short, messages go unnoticed. Through direct observation and informal interviews in Gurupá, we identified three basic types of programming in which this is most likely to happen: merchandising or product placements as a form of advertising; social merchandising in which social messages designed to educate the masses are woven into the story lines; and intertextual references in the form of stories, people, or events discussed in other media and then referred to on television. A discussion of each follows.

Merchandising and Product Placement

Merchandising and product placement are forms of advertising that incorporate consumer items or services into a program, thereby increasing their visibility and marketability (La Pastina 2001: 541; Vink 1988: 236). On Brazilian television this practice dates to the late 1960s (Herold 1988; Straubhaar 1991). According to La Pastina (2001: 541), "These insertions are not intended to break away from the narrative but to be an integral part of the text, attempting to create an organic relationship between the advertised product and the narrative, encouraging viewers to 'read' the product as a quality of the characters using and approving it."

In Gurupá I observed scores of such cases while watching television with consultants and acquaintances. To ascertain whether my fellow viewers noticed the merchandising, I asked during the broadcast or shortly thereafter if they had noticed the product placements and if they were familiar with the product. In some instances the viewers were aware of the advertisement and readily commented on the quality or price of the item. Shampoos, soft drinks, beer, and iPods are a few examples I recorded. Some even reported changing their normal consumption habits in order to use the product. In these cases viewers heeded the message and altered behavior. In many other cases, however, viewers missed the merchandising, typically those targeted at wealthier audiences—in other words, things and services that are unaffordable, cannot be easily found locally, or are not of much use in people's day-to-day lives. A few examples are dietary supplements, weight loss pills, plastic surgery, pet foods, expensive cars, expensive clothing, banks, computer technology, and tutoring services.

I recorded one example of missing product placement during a telenovela I watched with Socorro, the nineteen-year-old store clerk, and her family. During the show a couple engaged in conversation began walking down a city street. They paused under a bank sign and then continued down the street, never stopping the conversation. The camera, however, left the couple and focused on the bank sign for a few seconds, after which it caught up with the pair as they continued down the street. When I asked about this scene, Luis, Socorro's father, protested that this bank had operated in Gurupá a few years ago but closed and moved away. He grumbled that when the economy became slow in the area the bank just left. He felt it did not do anyone any good. When I mentioned that the focus on the sign was a product placement designed to get viewers to use the bank's services, he scoffed and commented, "Don't you think that is worthless? There are no banks here now, so why bother."

On another occasion I watched a telenovela in an interior hamlet with about twenty residents of all ages. The communal diesel generator was turned on just for the show, and the crowd gathered in front of the community's only functioning TV set. Near the end of the episode a laptop computer became the focus of a product placement. The characters talked about the ease of its use, its lightness and portability, all the while clearly showing the brand name to the camera. After the show I asked viewers what they thought of the laptop, and they responded with words like *legal* and *barcana*, slang that can be glossed as "cool." When I mentioned that the computer was shown as a product placement advertisement as a way to entice viewers to buy it, the group responded with amusement. One youth chuckled, "*Égua* [Golly], I would have to win the lottery to buy one." A middle-aged woman turned to advise me, "Things like that on television are for the rich who live in the cities, not for us poor people here in Gurupá."

Puzzlement and amusement are the typical responses I received when questioning viewers about missed product placements. In most cases the viewers saw the products and services as part of the story line and not as commodities to be consumed. For these viewers product placements are props demonstrating the prosperity and glamour of the urban privileged class and symbols of progress and modernity. The viewers simply do not recognize them as items or services that they might consume. La Pastina (1999: 30, 192) comments on this same phenomenon in Macambira, pointing out that viewers need to have a basic awareness of capitalist culture and exposure to the items or services in order to read and understand product placements. Most people in La Pastina's study, like the people in Gurupá, simply see product placements as integral parts of the telenovela narrative, or they do not see them at all (192).

La Pastina (194) also reports that although viewers in Macambira frequently missed the product placements, they did pick up on the wealth disparities demonstrated by their consumption. Viewers reacted to the indicators of wealth and modernity with a deepening sense of their marginalized existence, compared to the Brazil seen on television (for similar observations in Egypt, see Abu-Lughod 2005). This experience, La Pastina maintains, creates sentiments of injustice and inequality, as viewers do not have access to the goods and lifestyles demonstrated on television. By contrast, the Gurupaenses I talked to did not openly express these feelings of injustice or inequality while discussing products shown on television. Instead, they expressed excitement and wonder and perceived these items as important markers of development. They are seen as desirable, although not within people's reach to consume, at least not yet.

To pursue the topic of wealth disparities and merchandising further, we asked why telenovela characters have so much wealth while people in Gurupá do not. In the 1999 survey among those who responded to the question, 6.4 percent were unsure, 45.2 percent felt the programs were unrealistic, and 48.4 percent said the characters depicted had good-paying jobs or lived in rich places—meaning they understood the demographic misrepresentation of the show that favors wealth over poverty. In the 2009 survey only 1 percent were unsure, while 26.7 percent said the telenovelas were unrealistic, 42.7 percent cited demographic misrepresentations, and 29.7 percent responded they were just different realities (an answer that overlaps the previous two). During the surveys and during informal interviews with consultants, we recorded no articulation of marginalization or social injustice as La Pastina did. Why the difference?

Abu-Lughod (2002: 377) proposes one possible answer. In her research in Egypt she notes that the ways in which viewers are positioned within modernity are at such odds with the visions that urban middle-class professionals promote through television that selective readings become a necessity. She suggests that television creates its own separate world that is only a part of the daily lives of the villagers. She maintains that what viewers witness through programming can only supplement but never supplant the world that already exists. Nor is television simply a fantasy escape; it is a separate sphere of existence (Abu-Lughod 2002: 387).

Similarly in Gurupá the gap between the world of the telenovela, for example, and that of Gurupá is so vast that a logical connection between the two may be impractical. In this sense television becomes a separate existence, very entertaining but otherwise not very connected to day-to-day life. When viewers are confronted by material wealth and complex technology on television, they are understood as things from a different time and place—foreign to their life but maybe possible to have in their future.

There may be other forces at work in Gurupá that mitigate against feelings of marginalization and social injustice. The most important of these are the significant improvements in lifestyle experienced by most Gurupaenses over the past decade (see Chapter 5). By Brazilian standards Gurupá is still a poor place, but relative to its previous conditions the community has experienced tremendous improvements. This is also reflected in the people's basic optimism about the future. Feelings of inequality and injustice, generated by observing the affluent lifestyles and advertisements on television, are blunted by these changes, at least for the time being.

Social Merchandising

Social merchandising is a practice common in Brazilian telenovelas, dating to the early 1970s, in which contemporary social and political issues are written into story lines (Fernandes 1994). According to La Pastina (1999: 12, 34), social merchandising reconfigures traditional melodramatic narratives into deliberations on current concerns arising from the Brazilian elite's political agenda. The process is based on the model of product placement, but instead of selling consumables the idea is to "sell progressive views" through entertainment-education programming about current and often controversial subjects (La Pastina 2004; Almeida 2003; Prado 1987). The messages may even overlap with reality, as when real-life people appear in telenovelas, playing themselves (La Pastina 2004: 311).

The topics examined over the past two decades in telenovelas include abortion, racism, homosexuality, adultery, gender roles, religion, smoking, drug abuse, mental health, street children, missing children, child labor, illegal immigration, elder abuse, HIV/AIDS, breast cancer, street crime, leukemia, political corruption, land rights, and the Internet (La Pastina, Patel, and Schiavo 2004). We found that television viewers in Gurupá pick up and understand some of these social messages, although they are typically localized (see Chapter 5's discussion about child labor). However, viewers overlook many other messages. Paralleling missed product placement, the missed social merchandising is simply not grasped, or at best is seen as tangential to the story line, with very little meaning to the viewer. The main reason for missing the messages is a lack of cultural capital or too little cultural proximity to understand and thereby enjoy the program. For some the link to local reality in Gurupá is so incongruous that the social messages might as well be beamed from another planet. Viewers in these cases are often inattentive to the story line, or they may give up watching the program entirely.

From participant-observation during televiewing and through informal interviews, we found that telenovelas filmed in the south of Brazil that deal with the dramas of urban middle- and upper-class families of European descent are among the most difficult for Gurupaenses to understand and enjoy, and the most likely to result in an inattentive audience. This pattern only worsened in the 2000s as Stage II viewing habits evolved to include multitasking during programs and televiewing fatigue and saturation. As a result, uninteresting or boring shows from the local perspective, or slow-paced scenes of otherwise entertaining shows, receive scant or intermittent attention. When social merchandising falls within one of these categories, the basic message eludes the inattentive viewer.

I observed one such case during the 2003 airing of the telenovela *Mulheres apaixonadas* (Passionate Women). Social merchandising written into the programming included critiques of domestic violence, female alcoholism, prostitution, violence in the streets, elder abuse, and lack of attention to organ donation and breast cancer. For most Gurupaenses, however, these messages were ineffectual because very few followed the program. The telenovela was unpopular with those who were unable to identify with it. Among the negative comments I collected during its broadcast were the following: "It is weak and I don't like it"; "It's boring, no action"; "I don't need to see another novela about rich people's problems"; "No one acts the way people on the novela act, it is too unreal."

I also recorded levels of unpopularity through several weeks of walk-throughs in the town to see who was watching television (see Chapter 3). At six o'clock, during the first Globo telenovela, very few people were watching television. Many were out in the streets enjoying the end of the day's heat, talking and visiting, or in the back of the house performing chores. By contrast, the seven o'clock telenovela, *Kubacana*—set in pre-revolution Cuba with many rural scenes—was fairly well watched. This level of viewership continued through the national news. When *Mulheres apaixonadas* came on around 9:00, however, most TV sets were turned off, or left on with no one watching, and people busied themselves with other activities.

When I tried to engage people in discussions about the social merchandising in *Mulheres apaixonadas*, very few understood the references, or they responded in ways that gave no acknowledgment to the telenovela. For example, when I asked whether a national system for donating organs was a good idea, which was a suggestion presented in the show, I was met with puzzled looks. More than one person responded that the idea sounded like organ theft. One teenage girl told me, "You mean that people sign a piece of paper so that other people can steal their body parts and send them overseas? I think that is criminal." I also tried to engage people in conversations about elder abuse, also covered in the telenovela. However, I could find no one among my consultants who thought abuse of one's older relatives was likely. Milton, my research assistant, responded to my question about elder abuse by saying, "Who would not take care of their grandparents or parents? Who would not feed them, get them medical help, or visit them every day? Who would ever hit an elder? This is not possible."

In other cases of missing social merchandising, the principal problem is focusing on unintended messages. One example I recorded occurred during the telenovela *América* (2007). The show was designed to demonstrate the dangers for Brazilians illegally migrating to the United States in order to curtail the practice. Before the telenovela few people in Gurupá had ever contemplated leaving the country for work (the local migration patterns are regional, with very rare examples of individuals venturing to the south of Brazil), so for most the message was unclear and largely irrelevant. For others, however, the show piqued interest in the United States by showing the quality of life there. It also explained different ways to get there, legally and illegally. As mentioned in Chapter 5, during the running of the telenovela I was approached by Gurupanese youth asking how I traveled back and forth to the United States, how much it cost, how they could get a passport, and if I knew how they could sneak across the border from Mexico and find a job. This interest was not unique to Gurupá. It was a scenario repeated throughout Brazil, which corresponded to a spike in Brazilians entering the United States, and staying, without legal documentation.

Intertextuality, or the practice of using one text implicitly or explicitly to refer to another, when used in the context of television refers to one program cross-referencing another program's plot, characters, settings, and so forth. The concept can be expanded to include references to other media or other sources of information (e.g., news, films, music, books, Internet, folktales, gossip), although this might best be labeled extratextuality (White 1992). Ott and Walter (2000) distinguish two broad types of intertextuality: slippage in meaning between the text and reception by an active audience, or polysemic readings; and purposefully placed references in programming to attract audiences. In each case viewers' cultural capital greatly influences their ability to comprehend extra- or intertextuality, or in the cases presented below, to simply miss it.

I observed viewers missing intertextual messages as a form of slippage on many occasions. Missing merchandising and social merchandising fit the description to a certain extent. In a narrower context I encountered degrees of uncertainty and misclassification for certain objects not characteristic of the local setting. One repeated example is snow. While watching programming depicting snow in northern climates, I have been struck by the number of people commenting they have seen snow in Gurupá. When I press for more information, people tell me it often occurs early in the morning, on the water, on land, and in the treetops. I have tried to distinguish snow (*neve*) from mist and fog (*névoa, nevoeiro*) in these conversations. I mentioned that snow is similar to the ice that accumulates in a freezer. During the cold season where I live, I explained, it falls all over the place. Despite my detailed explanation, Gurupaenses generally think of snow in terms of that with which they are familiar—fog and mist.

Another case of slippage occurred as I watched the movie *Shrek* (2001) with several other adults one afternoon. The animated film was dubbed into Portuguese. During one of the advertising breaks I asked what manner of creature Shrek was. My fellow viewers puzzled over this for a while, then came up with a collective answer: "He is a frog [*rã*]." When I tried to explain that in fact he is supposed to be an ogre (*ogro*), I was met with blank stares. Not satisfied, I pulled out my Portuguese-English dictionary and read off the various translations for ogre: *bicho-papão* (bogeyman), *monstro* (monster), and *gigante que come gente* (giant who eats people). None suited the group, since Shrek was not particularly scary or eating people. They continued to call him a frog.

Upon further reflection, the classification makes sense. None of these people were versed in European fairy-tale creatures, but they were well aware of stories and legends about rain forest fauna. The frog is the closest fit to the cartoon character. However, by classifying Shrek as a frog, the intertextuality written into the story and plot is lost. The same is true, of course, for most of the other fairy-tale characters (from the gingerbread man to Robin Hood) that have no referent in the local culture.

Other examples of missed intertextuality I observed, also in cartoons, were episodes of *The Simpsons*. The show, likewise dubbed into Portuguese, is of interest to adults and children. As I watched with my consultants, I tried to pay attention to what creates laughter. Clearly the oddly drawn characters get attention. Slapstick and self-deprecating humor elicited chuckles as well. What is repeatedly missed is the humor created by parodic allusion—meaning the inclusion of a caricature or spoof of another text in a story line that "seeks to amuse through juxtaposition—a goal that is enhanced by the reader's recognition of the parodic gesture" (Ott and Walter 2000: 436). It is common practice in *The Simpsons* to incorporate popular cultural references as well as to parody other television programs, movies, and the U.S. and world news (Ortved 2009: 7). References to a Hitchcock film, the appearance of Michael Jackson, the mocking of General George Patton, kidnappings for ransom in Rio, and thousands of other examples of intertextuality and extratextuality are part of the appeal of the series in the United States. Nearly all of this, however, is missed in Gurupá. *The Simpsons*, in Gurupá, is just a quirky cartoon that receives limited attention and even less TV-talk.

Since *Shrek* and *The Simpsons* are culturally exotic texts to viewers in Gurupá, it is not surprising that people have problems identifying their extra- and intertextual references. The same problem, however, also occurs with Brazilian productions, although to a lesser extent. In many telenovelas, extra- and intertextual references are made that tie the show to real-time events and public figures. In fact, sometimes the lines between fact and fiction are blurred. La Pastina (2004: 303) gives examples from the telenovela *O Rei do Gado* (1996–1997) in which news headlines were written into the plot. The show highlighted the topics of violence against peasants and the landless movement's tactics to legally claim unused land. As part of its social merchandising campaign, characters in the telenovela protested vehemently for land reform and political reform. The blurring of fact and fiction occurred as two real-life senators from the Workers' Party played themselves in an episode depicting the funeral of a fictitious Senator Caixas who was assassinated by agents of large landowners while trying to mediate land conflicts. In the episode the real-life senators talked to reporters and eulogized the fictitious senator and his struggle for land reform (313). In this way the news became the telenovela as the telenovela also became news—a process La Pastina labels extratextual self-reflexivity (304).

When I queried people in Gurupá about the mock funeral in the telenovela, and the role that the real-life senators played, no one made the connection. Every person with whom I discussed the telenovela completely missed the extratextual self-reflexivity. La Pastina reports the same scenario in his study. He attributes missing extratextuality to viewers' lack of knowledge about current affairs: "[The viewers] needed access to objectified forms of cultural capital such as news, magazines, newspapers, and exposure to a broad range of television programs, as well as experience outside the local community. These objectified forms of cultural capital are central for the building of embodied cultural capital that can conversely be used to decode cultural texts" (322). But in Macambira, as in Gurupá, most people do not have access to the requisite media to understand the extratextual self-reflexive messages. Therefore, the messages are missed.

Although viewers miss extratextual messages, they often incorporate the meanings of the story into their daily lives. For example, La Pastina finds that viewers in Macambira were able to apply the notion of the honest Senator Caixas to local politics. Many used him as a model to assess local politicians and their flaws (La Pastina 2004: 318–319). I also found similar cases in Gurupá of people taking stories from the media and applying them locally, though they had missed the extratextual meanings. One example occurred after the contested 2000 U.S. presidential election between George W. Bush and Al Gore. Brazilian news ran numerous stories about the electoral college system, the complexities of vote recounting, and the legal challenges. When I arrived in Gurupá the following June, I was asked repeatedly how the electoral college system worked and why a powerful democracy like the United States did not have a simple one-person, one-vote system. I spent hours explaining the system to the best of my ability but never once was able to convey its logic. The people I talked to were sure there were shenanigans and corruption behind the process. Viewers in Gurupá simply missed the logic of the system and the rationale for the events that followed. Despite the confusion, people did take the story and use it to reference local events. Bena, a hotel owner in his seventies, lamented the defeat of Gurupá's former mayor, Cecília, in the last election. The vote was close. Bena referred to Gore's decision to stop the recount process in the United States, saying Cecília could have pressed for a recount, but like Gore she had had enough and ended the dispute gracefully.

Ignoring Interpellation

During our research we recorded a number of cases in which viewers noticed the messages included in programming but ignored them (Figure 6.1). These viewers interpreted the messages as uninteresting, irrelevant, secondary, unintelligible, nonserious, or plainly false and then disregarded them. No attempt was made to contest the messages or articulate alternative narratives. When viewers ignore the messages, the potential for influencing viewer perceptions, worldviews, or behavior is greatly diminished. Among the types of ignored messages we observed most frequently were ones showing or promoting viewpoints, customs, tastes, and celebrations designed to promote national identity. As discussed earlier, much of what constitutes national identity on Brazilian television is the idealized middle- and upper-class culture of southeastern Brazil.

Figure 6.1. Television nonviewing in the Dias home. Photograph by R. Pace, 2010.

Customs

One example of ignoring program content we observed is the custom of kissing cheeks when greeting and leaving. In much of Brazil this is a common practice among friends and families and is often extended to acquaintances as well. It occurs between women and men—and among women—of all ages. To give a kiss in greeting or leaving (*dar um beijo*), two people touch cheek to cheek (ideally physical touching of faces but sometimes only an approximation and usually without embracing bodies) and kiss (sometimes one kisses the cheek while the other receives; sometimes no one is actually kissed but the lips make the sound of a kiss). A kiss on one cheek, followed by a second kiss on the opposite cheek, is common. Three cheek kisses indicates greater affection. All types of programs show the "kiss-kiss" in all kinds of contexts on Brazilian television. Viewers are exposed to the practice frequently and repeatedly. Arguably, it marks Brazilian national identity, or at least the urban middle- and upper-class identity depicted most frequently on television.

Despite the ubiquity of the "kiss-kiss" on television and throughout much of Brazil, the practice is not regularly performed in Gurupá. Hugs (from full embraces all the way to grasping arms and patting on the back) are common, as are handshakes and giving blessings (parents or godparents bless those younger when departing—or at 6:00 p.m. when the church bells ring—by making the sign of the cross over the recipient, raising a hand with the palm forward toward the recipient, or touching the recipient's hand while repeating, "God bless you"). I asked consultants about the apparent lack of cheek-kissing in Gurupá. All agreed that the standard Brazilian custom enacted constantly on television is not practiced by most Gurupaenses. When asked why, they said it is not the local custom (*jeito daqui*). When asked what it means to observe people greeting and leaving with cheek-kissing on television while not doing it personally, most shrugged and said it means nothing. Milton, my assistant, summed up the sentiment: "Look, Ricardo, there are lots of things people do on television that we don't do. We don't drive big cars, we don't do jobs like they do, and we don't kiss like them. It doesn't mean much, they are the way they are, we are the way we are."

Straubhaar (2007: 235) comments on this type of response, citing La Pastina's work in Macambira. Viewers interviewed in rural Brazil understood the gap in norms and behaviors between small town and city, as well as between different regions. These viewers saw television "reality" as remote and uncharacteristic of their own lived experiences. In the case of Macambira, this created a feeling of marginality on the part of some viewers (La Pastina 1999: 194–195). In Gurupá, as indicated in the quote above (and in the above discussion of consumption), it is more likely to be seen as simply different.

Tastes

Another example of ignoring television's messages is in consumption of national dishes featured in programming. For Gurupá, *feijoada* is one such meal. Considered the national dish of Brazil (Peterson and Peterson 1995: 30, 84), feijoada is a highly prized stew of black beans and a variety of smoked and sun-dried meats, with pork one of the most favored. The meal originated as a slave dish on the sugar plantations of Bahia and, as such, includes all the less desirable parts of the pig (parts discarded by the masters, like ears, tails, and feet). The meal takes hours to prepare and is typically eaten on Saturdays with friends and family. Its consumption is strongly linked to Brazilian national identity.

In Gurupá, however, feijoada is a rarity. In three decades of research I have never seen it eaten. I asked my consultants why the meal is not common. Most shrugged and had no answer. A few who articulated answers mentioned that "it is too heavy to eat in the heat of the day," "there is no tradition of eating it here," and "we prefer our *tacaca*" (a regionally cherished soup of dried shrimp and tapioca and seasoned with tucupí sauce derived from manioc [Peterson and Peterson 1995: 14]). As with the kiss-kiss, feijoada is not part of the local tradition and its presence on television, regardless of whether it is an indicator of national identity, is simply disregarded by viewers.

Musical preference is another case of ignoring national cultural tastes. Brazilian television showcases many forms of music, but Brazilian pop (*música popular brasileira* [MPB]) and international pop receive by far the most airtime. The telenovelas incorporate the latest pop hits into story lines with particular songs used with particular characters as their theme songs. From the telenovela flow, the songs are played on radio and released as CD collections under the logo of the telenovela (La Pastina 1999: 182–184). They are widely consumed and the songs played repetitively throughout much of Brazil, sometimes for years. Despite the promotional blitz that surrounds the television music, almost none of it is played in Gurupá. I have rarely heard MPB and international pop played on the three local radio stations, never heard it played on the town's public address system, infrequently heard it played in the dance halls, and never heard it played at concerts. And, walking down the streets and listening to the sounds coming from houses, I have seldom heard the music.

What is ubiquitous in Gurupá, in contrast, are *brega* and *carimbo*, both fast-paced music with accordions and electric guitars that are found throughout the North and Northeast of Brazil. These genres are known for their rural roots and are frequently interpreted as cheesy, tacky, or hickish by their detractors. A more recent version is *techno-brega* and *melodia*, even faster-paced, dance-oriented styles that rely on synthesizers. In Gurupá nearly all live shows in dance halls are techno-brega or melodia since a performer can dispense with a band and rely on a keyboard or two for accompaniment. Over all, regional preferences in music are clearly dominant and national preferences are secondary or ignored. Even though Gurupaenses are inundated by MPB and international pop music on television, they in large part ignore them.

Saints and Celebrations

Yet another case of missing calls for national identity occurred during the 2001 broadcast of the telenovela *A padroeira* (The Patroness). Part

Figure 6.2. Saint Benedict procession. Photograph by R. Pace, 2011.

of the story line retold the history of Nossa Senhora de Aparecida (Our Lady of Apparition), Brazil's patron saint, whose image was discovered by three fishermen in the Paraíba do Sul River in São Paulo in 1717. The telenovela recounted miracles attributed to the Virgin and the beginning of the Aparecida cult in Brazil. When I asked my consultants about the show, all were familiar with the story and recognized the Virgin as Brazil's patron saint. When I next asked if Our Lady of Aparecida is more important than Gurupá's Saint Benedict—since she is the national patron saint—the answer was unanimously "No" (Figure 6.2).

For example, Milton told me, "She is more important in São Paulo [where the statue was found and where the basilica is located]. Here it is still Saint Benedict." Chico, Cecília's husband, said, "People in Gurupá have Saint Benedict. He was chosen by the slaves, by the poor, so he is ours." Ana, proprietor of a boardinghouse, in her forties, informed me, "Each place has its saint. Here it is Saint Benedict. What is your town's saint?" Carmita, Bena's wife, added, "Saint Benedict takes care of people here; Our Lady of Aparecida takes care of people in other places." In all responses there is a politeness toward the Virgin, but clearly the local trumps the national. Aparecida is all but ignored. Even the October 12 national holiday for the Virgin is overlooked—in part due to the overriding celebration of the Círio in Belém (second Sunday of October) in honor of the Virgin of Nazareth, in which people from Gurupá often participate.

Perhaps the most illuminating example of ignoring television programming—especially its call for national identity—is the downplaying of Carnaval in Gurupá. In most of the rest of Brazil Carnaval is a major event that celebrates national culture (DaMatta 2001: 26–27). The country indulges in innumerable celebrations in the weeks preceding the holiday and then reaches a festive frenzy during the four main days of Carnaval. All of this is televised in great detail in hundreds of hours of coverage from all the major cities. For Gurupaenses living in town, since the late 1980s the viewing of these festivities on television has been unavoidable.

Despite exposure to the pageantry and national pride featured in the celebration, Gurupá's Carnaval is a relatively meager event. There are dances, parties, and an occasional dance block or two that parade around the town accompanied by a makeshift samba band, but the event pales in comparison to other, more popular local celebrations, which draw much larger crowds. In the 1999 survey we asked respondents to rank their favorite celebrations. Carnaval ranked last on a list that included Christmas, the festivals of Saint Benedict and Saint Anthony, and Independence Day. By 2009 the celebration crept up in the local rankings, possibly due to television exposure. Yet no one ranked it as the most important event, and only 8 percent said it was the second most important event, followed by 40 percent for third, 18 percent for fourth, and 34 percent for last place.

I was puzzled by this uninspired attitude toward the quintessential Brazilian event. I asked my consultants why Gurupá does not celebrate Carnaval as much of the rest of Brazil and received four categories of replies: (1) the event is unaffordable because the local government does not sponsor it by providing money for decorations or the simple but colorful T-shirts that the dance blocks use as costumes; (2) it follows too closely the most important local celebration, that of Saint Benedict in late December, so people do not have the resources, or desire, to celebrate; (3) there is no history of celebrating Carnaval in the community, so why start now; and (4) it is the peak of the rainy season, which not only soaks the environment with numerous daily downpours but also dampens the spirits, leaving little will for revelry (also see Wagley 1976: 187). Against these odds, television interpellation seems to have created only a tepid desire to celebrate this important show of national identity.

In contrast to the local indifference toward Carnaval, we found that

Gurupaenses openly and enthusiastically embrace a very hyped-up, carnavilesque expansion of the June Festivals (*festas juninas*) first established during the rubber boom. These festivals honor Saints Anthony, John, and Peter and also celebrate Brazil's rural identity. They are most popular in the North and Northeast but are celebrated throughout the country (Wagley 1976: 203–204). The monthlong event typically consists of bonfires, fireworks, regional foods, religious processions, "country" music, popular theatrical performances, and dances such as the quadrilhas (see Figure 5.3).

In Gurupá the quadrilhas have become competitions between different public schools or, on an advanced level, between rival dance squads and the surrounding towns (Gurupá usually has four dance teams). The squads are named, not infrequently, after favorite telenovelas. They consist of twenty to forty youths who practice their dance steps for months in preparation for the festivities. Their costumes are costly elaborations of stereotypical rural folk dress, although other themes may be used (e.g., indigenous populations). The dances are flashy, carefully choreographed, and performed to regional music—brega and *forró* (a traditional music played with a trio of drum, triangle, and accordion). The money, time, effort, enthusiasm, and camaraderie involved in the quadrilhas parallel those of the Carnaval dance blocks in other parts of Brazil.

Why do many Gurupaenses choose the June Festivals over Carnaval? This is possibly due to its association with rural roots; its association with the Northern and Northeastern identity as experienced through the musical, gastronomic, and dance traditions, much of it brought to Gurupá during the rubber boom; its occurrence during the dry season when outdoor activities are much easier; and/or its overlap with the community's celebration of Saint Anthony. Whatever the reason, it is clear that television's call for Brazilian identity through Carnaval is no match for the largely untelevised regional and rural attraction of the June Festivals.

Race

Much has been written about Brazil's system of racial classification whereby people are grouped by phenotype (physical features) and socioeconomic status (Harris 1970; Kottak 1967). The system is known for its fluidness, since individuals can change their race by altering their appearance (e.g., getting a suntan or changing hair color) or shifting their socioeconomic status (i.e., the notion that acquiring money whitens an individual). It is also known for its descriptive complexity, with numerous terms to account for phenotypical combinations. For example, in a study by IBGE in 1976 (see IBGE 1999) census poll takers recorded 134 different terms for skin color and other associated phenotypes throughout Brazil. Harris (1970) elicited 492 terms by using black-and-white drawings of people with different skin shades, facial features, and hair types. Kottak (1967) reports over 40 classifications used in the small fishing village of Arembepe in the Northeast, although people used these terms inconsistently.

Other scholars, however, maintain that the multiple racial categories reported in the literature are exaggerations and that most of the terms are simple color and feature labels that describe individuals' appearance but do not classify people into races (Sheriff 2001: 45, 54). This viewpoint greatly reduces racial classifications, sometimes to a simple bipolar conception of racial identity (white and black).

Regardless of the true nature of Brazilian racial classification, television programming incorporates many descriptive terms to label people's appearance. Among the most commonly used terms are *mulato* (a mix of white European and black African), *moreno* (tan), *branco* (white), *negro* or *preto* (black), *pardo* (dark brown), *japonês* (Asian), and *índio* (Native American/Indian). There are modifiers used as well, such as *claro* (light) and *escuro* (dark) for skin color. Most people appearing on television are of European descent (*branco*), while people of mixed and African descent typically have minor, stereotypical roles as servants and manual laborers.

Our interviews and observations revealed that people in Gurupá possess a variant racial classification. Only three labels common in national discourse are used consistently: preto, moreno, and branco. A fourth term, *caboclo* (mixed), is not commonly used in national discourse. "Caboclo" is a label that attempts to account for mixtures of blacks, whites, and descendants of the indigenous populations. In other parts of Latin America the term *mestizo*, referring to people of European-indigenous descent, might be used for this group, although it does not typically extend to those who also have African descendants. The Brazilian term *cafuzo* refers to people of African-indigenous descent, but it is not widely used and does not include Europeans. Both cafuzo and *mestiço* (the Portuguese word for "mestizo") are not commonly used in Gurupá.

When Wagley (1976: 130) studied Gurupá's racial classification in 1948 he found that "caboclo" had a narrower definition, that it was reserved for people with "Indian physical features." The key diagnostic feature for this group is hair. The caboclo has black coarse hair on the head and "three hairs on his chin for a beard[,] and his hair stands on end despite all efforts to comb it" (130). Skin color and facial features in the Gurupá system are not key diagnostic features since they are seen to be deceptive—meaning they are traits that overlap racial classifications. Wagley also found that the term is used inconsistently. For example, he asked eleven of his consultants to classify the vice-mayor, whom he considered to be a "portly man whose mixed ancestry is clearly of all three racial stocks, but his appearance is more that of a European Indian mestizo." Five called him caboclo; six called him branco (134).

By the 1980s, when I started research in Gurupá, people still classified individuals as caboclo, but the term had become more problematic and controversial, less likely to refer to phenotype and more likely to be used for social class. Some refrain from using the label altogether because of its derogatory connotations (see Pace 2006; Lima 1999). Others use the term for geographic references (a caboclo is anyone from the state of Pará or from the rural part of Pará), for social class (caboclos are the poor and uneducated), or for subsistence lifestyle (analogous to *ribeirinhos* [riverbank dwellers], agro-extractivists, or peasants). The multifaceted nature of the term makes it difficult to discern whether a person is using the label to refer to race, social class, geographic origin, lifestyle, or even as a descriptive term or an insult.

For example, while in Jocojó (one of Gurupá's interior hamlets and also a quilombo) in 2002 I asked Mauro, a subsistence farmer in his early thirties, if there is any indigenous blood among the people of Jocojó. He said yes, you can see it in the faces of people. I asked how he classified these people in terms of race. He said there is no special word for Indian features. I asked if *caboclo* meant "Indian." He said no. I next asked if a caboclo is a negro. He said they are the same thing; only the hair is different, straight versus kinky.

In a conversation with Ana, proprietor of one of Gurupá's hotels, I asked what a caboclo is. She said it can be a preto, branco, or moreno. They all fit. I asked if there is any label for people with Indian features. She said no but then added that maybe you can use "moreno" but with straight hair. In my notes from 1985 I recorded a variant view from a neighbor named Manuel, a handyman in his fifties at the time. He told me, "A caboclo has Indian features; a caboclo is moreno."

Despite people's increased exposure to television and greater access to national discourses about race, the use of the term *caboclo* continues while other terms such as *mulato, mestizo,* and *pardo* are persistently ignored. Part of the underlying rationale, we hypothesize, is the need to deal with a very even tripartite mixing of peoples, African, European, and indigenous. The widespread expression of these mixed phenotypes does not occur in most of Brazil, due to the nearly complete demise of the indigenous population. As a result, national terms commonly used for race and/or individual physical description are insufficient to account for indigenous traits mixed within the population. Thus alternative terms must be used.

A second underlying rationale for this system is the predilection to disavow both indigenous and African heritage. Being called an índio is typically understood as an insult (Wagley 1976: 141). Alfredo, a church functionary in his late fifties, commented in 2002, "Until very recently we considered Indians to be *bichos* [beasts] from the stories we heard. No one wanted to identify with them." In a similar manner, people deny or are unaware of their African ancestry. Gabriel, a seventy-two-year-old religious leader in Jocojó, told me in 2002 that until recently no one in his family knew they were descendants of slaves and blacks. He said, "No one called themselves negro or descendants of slaves. That would be an insult. We saw ourselves as pretos, morenos, and caboclos but never as negros." The denial of heritage is likely associated with the lack of use of the terms *mulato*, *pardo*, and *índio*. *Caboclo*, by contrast, is a neutral term in this regard, as are *preto* and *moreno*, which can refer to colors and features and not necessarily, or overtly, to "race" in Gurupá.

By 2000 there were shifts in the racial classification system in Gurupá. The changes were the result of incipient acknowledgment of indigenous and African ancestry. In both cases, this newfound awareness is tied to claims of landownership on the basis of ethnicity. This right was established by Brazil's 1988 Constitution. Decree 78 guaranteed ethnic minorities the right to own the land upon which they live and work. The law applies to indigenous groups as well as to groups descended from African slaves. For the latter, the important criteria are the establishment of a slave refuge, or quilombo, before 1888, the date of the abolition of slavery; continuous occupation of the territory since; and preservation of cultural heritage (such as with religion, music, and dance). The inhabitants are known as *remanescentes de quilombos* (remnants of fugitive slave refuges), *quilombolas*, and negros. By the late 1990s the governor of Pará pushed hard for the establishment of quilombos in the state. Gurupá's Padre Giúlio first brought the idea to the municipality, while FASE and the rural union quickly followed up and began the legal work. By the mid-2000s, 85,468 hectares—or nearly 10 percent of the municipality—was classified as a quilombo (Trecanni 2006: 607).

Living in a quilombo, however, requires the recognition of African ancestry. When I talked to members of quilombo communities in 2001 and later, they sheepishly, if not begrudgingly, talked of being negros in a positive sense. For example, Doca de Castro, an agro-extractivist in his forties from the quilombo Maria-Ribeira, stated, "I am negro." He continued, "Twenty-five years ago I would have been embarrassed to admit being negro. People then, and now, use the term *preto*. But African and slave ancestry was always hidden. No one spoke of it openly." During this same conversation Jean-Marie Royer, a French anthropologist who conducted research in Maria-Ribeira in 2000 and now resides with his wife and two children in Gurupá, commented that before the offers of land for quilombos no one would acknowledge slave descent or being negro. A year earlier, Paulo Oliveira from FASE mentioned to me that people in Gurupá were not so much developing a cultural awareness of being negro as political awareness that the land is theirs because their ancestors were slaves. The important point here, in relation to the media, is that the principal source of information challenging the racial classification system has came from NGOs, the church, the government, and the rural union. Television plays a minor role in this regard.

Social Class

A final case of ignoring television messages is the delineation of social class and ideas for mobility. Brazilian television depicts class distinctions through symbols of affluence and taste. It also sets forth a strong message that social mobility is accomplished by luck, rich benefactors, or marriage, but rarely hard work. It is particularly clear in the story lines of telenovelas and on news broadcasts that class-based social movements are rarely responsible for improved standards of living. This view has been tempered somewhat in the late 2000s with the successes of President Lula's Workers' Party policies of wealth redistribution (e.g., subsidies for the poor, young, and elderly).

By and large, Gurupá viewers watching these representations understand them and find them interesting but largely dismiss them as irrelevant to local life. Their interest stems from the depictions of previously unknown lifestyles of the affluent. Viewers in Gurupá are fascinated by the wealth and the activities, so they watch and learn about middle- and upper-class norms. Just as La Pastina (1999: 151) finds in Macambira, people "were curious to see where these characters ate and entertained themselves, and how they dressed, spoke and worked." According to

Kottak (2009: 135–136), this process actually improves social navigation skills for viewers. If they come into contact with the more affluent members of society, understanding their class-based norms and behaviors allows them to be less reluctant and less uncertain in their interactions.

We found that despite their curiosity about the middle and upper classes, Gurupá televiewers ignore televisual representations when they discuss local social class categories and interactions. As mentioned in Chapter 3, Wagley (1976: 105) described the social system he observed in the 1940s as a deteriorated two-tier system divided into four subsections. On top was the first class (gente de primeira), comprising merchants, large landowners, professionals, and civil servants. Below them in the second tier were the lower-class town dwellers (gente de segunda), the lowly paid clerks, and semiskilled labor (e.g., masons, carpenters) who might also engage in some agro-extractivism. Next were the terra firme farmers (Gente de Sítio), followed by the várzea extractors.

By the 1980s this system had decayed further. People I talked to insisted there were no longer any representatives of the first class. Sebá, a retired subsistence farmer in her sixties, told me in 1985, "There are no longer first class people in Gurupá. But there are people from the second and third class. Second class is higher up. They came in after the first class people died off. Third class is the poor. The poorest of the poor have no certain job. The better-off poor have nice houses." Zeca, the former prosecutor, echoed this viewpoint, adding:

> Today there are no more first class people. There are people of the first selection [gente de primeira seleção] and second selection, who are lower. These divisions are not classes as before. The first and second classes of old functioned by rigorously separating people. For example, dances were held in which class boundaries were not crossed. Today the first selection is small; the second is big.

Zeca's wife, Beija, interjected, "There are no social classes today. There is no separation within society. The difference today is only money."

When we asked people how they distinguish social rankings, whether by class or another measure, we inevitably heard three general qualities that separate people. One is money, as in Beija's comment above. Money, however, is the least important of the three in determining social rank. As Bena commented to me, "Any caboclo can sell land and have some money. But he will spend it and end up poor again." What is more important, according to Sebá, is knowledge and training so people have the know-how to improve themselves and find solutions to problems. Education is part of this, but acquiring a profession is the ultimate goal. Others we talked to also commented on job selection. There was a common division between manual labor and using one's knowledge to direct others to do manual labor. In this context owning a business is considered ideal and prestigious. Others work for the owner, who collects the money. This attitude is evident in the high number of dance halls in town, most of which sit idle year-round. But they are, nonetheless, important symbols of prestige and affluence for the owners.

The third trait is prestige. Many report that a person is of higher standing if he or she is known (*conhecido*). This often includes people with political power as well as those with large social networks, for example, patrons with many clients or godparents with scores of godchildren. In these cases the family name can help elevate or lower a person's status.

These folk conceptions contrast sharply with the images of wealth and power depicted on television as social class markers. Since wealth is far more limited in Gurupá, the idea of class ranking must be based on different criteria. Television wealth is unattainable and unrealistic to most viewers in Gurupá, as are the high levels of education and wide range of well-paying jobs. As discussed above, wealth, higher education, and well-paying jobs are seen as important markers of development and are desirable, but they are understood to be beyond viewers' ability to consume or obtain. They are ignored in the local system of classification.

Notions of how to obtain social mobility also differ from television texts. Nearly all paths to mobility shown on television require personal connections to someone with power, influence, or wealth (see Chapter 2). Personal traits such as education, intelligence, hard work, or even good looks are not sufficient in and of themselves for mobility. In Gurupá the lack of wealthy and powerful people truncates these avenues. There are no rich to marry, or to discover missing ties to, or to be a benefactor. By contrast, in the discourses I recorded, social mobility is always framed in the context of gaining a desirable profession, either through training or education. Once this is obtained, however, people assume one will have to leave Gurupá because there are so few job prospects in the community. In other words, social mobility requires geographic mobility. Never mentioned is luck, or winning the lottery (which is not available in Gurupá). People also do not assume that hard work leads to mobility, especially for the agro-extractivists. This is one of the few congruencies with television's messages.

Resisting Interpellation

On various occasions we witnessed resistance to television messages. In such cases the texts are understood as false, misleading, or a threat to the preferred or accepted worldview. Unlike the cases of ignoring messages, the response is to subvert the texts by articulating alternative viewpoints. These viewpoints draw from other sources of available information such as churches, political parties, unions, family members, and friends. Interestingly, the number of examples we found of resisting television messages are far fewer than the cases of heeding, missing, and ignoring. People in Gurupá, at this stage in television exposure, do not appear to have developed the habit of challenging the authenticity or authority of programming, at least on a frequent basis. Trust in the medium is high, and without substantial alternative sources of information about the world beyond Gurupá there is little basis to resist the messages. Viewers perceive television as a reliable window on the rest of the world and are eager to absorb what is presented. Information that does not appear to fit local realities is more than likely missed or ignored rather than resisted. Still, we did record two examples of people resisting the messages articulated on television. In both cases television's messages collided with strongly held local beliefs.

Belief in the Local Supernatural

In Amazônida culture a variety of supernatural beings are believed to inhabit the rivers and forests, many of them of indigenous origin. Known as *bichos encantados* (enchanted creatures) and *bichos visagentos* (magical beasts), they appear in the form of animals, with some having the ability to take on human form (Galvão 1955; Slater 1994). Telling personal stories of encounters or near-encounters with these supernatural entities is a way to understand the rain forest and humanity's place within it. It may also function as a supernatural warning to those who overexploit rain forest resources, and it is clearly a way to explain chance and misfortune. I have heard Gurupaenses tell many of these stories, often in the still of the night or while deep in the forest for maximum effect. With increasing exposure to television, however, we found shifts in the stated beliefs about these beings. Table 6.1 lists the responses to queries on the existence of bichos encantados over the years. During this time a number of television programs, movies, and school textbooks specifically discussed bichos encantados. In general, the programs present beliefs in these creatures as

Table 6.I. Belief in the Existence of Supernatural Beings

	Cobra Grande (%)	Boto Transformation (%)	Curupira (%)
1986	89.8	68.1	62.3
1999	76.6	55.3	40.9
2009	82.2	56.4	47.5

regional folklore and superstition, characteristic of uneducated and backward populations (Slater 1994: 39, 221). This viewpoint appears to have taken a toll on public opinion but not uniformly.

The first supernatural entity is the cobra grande, the giant snake or anaconda. It typically grows too large to support its weight on land and must move into the water. Once in the river, it wreaks havoc on anyone in or on the water, sinking boats and drowning or devouring survivors. It almost always appears at night, with its head raised just above the water, and people observe it as brightly glowing red eyes or as a blue flame streaking across the water. In more elaborate versions of the story, the creature may transform itself into a brightly lit riverboat with people aboard (Galvão 1955: 98–99; Slater 1994: 160). I recorded many stories of encounters with the cobre grande. No one I talked to, however, believed in the more elaborate versions of transformation.

Another entity is the boto, or freshwater dolphin. This bicho encantado is said to have the ability to transform into attractive human forms. The male boto is known to appear at festivals and dances, dressed in white, usually wearing a hat to cover his blowhole. Women cannot resist his charms but typically end up pregnant. Female botas are equally seductive, and men falling for their charms are said to drown as they attempt to have intercourse underwater. Some humans, however, are taken by the boto to an underwater mystical city (*encante*) where they live out their lives, transformed into botos themselves (Galvão 1955: 96–97; Slater 1994).

The final being considered here is the curupira, a small, dark, childlike creature whose feet are turned backward. It is considered a powerful forest guardian that entraps humans who abuse nature, as in overhunting. These humans, on seeing the curupira's footprints, try to escape by going in the opposite direction, only to run into the awaiting beast (Galvão 1955: 99–101; Slater 1994: 138–141). Over the years I have talked to three people in Gurupá who insist they have seen the creature. Sebá, the retired midwife, for one, told me the Goeldi Museum from Belém actually came and captured one in Gurupá in the 1970s.

As Table 6.1 indicates, between 1986 and 1999 there was a decline in the stated belief for each of these entities. Belief in the curupira shows the greatest decline, which happens to correspond to the inclusion of a generic version of the creature in school textbooks' folklore section. This curupira is an índio youth, complete with warpaint and feathered headdress, with its feet turned backward. The pan-Brazilian form is presented as fantasy, similar to the representations of Bigfoot in the United States. By the 2009 survey, reported belief in the cobra grande rose well above the 1986 level, corresponding to the popular *Anaconda* movies shown on Brazilian TV (1997, 2004, 2008). Belief in curupiras also increased, and acknowledgment of shape-shifting botos increased slightly.

When I asked my key consultants about these changes, they associated the initial decline in belief with negative depictions in the media. At the same time they insisted that more people believed in these beings than answered affirmatively on the interview schedules. Our research assistants likewise commented on their suspicions that some respondents felt uncomfortable admitting they believed in these creatures. When I asked about the 2009 resurgence in belief in cobras grandes, increase in belief in curupiras, and slight increase in belief in botos transforming, the consultants suggested that many Gurupaenses reason that outsiders creating television shows or writing books about Amazon creatures do not really understand the local reality. Perhaps, they suggest, if these outsiders stay in the rain forest longer, they too will encounter these creatures (for similar comments, see Slater 1994: 221, 223). Others remarked that the creatures were more numerous in the past and might now face extinction, but they do exist. As for rising belief in the cobra grande well above 1986 levels, they cited the four *Anaconda* movies as reinforcing belief in the creature, even though the films were written as fantasy.

What is being expressed through these viewpoints, we hypothesize, is a reaffirmation of regional identity through resistance to the preferred televisual and textbook messages. For many in Gurupá, the persistence, or reassertion, of regional views and regional identity contests national sensibilities relating to the rain forest supernatural. Even though our figures show declines for botos and curupiras over the years (although we suspect that belief in these beings is underreported), there is a steady core of respondents willing to tell us that the creatures exist. The strong belief in the cobra grande may also signify strong local beliefs in the entity, deeply rooted in cultural belief and recently bolstered by the depictions of the creature in movies. Even though the *Anaconda* movies are understood as fiction, people in Gurupá read the texts as an affirmation of the creatures' existence, unlike their readings of other media depictions of botos and curupiras.

Political Preferences

Media researchers have long debated the influence of televised political messages on public opinion, and particularly on voting behavior. For Brazil, the special relationship between Globo, the political system, and viewers leads some media analysts to suggest an alternative model of media power. Straubhaar (1989: 140–141), for example, notes that unlike other Latin American media, Brazilian television has evolved to the point where it wields tremendous influence over not just the formation of popular opinion but over government decision making and policy formation as well. Sodré (1977: 128), as mentioned in Chapter 1, regards Brazilian television as a powerful creator of hegemonic cultural views that controls discourse through a monopoly on speech (partly through the aesthetics of the grotesque) that basically neutralizes the possibilities of popular expression. Reis (2000: 204) comments, "My personal experience as a Brazilian television viewer and analyst leads me to believe that, to this day, broadcast TV still has an immense influence on virtually all aspects of Brazilian culture and society. . . . Brazilians across the board often refer to something they saw on *Jornal Nacional*—Rede Globo's most watched evening newscast, or on one of the soap operas."

One of the most intense debates over media influence and politics centered on the presidential elections of 1989. The majority of political and media analysts agree that the Globo network slanted its election coverage in favor of the conservative candidate, Fernando Collor de Mello (Straubhaar, Olsen, and Nunes 1993: 123). Arguably, the biased coverage was influential in swaying the close election in Collor's favor. The majority of Gurupaense voters, however, were undeterred by Globo's favoritism and voted in the initial and runoff elections for the Workers' Party candidate, Luiz Inácio Lula da Silva. In fact, Gurupá was the only municipality in all of Brazil where Lula carried both the initial and runoff elections.

Why did Gurupá differ substantially from neighboring municipalities that voted for Collor, as well as much of the rest of Brazil, in persistently rejecting the conservative message they heard on Globo? The answers lie in the messages from alternative sources of political information, particularly the religious and politico-economic discourses emerging from the

Catholic Church and the rural labor union (Pace 1998). Both of these institutions were strongly influenced by liberation theology. As taught by the community's priest and church laity, religion and politics were intertwined, forming a critique of local and national injustices (including the structural sins of capitalism) with a corresponding call for peaceful but forceful protest to challenge and change abuses. By the late 1980s, following much organizational work, social-consciousness raising, legal action, and public marches, an explicit political culture of resistance had emerged that was critical of conservative political ideologies but very supportive of oppositional/leftist views. The messages from the priest, church laity, and rural union members worked in favor of Lula's Workers' Party and, in the end, were more powerful than Globo's favoritism.

CHAPTER 7

Conclusion

In the preceding chapters we documented the range of changes associated with the introduction of television to the Amazonian community of Gurupá. Employing an ethnographic approach and three surveys spanning a twenty-seven-year period, we analyzed the arrival and subsequent spread of the medium. Using a middle-ground theoretical approach, we gauged the relative strength of television influence vis-à-vis viewers' ability to mediate it. We observed and delineated patterns of viewers' responses in terms of behavior, social identity, and worldview while situating changes—and resistance to changes—in the greater sociocultural context of Gurupá. The results are a comprehensive analysis of televiewing in Amazônia that serves as a unique resource for comparative, cross-cultural media research.

Throughout the book we looked for balance between media power and viewer agency as experienced in daily life. An important conclusion from our study is that careful analysis of audience agency does not automatically negate the potential to identify media influence. To the contrary, by developing a framework for viewer response—heeding, missing, ignoring, and resisting—combining it with the concepts of cultural capital and cultural proximity, and observing changes over three decades, we have been able to observe a wide range of positive and negative responses to media messages. Our study has been aided by the ability to isolate television's impact in Gurupá, given the remoteness of the community, both geographically and culturally, and its technological limitations, which confines television viewing for the majority to one station, Globo. The lack of access to the Internet during most of our study period, the narrow regional focus of available radio stations, and the low literacy rates and low consumption rates of newspapers, magazines, and books also have allowed us to isolate television's impact from other sources of media.

Through the work of key Brazilian and Brazilianist media scholars, we identified preferred messages repeatedly transmitted by television programming over several decades. We dealt with the complexities of polysemic readings by relying on scholarly research and, most important, the actual readings of programming by people in Gurupá. What we have found are four general messages engaging viewers. The first is presented in consumerist texts that attempt to structure the nature of consumer desire and offer possibilities to satisfy it. These texts occur in straightforward advertisements or in product placements in programming. The second message comes from national texts designed to construct pan-Brazilian identity. Key to the formation of national identity is the dissemination of idealized representations of race, class, and gender based on cultural patterns of the middle and upper classes in urban southeastern Brazil. The third general message is delivered in development texts that focus on the need for capitalist industrialization and the replacing of traditional and agrarian patterns with progressive urban and modern ones. Development can signify industrialization, improvements in standards of living, and economic growth. Developmentalist texts also warn of ensuing perils, such as crime. Fourth, political texts communicate political messages supportive of those in power, although allegiances shift as political regimes come and go.

Given the rich historical and ethnographic material available for Gurupá, we devoted considerable space to the description of the socioeconomic setting and the historical precedents leading to the formation of the current Amazônida culture. We traced the contributions of the indigenous, European, and African populations, ranging widely from environmental adaptation and subsistence food technology to supernatural belief. From this longitudinal base, we were able to situate media impacts in the context of both long-standing and recent forces operating in the community.

Our ethnographic work began by describing television's introduction and spread in Gurupá. We used Kottak's five-stage model to describe television's impact throughout Brazil, focusing on Stages I and II for Gurupá. Using Peterson's analysis of media engagement, we focused on five dimensions of viewership. The first dimension involves technological constraints to televiewing. In Stage I televiewing is limited by high costs, poor reception, electricity rationing, and the risk of lightning strikes. By Stage II the accessibility of cheaper television sets and the installation of the municipal satellite dish leads to the rapid spread of televiewing. Those who can afford private satellite dishes have access to multiple channels.

For the vast majority, however, reception was limited to Globo—the only licensed channel for the municipal dish until 2010.

The second dimension examines social class standing and viewership. In Stage I television ownership and viewership parallel the social class hierarchy. The middle class owns the TV sets and the working class gains access through asymmetrical ties to individuals and families. Even proximity to the television set itself reflects social hierarchies—with viewing proximity sometimes used as a reward for proper subservience. By Stage II increasing ownership among working-class families in town blurs class distinctions in television access—although many poorer families are still relegated to watching television in the homes of others. Television ownership and viewership in the interior, by contrast, continue Stage I patterns because of the costs to acquire diesel generators, antennas, or satellite dishes. The third dimension is the signification of television as a material object and a communication modality. Although there are some minor changes in signification between Stages I and II, on the whole television remains a prized possession, prominently displayed in front rooms with doors and windows open to the street for passersby to see (except at night in Stage II). In both stages television indicates movimento and modernity, and positive attitudes toward the medium remain high, reaching a 99 percent approval rating in 2009.

The fourth dimension of viewership examines the gradual displacement of public activities. In Stage I Gurupá's nightlife all but ends with the arrival of television. By Stage II and corresponding viewing saturation, nightlife returns as many people ignore programs. Only large, community-wide events are delayed until the last telenovela ends.

The final dimension of televiewing focuses on habits of spectatorship. With expanded ownership in town, audiences of mixed social class backgrounds in Stage I transform into relatively segregated and homogeneous group viewership (i.e., poor with the poor, middle class with the middle class) by Stage II. The few exceptions to this pattern include mixed class viewing in public places, domestic workers watching with middle-class employers, and populations outside of town. The mixed age and gender audiences observed in Stage I persist into Stage II, however, with little or no apparent segregation apart from audience composition according to programming preferences. As people become accustomed to televiewing in the transition from Stage I to II, another noticeable change involves shifts away from silence and mesmerized gazes to movement, sporadic conversation, and multitasking.

In addition, the rules of public access to televiewing in private homes

Table 7.I. Viewer Response to Preferred Messages (Consumerist, National Identity, Developmentalist, and Political Texts)

Heeding	Missing	Ignoring	Resisting
TV-talk	Merchandising	Customs	Forest supernatural
Identity-talk	Social merchandising	Tastes	Politics
Awareness-talk	Intertextuality	Saints/celebrations	
Consumption		Race classifications	
Material display		Social class classifications	
Social identity			
National identity			
Gender roles			
Worldview			
Development			
Fear of crime			
Best place to live			

in town change. In Stage I public pressure mandates access to relatively scarce televisions—at minimum through open windows or doors to viewers in the street. By Stage II families in town expect some modicum of privacy during televiewing, due to community-wide television saturation. Public viewing (from outside a home) is no longer necessary or even desirable, since one can usually find easy access to television elsewhere—at a relative's, friend's, or neighbor's home. In short, televiewing in town transforms from a very public form of interaction into a more private event, with corresponding high rates of neighborhood and community visitation declining. This pattern, however, does not hold for the interior communities, where scarcity of TV sets results in the continuation of Stage I patterns.

In our discussion of the details of television's influence vis-à-vis viewer agency—as outlined in Table 7.1—we pointed out that our categories—heeding, missing, ignoring, and resisting—are heuristic constructions that are not always mutually exclusive. The variables listed also indicate that a majority of people demonstrate or express these behaviors/views, but there are always dissenters. We noted the lack of strong statistical variations in responses by social class, age, and gender. These findings, we suggested, stem from the relative social class homogeneity of Gurupá, the recent and rapid spread of television, and the primacy of social class over gender in terms of shaping responses. Despite these caveats, the changes we have identified over a span of twenty-seven years indicate the interplay between the power of the texts and the agency of the viewers.

Heeding Messages

In terms of heeding television's interpellation, or accepting media influence, we identified a number of observable behavioral changes and attitude shifts in worldviews and social identities. As we noted viewers' acceptance of messages, we also explored how they may negotiate meanings before integrating the texts into local realities. This is the process of localizing, indigenizing, or hybridizing the extralocal or national—a process through which the original meaning may be somewhat altered. We also explored just how profoundly or cursorily attitudes and behaviors had changed, especially when individuals had to act on novel ideas (e.g., the complicated case of gender role perceptions). Despite these caveats, a wide range of changes have been instigated by the dissemination of televisual messages.

We identified five categories of heeding, with several subcategories. Our data reveal that participation in television discourse communities provides viewers with novel information, or additional layers of awareness, to rethink all kinds of social identities, worldviews, and behaviors. In the case of identity-talk (one form of TV-talk), discourse becomes a way to establish links to national or regional cultures in real time. It may also establish social boundaries as viewers appropriate phrases and terms from programming and then use them to create codes to classify insiders and outsiders, as with the permutations of the term gringo. Viewers draw boundaries between the local and national, but not in predictable ways. As discourse used to understand new ideas, issues, or events, awareness-talk often involves interpretive speech to place the idea, issue, or event in a localized context. In each of these cases, unity and identification with the Brazilian world beyond Gurupá is the great attraction. Many, if not most, of the terms diffused by television are not particularly useful over the long term and fade from use, suggesting that use primarily links the speaker to real-time Brazilian identity.

Another easily identifiable category of positive response to interpellation is the consumption of products advertised on television. These advertisements and television programming in general attempt to structure the nature of consumer desire and offer possibilities to satisfy it. In Gurupá, however, consumers' weak purchasing power limits this influence. What they can afford are inexpensive consumables like shampoos, laundry detergent, cheap watches, beer, and only occasionally more expensive clothes. We found that consuming the affordable advertised goods is a powerful way to "materialize nationality" through the formation of an imagined community of consumption. Likewise, the material display of items or styles shown on television also indicates positive responses to interpellation. When people in Gurupá obtain and display these objects or styles, they engage in a process of identity construction that links them to national and supranational levels.

Accepting and appropriating social identities portrayed in programming are other examples of heeding television's interpellation. Whether identity is defined as a reflexive understanding of self, an ideological positioning of the social self within stratified society, or an ever-changing discursive construct, television provides much of the material used in identity construction through its representations of appropriate behaviors, norms, and attitudes. Television programming in and of itself does not construct identities for viewers but serves as a principal resource offering material to be accepted and/or transformed. We identified two cases where television programming creates observable changes. One was in the formation of nationalistic identity, especially noticeable when contrasted with representations of foreign otherness (e.g., in international news or telenovelas in overseas settings), which stimulated discussions on "Brazilian ways" versus "foreign ways," or even "local ways." The second change involved gender identities. Exposure to the possibilities of expanded gender roles in television programming, especially for women, was associated with shifting opinions on liberal attitudes toward women employed in public spaces. These changes occurred in tandem with Gurupaense women taking on many public roles. At the same time, there were limitations, as many women were expected to perform domestic duties in addition to their newfound opportunities. We also noted that shifts in gender appropriateness for local jobs are more closely linked to the enfranchisement and egalitarian messages emanating from the Catholic Church and repeated in the rural union and Workers' Party. In addition, we found conflict between egalitarian views on domestic gendered tasks and largely nonegalitarian attitudes toward household economics. In other words, we suspect that in certain cases, at the most basic level, the machismo-marianismo pattern persists, despite the liberal messages to the contrary coming from television and the real-life experiences of women who work in the more traditional realms of men.

Television also has shaped worldviews. We found three cases where Gurupaenses' worldviews closely mirror the viewpoints shown on television. The first includes opinions on development. The shifts in definitions, from jobs and industry to social development and technology and then growth and technology, reflect changes in national discourses. Local realities also play a role as the national is localized and the particulars of development reflect local possibilities Sometimes, however, localization leads to inconsistencies and contradictions.

As in the case of the Belo Monte dam, Gurupaenses are in fact heeding two preferred messages: developmentalist and environmentalist. The two messages are at odds in the media and in politics, so when heeding these messages Gurupaenses must negotiate the inherent contradictions involved. As the national is localized, in terms of the dam's development potential and environmental impact, the contradictions will be dealt with, ignored, and/or rationalized.

Fear of crime is another example of the impact of heeding television's messages on worldview formation. People in Gurupá express high rates of anxiety about crime in distant urban places such as São Paulo and Rio, as well as in Belém. This fear originates primarily from television images and stories. The explicitly detailed depictions of crime and violence, repeatedly shown, drive up viewers' fear levels. These fears are then transposed to Gurupá with great exaggeration. We speculate that general perceptions of crime tend to be framed within the national TV discourse, with a focus on considerable violence and danger. Perceptions about actual behavior like walking the streets at night or the best place to live call for local views and actual experiences. The framework is local, not national. People heed the national interpellation on crime—but not always and not in predictable ways.

Viewers' shifting opinions on the best places to live also draw heavily from television's messages. The steady drop in a preference to live in large Brazilian cities and the rise in Gurupá's desirability are linked to depictions of crime, as well as reports of unemployment and poverty broadcast in the news. These images are not countermanded by telenovela representations of affluence and modernity in these same places. The particular case of the telenovela *América* and the rise in positive opinions about life in the United States is a clear example of television's influence, even if opinions change as memory of the telenovela fades.

Missing Messages

Although we documented the ways that Gurupaenses heed messages as they try to imitate behavior, consume goods, copy social identities, and alter worldviews as best they can, there are clear limitations. We found cases in which viewers lack the necessary cultural capital and cultural proximity to recognize and understand what writers and producers wish to communicate. We identified three categories of messages typically missed. The first is product placement. Gurupaense viewers typically miss the items and services targeted for wealthier audiences. In most cases, they see them as part of the story line and not as commodities to be consumed. For these viewers, product placements are props demonstrating the prosperity and glamour of the urban privileged class and/or symbols of progress and modernity. The viewers simply do not recognize them as items or services that they can potentially consume.

We asked whether viewing wealth and prosperity on television far beyond what is obtainable in Gurupá leads to feelings of marginality and deprivation. Unlike other studies in Brazil, we did not find such feelings. Instead, we postulated that the gap between the ideal consumer world of the telenovela and the experienced life in Gurupá is so vast that a logical connection between the two is impractical. Television becomes a separate existence, very entertaining but otherwise not connected to day-to-day life. When confronted by material wealth and complex technology on television, viewers understand these ideas as things from another time and place—foreign to their life but perhaps plausible in their future.

A second category of typically missed messages is social merchandising. These messages reflect the viewpoints of the urban middle and upper classes on wide-ranging topics like abortion, racism, homosexuality, drug abuse, mental health, child labor, illegal immigration, political corruption, and land rights. We found that television viewers in Gurupá may understand some of these social messages—although they are typically localized—but on the whole overlook most of them. In this case viewers simply do not grasp the concepts, or they see them as tangential to the story line, with very little meaning. The main reasons for missing the messages is a lack of cultural capital and/or too little cultural proximity to understand what is presented. Viewers in these cases are often inattentive to the story line or may give up watching the program.

The third category is intertextuality/extratextuality. We found that it is very common among televiewers in Gurupá to overlook these cross-references. Missing intertextual messages occurs most often with foreign programs but also with domestic programming. In both cases viewers need access to multiple forms of media and exposure to a broad range of television programs, as well as experiences in places and events outside the local community, in order to decode intertextuality. Interestingly, we found that even though viewers miss intertextual messages, they may nonetheless incorporate variations of the references into their daily lives.

Ignoring Messages

In cases of ignoring, the audience perceives the preferred messages but deems them uninteresting, irrelevant, secondary, unintelligible, nonserious, or plainly false. In terms of tastes and customs, the preferred patterns of behavior shown on television represent the lifestyles and habits of the middle and upper classes of southeastern Brazil and are clearly less appealing than regional patterns already in place, sometimes for centuries. We found a preference for locally important saints, regional festivals to the exclusion of Carnaval, and the regional construction and conception of race over those promulgated in national discourse. We also found that preferences for locally important sainst supersede interest in saints celebrated and televised nationwide. One of our most curious findings was the devaluation of Carnaval—the ubiquitous and quintessential expression of Brazilian identity prominently shown on television—in favor of the regional June Festivals that celebrate saints, rural culture, and Northern/Northeastern identity, which are far less likely to be televised.

The construction and conceptualization of race was another example of ignoring television's messages. We found that Gurupaenses disregarded many descriptive terms used in national race discourse (e.g., pardo, mulatto, mestiço), selecting only three commonly used terms to indicate skin color (preto, moreno, branco). They then added a fourth, caboclo, which is a term used to account for phenotypical mixtures of blacks, whites, and, in particular, descendants of the indigenous populations of the region, who are uncommon in other parts of Brazil. This classification system varied significantly from the pan-Brazilian typology presented on television.

By 2000 shifts in the racial classification emerged in the form of incipient acknowledgment of indigenous and African ancestry. Particularly in the case African ancestry, this newfound awareness is tied to claims of landownership. It is not clear if people are developing a cultural awareness of being negro or simply developing a political awareness that the land is theirs because their ancestors were slaves. The important point that we make, in relation to the media, is that the principal source of information enabling shifts in the racial classification system has come from NGOs, the church, the government, and the rural union, with television likely playing only a minor role.

The conceptualization of social class is a final example of ignoring television's interpellation. Despite viewers' curiosity about and careful scrutiny of middle- and upper-class lifestyles widely shown in television programming, when Gurupaenses talk about social class classification and interactions, they tend to ignore these televisual representations. Instead they focus on a much-reduced social scale (IBOPE's B3, C, and D) that ranks people on the basis of three general categories: money, knowledge/training in order to obtain a profession, and prestige (which includes a large social network). These folk conceptions contrast with the images of wealth and power depicted on television as social-class markers. Since wealth is far more limited in Gurupá, class ranking is based on different criteria.

Social mobility likewise varies. For example, nearly all paths to mobility shown on television require personal connections to someone with power, influence, or wealth. In Gurupá, however, the lack of wealthy and powerful people truncates these avenues. By contrast, social mobility is always framed in the context of gaining a desirable profession, either through training or education. Once this is obtained, people assume one will have to leave Gurupá since there are so few job prospects in the community. In other words, social mobility requires geographic mobility.

Resisting Messages

We uncovered only a few instances of resistance to television messages. Our hypothesis is that people in Gurupá infrequently contest the authenticity or authority of programming since they lack the cultural capital to challenge most televisual messages. There is one exception: belief in forest supernatural beings, despite television's representations of these entities as folkloric and imaginary. This persistent belief is likely an affirmation of regional identity and overt resistance to preferred televisual texts promoting national sensibilities.

A second case of resistance involves politics. In the 1989 elections Gurupá was the only municipality in all of Brazil where Luiz Inácio Lula da Silva won both the initial and runoff elections. Since this time the majority of the municipality has staunchly supported the Workers' Party, even though television programs, especially those broadcast by Globo, opposed it, at least until Lula took office. Gurupá's uniqueness in comparison to surrounding municipalities, and much of the rest of Brazil, derives from the political activism of the rural union and the Catholic Church, both of which advocate the religious and politico-economic discourses on social justice, particularly liberation theology.

In all cases in which television messages missed their mark, the degree of cultural capital possessed by viewers and the proximity of the text to local realities are key elements that shape reception results. Straubhaar (2007: 195 ff.) provides a framework for understanding and gauging viewer responses in the context of choosing between national, transnational, and global television programs, which is relevant to our findings. He begins with the supposition that much of a viewer's cultural capital is rooted in the local or subnational region, despite the impact of globalization (198). Local culture, therefore, will often supersede national culture in terms of viewers' perceptions and worldviews. Particularly in situations where educational systems are weak, people's ability to travel or otherwise experience the outside world is limited, and family and personal networks are key sources of information, the local will overshadow the national and international in terms of mass-media choices.

Straubhaar sets up a continuum in which

> at one extreme, lower class audiences have localized networks that stress localized cultural capital and a localized version of cultural proximity, preferring local music to national music for example. At another extreme, elites often have family and school networks that are global, leading them to direct personal experience with global friends and contacts, perhaps to minimize cultural proximity, acquire a more globalized sense of personal identity, and pursue what they see as more cosmopolitan or global media choices. (2007: 203)

Gurupá fits in the lower end of the continuum. Missing, ignoring, and resisting preferred messages, crafted as national messages based on lifestyles of the middle and upper classes in the Southeast of Brazil, becomes an expression of regional identity. These persistent regional patterns signal an important disjuncture with the forces of nationalistic homogenization. In fact, ignoring and resisting preferred messages might actually trigger a better-defined regional identity.

Media Influence and Theoretical Polemics

Our qualitative and quantitative data, carefully situated in the ethnographic context, provide ample evidence of the nuances of message reception. Yet, given the polemical character of discussions to date, we anticipate critiques, especially from those who might challenge this study's positivistic leanings.[1]

Couldry (2010: 41), for example, maintains that the relevant questions about media are, "What types of things do people do in relation to media?" and "What types of things do people say in relation to media?" No longer should we make straightforward inquiries such as "What do media do to people and cultures?" or even "What do people do in response to media?" (Bird 2010: 86). While the former set of questions are lucid and lead to rich findings—and we actually ask them in this research—the unnecessary dilution of the second set of questions and their search for causal relationships is unfortunate. Such questions are answerable, as we show in our work, when gleaned from ethnographic research (including both quantitative and qualitative methods) by nuanced probing.[2]

The media researcher Rajagopal (2001) raises a number of important points on media influence in his treatise on Indian politics and television. His comments and critiques are both germane and challenging to our approach and merit some discussion. Rajagopal acknowledges that television has significantly changed the political climate in India, but he maintains that

> to thereafter treat [television] as center and source point of influence is misleading. A critical theory of the media cannot have the media as its center. . . . There is an institutional break between production and reception, and between the dispersed regions of message interpretation and the indirect modes of its use. Accordingly, no law-like patterns of influence are likely to be discerned. . . . Television's influence has, then, to be presumed rather than discovered, contra media effects research, as the backdrop, stage, and vehicle of social interaction. (24)

We contest these assertions as being overly dismissive. For example, stating that a critical theory of media cannot have the media as its center and source of influence overstates the case and is counterintuitive to ethnographic studies like ours. By definition ethnographies "highlight the interconnections between media practices and cultural frames of reference . . . [treating media as] simply one aspect of contemporary social life, no different in essence from law, economics, kinship, social organization, art, and religion" (Askew 2002: 10). The focus of our study is television but situated within a broad and complex framework that considers sociocultural factors so as to understand and contextualize its influence.

Rajagopal states that the disjuncture between the production and the reception of messages and between interpretation and indirect modes of use results in no lawlike patterns of influence likely to be discerned. His point assumes polysemic readings and aberrant interpretations (Eco 1990) as the norm.[3] But in this study we identify and measure a number of messages over time that not only resonate among the population and change attitudes but lead to behavioral changes as well. While media scholars may debate the multiple meanings of texts and the probability of adherent readings by viewers, televiewers in Gurupá respond in patterned and observable ways as they heed television's interpellations.

Of course, Gurupá viewers do not heed all messages. We have presented many detailed examples of television messages going askew—missed, ignored, or resisted. The mismatch between preferred message and viewer interpretation delineates the limits of media influence. Details of viewers missing, ignoring, and resisting messages provide critical data indicating just how active audiences can be and under what circumstances they are active.

Returning again to Rajagopal, he maintains that "television's influence has to be presumed rather than discovered, contra media effects research, if it is to be understood" (2001: 24). Although this assumption is supported by many (see, e.g., Hughes-Freeland 2002: 681), it unnecessarily rejects or ignores empirical evidence from other approaches that identifies such influence. In the pages of this book we "discover" television's influence in the community. The key to discovery in our case is a longitudinal, ethnographic, and quantitative approach. The relative isolation of Gurupá (geographically, culturally, and technologically) allows us to pinpoint television's impact, separating it from other forms of media. The rich ethnographic data we possess also allow us to understand how televisual messages are contextualized, as well as challenged and rejected by the local culture.

Will our research and similar studies collectively lead to the identification of "lawlike patterns of influence"? Is there a chance that middle-ground approaches will reveal parallel patterns of influence as well as viewer agency across cultures? If researchers heed the mantra of polysemy and refrain from the quest for discovery of effects/influence, then we will never know. If, on the other hand, we take concepts such as cultural capital and cultural proximity and situate them in longitudinal and ethno-graphic contexts, then basic patterns may begin to emerge. At least we can hope to achieve what Kitzinger (2004: 194) describes as a "nuanced understanding of how media influence operates (i.e., when and under what circumstances), at all times maintaining a clear conceptualization of who is trying to communicate, what, to whom, and why." It is our hope that this study may contribute to this process.

Notes

Chapter I

1. In this book we use the first-person-singular pronoun *I* to refer to Richard Pace—who has been conducting ethnographic research in the community of Gurupá for nearly three decades. The first-person-plural pronoun *we* refers to the coauthors Richard Pace and Brian Hinote jointly—the latter of whom began research in Gurupá in 2009. When referring to the administration of the interview schedules, "we" is also used to include the two research assistants from Gurupá, Edson Palheta Texeira and Milton Dias.

2. We use only the first names of our consultants in this work, in part due to the local tradition wherein everyone is on a first-name basis and in part to conceal identities. We use first and last names when referring to other researchers and the priest. All the place-names and names of rivers are real.

3. Until the beginning of the 1990s there were very few ethnographically based cross-cultural studies of television. A few exceptions were Granzberg and Steinbring 1980; Williams 1986; Murray and Kippax 1978; and Kottak [1990] 2009. There has been, by contrast, a significant body of cross-cultural literature in mass communication research, such as Leibes and Katz 1991; Lull 1988, 1990. These studies, however, use methodologies developed in the cultural context of Europe and North America, particularly in terms of discourse styles and social interactions such as formal interviews and surveys. According to some scholars, these methods can distort and invalidate findings (Ginsburg 2005: 19–20; Peterson 2003: 10).

4. Parts of *Amazon Town TV* incorporate previously published material by Pace: Chapter 1 uses sections of the theoretical discussion from Pace 2009; Chapter 3 includes material adapted from Pace 1998; Chapter 4 uses sections published in Pace 1993; and Chapters 5 and 6 contain material published in Pace 2009. All these texts are reproduced here with permission of the original publishers (Lynne Rienner, Wiley-Blackwell, and the University of Pittsburgh Press).

Chapter 2

1. For Tables 2.1, 5.5, 5.10, 5.11, 5.21, and 5.23 the data do not sum to 100.0% because not all categories are reported (e.g., "Don't know," "Neither," "Other," etc.). For Tables 4.1, 4.2, 5.2, 5.3, 5.4, and 5.18 the data do not sum to 100.0% due to rounding.

Chapter 3

1. Extreme poverty occurs for families with total income that is less than the cost of a basic food basket—which is equivalent to the FAO minimum daily caloric intake of 2,288 per household member.

Chapter 4

1. These estimates were based on a nighttime walk-by survey in which I looked for, or listened for, television broadcasts. Since most homes had their sets in the front rooms, often visible through windows and doors opening onto the street, I was able to get a good glimpse of who had and who did not have television. Since people could be out of the house or a set could have been located in a room not visible or audible from the street, I may have undercounted the number of sets.

2. During the research period there were no glass windows or screens used in homes. Wooden shutters covered window openings.

Chapter 5

1. This is a behavior Straubhaar (2007: 222, 230) labels "multilayered cultural identification," through which viewers may shift from local, subnational, regional, national, supranational, or transnational levels of identification.

2. For most of these categories listed there is no significant difference in the responses between men and women—except for the categories of small business owner and driver, which, interestingly, women rank as more appropriate for men than the sample average.

3. Peterson (2003) refers to this type of thinking as the bifocal principle. He writes that bifocality is "the ability to move back and forth between the local world of everyday experience and the larger world of virtual experience represented to us by various media. It further assumes that we relate these two dimensions of experience to one another. We understand the wider world presented to us in terms of our local worlds, and we understand our local worlds as shaped by forces in the wider world" (264). In the current case of crime perception in Gurupá, however, people occasionally look through the wrong lens, resulting in a blurry take on the world.

4. The divergence in percentages reported in Pace (2009) and here is due to an additional thirty interview schedules administered in 2009. The increase in favorability for Gurupá from 37 percent to 48.5 percent between the two data sets may be reasonably attributed to the time lapse following the telenovela *América*. Without the reinforcement of the telenovela's culturally understandable depiction of life in the United States, the culturally problematic representations more common in the Brazilian media dominated, resulting in erosion of favorability.

Chapter 7

1. Symptomatic of this polemic is Nugent's (2007: 134–135) tortuous apologia to the cultural studies readership for including raw data, tables, and charts in his analysis of photographs of indigenous populations in the Amazon in his otherwise "mainstream" interpretivist approach in visual anthropology. He writes, "Earnest discussion of method may induce a vegetable-like state among the normally alert and invocation of numbers in the course of cultural interpretation of images may be seen as a needlessly transgressive gesture, typically a kind of pathetic recourse to debased scientism" (2007: 134). Still, he compromises and includes twenty-six pages of "counting things" so as not to be burdened with gaining publisher permission to reproduce images and ". . . simply the convenience of being able to generalize over a finite body of data without having to address each image individually" (134). He absorbs the "collateral damage" from the presentation of his raw data and charts "as a consequence of [the] caricature of the anthropological enterprise that insists on the centrality of the interpretist versus positivist split" (135).

2. It is our contention that much of the material from practice theory approaches to media engagement can be analyzed to show influence, if not outright effects—the latter of which Couldry (2010: 37) defines as "a convincing causal chain from the circulation of a media text, or pattern of media consumption, to changes in the behaviour of audiences." Couldry goes on to acknowledge the obvious—the intuitive link between literary text and behavior underlying much of media studies. He continues, "Why else study the detailed structure of a media text as your primary research focus unless you can plausibly claim that those details make a difference to wider social processes? But it is exactly this that is difficult to show" (37). Difficult does not mean impossible, and when such links appear, refusing to recognize them, or opting to use language that mutes or obfuscates such links, might have more to do with ideological renderings and overreactions to previous positivistic approaches than with solid epistemological grounds. A trillion-dollar advertising industry tied to television apparently has little difficulty finding these links and investing heavily in them.

3. Such a broad statement is invalidated by much of the research on agenda setting, framing, priming, and branding, which shows the contrary (Kitzinger 2004). Even Eco (1990: 7) states, "The rights of the interpreters have been overstressed [as if] interpretation has no context and there is a failure to examine the limitations or constraints of readings."

References

Abercrombie, N., S. Hill, and B. Turner. 1980. *The Dominant Ideology Thesis*. Boston: G. Allen & Unwin.

Abu-Lughod, L. 2002. "The Objects of Soap Opera: Egyptian Television and the Cultural Politics of Modernity." In K. Askew and R. Wilk, eds., *The Anthropology of Media: A Reader*, 376–393. Malden, MA: Blackwell.

———. 2005. *Dramas of Nationhood: The Politics of Television in Egypt*. Chicago: University of Chicago Press.

Afonso, L. 2005. *Imagens de mulher e trabalho na telenovela brasileira (1999–2001)*. Goiânia: Editora da Universidade Católica de Goiás.

Almeida, H. 2003. "Telenovela and Gender in Brazil." *Global Media Journal*. lass .purduecal.edu/cca/gmj/sp03/gmj-sp03_TOC.htm.

Althusser, L. 1971. *Lenin and Philosophy and Other Essays*. London: New Left Books.

Amaral, R., and C. Guimarães. 1994. "Media Monopoly in Brazil." *Journal of Communication* 44(4):26–38.

Appadurai, A. 1990. "Disjuncture and Difference in the Global Cultural Economy." *Public Culture* 2(2):1–24.

———. 1996. *Modernity at Large: Cultural Dimension of Globalization*. Minneapolis: University of Minnesota Press.

Araújo, J. 2000. *A negação do Brazil: O negro na telenovela brasileira*. São Paulo: Editora SENAC.

Armbrust, W. 1998. "When the Lights Go Down in Cairo: Cinema as Secular Ritual." *Visual Anthropology* 10:413–442.

Askew, K. 2002. Introduction to K. Askew and R. Wilk, eds., *The Anthropology of Media: A Reader*, 1–14. Malden, MA: Blackwell.

Barham, B., and O. Coomes. 1994. "Wild Rubber: Industrial Organization and the Microeconomics of Extraction during the Amazon Rubber Boom (1860–1920)." *Journal of Latin American Studies* 26:37–72.

Barker, C. 1999. *Television, Globalization, and Cultural Identities*. Philadelphia: Open University Press.

Barroso, M. 2006. "Waves in the Forest." PhD dissertation, London School of Economics.

Berryman, P. 1987. *Liberation Theology: Essential Facts about the Revolutionary Movement in Latin America and Beyond*. Philadelphia: Temple University Press.

Bird, E. 2010. "From Fan Practice to Mediated Moments: The Value of Practice Theory in the Understanding of Media Audiences." In B. Bräuchler and J. Postill, eds., *Theorising Media and Practice*, 85–104. Oxford: Berghahn.

Blay, E. 1981. *As prefeitas: A participação da mulher no Brasil*. Rio de Janeiro: Avenir Editora.

Boas, T. 2005. "Television and Neopopulism in Latin America: Media Effects in Brazil and Peru." *Latin American Research Review* 40(2):27–49.

Borelli, S. 2005. "Telenovelas: Padrão de produção e matrizes populares." In V. Brittos and C. Bolaño, eds., *Rede globo: 40 anos de poder e hegemonia*, 187–203. São Paulo: Paulus Editora.

Borromeu, C. 1946. *Contribução a história das paróquias da Amazônia*. Niterói: Escola Industrial Dom Bosco.

Bourdieu, P. 1984. *Distinction: A Social Critique of the Judgment of Taste*. Cambridge, MA: Harvard University Press.

Bräuchler, B., and J. Postill, eds. *Theorising Media and Practice*. Oxford: Berghahn.

Brondízio, E. 2008. *The Amazonian Caboclo and the Açaí Palm: Forest Farmers in the Global Market*. New York: New York Botanical Garden Press.

Bruneau, T. 1982. *The Church in Brazil: The Politics of Religion*. Austin: University of Texas Press.

Bunker, S. 1985. *Underdeveloping the Amazon: Extraction, Unequal Exchange, and the Failure of the Modern State*. Chicago: University of Illinois Press.

Butler, J. 1997. *Excitable Speech: A Politics of the Performative*. New York: Routledge.

Canclini, N. 1988. "Culture and Power: The State of Research." *Media, Culture and Society* 10:467–497.

———. 1995. *Hybrid Cultures*. Minneapolis: University of Minnesota Press.

———. 1997. "Hybrid Cultures and Communicative Strategies." *Media Development* 44(1):22–29.

Chibnall, S. 1977. *Law-and-Order News: An Analysis of Crime Reporting in the British Press*. London: Tavistock Press.

Clark, W. 1991. *O campeão de audiência*. São Paulo: Editora Nova Cultural.

Cleary, D. 1998. "Lost Altogether to the Civilised World: Race and the Cabanagem in Northern Brazil, 1750 to 1850." *Society for Comparative Study of Society and History* 40(1):109–135.

Comstock, G., S. Chaffee, N. Katzman, M. McCombs, and D. Roberts. 1978. *Television and Human Behavior*. New York: Columbia University Press.

Coomes, O., and B. Barham. 1994. "The Amazon Rubber Boom: Labor Control, Resistance, and Failed Plantation Development Revisited." *Hispanic American Historical Review* 74(2):231–257.

Corner, J. 2000. "'Influence': The Contested Core of Media Research." In J. Curran and M. Gurevitch, eds., *Mass Media and Society*, 376–397. London: Arnold.

Costa, C. 2000. *Eu compro essa mulher: Romance e consumo nas telenovelas brasileiras e mexicanas*. Rio de Janeiro: Jorge Zahar Editor.

Couldry, N. 2010. "Theorising Media as Practice." In B. Bräuchler and J. Postill, eds., *Theorising Media and Practice*, 35–54. Oxford: Berghahn.

Creeber, G. 2006. "Introduction and Decoding Television." In G. Creeber, ed., *Tele-Visions: An Introduction to Studying Television*, 1–11, 44–59. London: British Film Institute.

Creswell, J. 2009. *Research Design: Qualitative, Quantitative, and Mixed Method Approaches*. Thousand Oaks, CA: Sage.

DaMatta, R. 2001. *O que faz o Brasil, Brasil?* Rio de Janeiro: Rocco.

———. 1987. *A casa e a rua*. Rio de Janeiro: Rocco.

Descartes, L., and C. Kottak. 2009. *Media and Middle Class Moms: Images and Realities of Work and Family*. New York: Routledge.

Di Paolo, P. 1990. *Cabanagem: A revolução popular da Amazônia*. Belém: CEJUP.

Dutra, M. 2005. *A natureza da TV: Uma leitura dos discursos da mídia sobre a Amazônia, biodiversidade, povos da floresta*. Belém: Núcleo de Altos Estudos Amazônicos (NAEA), UFPA.

Eco, U. 1990. *The Limits of Interpretation*. Indianapolis: Indiana University Press.

Fairclough, N. 1995. *Media Discourse*. New York: E. Arnold.

Faria, V., and J. Potter. 1999. "Television, Telenovelas, and Fertility Change in North-East Brazil." In R. Leete, ed., *Dynamics of Values in Fertility Change*, 252–272. Oxford: Oxford University Press.

FASE (Federação de Órgãos para Assistência Social e Educacional). 1997a. "Marajoí: O rio do mururé e do açaí." *Boletim do Programa Gurupá* 1(3):2.

———. 1997b. Editoria. *Boletim do Programa Gurupá* 1(1):1.

———. 2002. "Brasil: Manejo florestal comunitário na Amazônia brasileira." FASE Projeto Gurupá, www.fase.org.br. Accessed December 2002.

———. 2006. *Manejo florestal comunitário: Experiências em Gurupá—Pa*. Belém: FASE.

Fernandes, I. 1994. *Telenovela brasileira: Memória*. São Paulo: Editora Brasiliense.

Follmann, J. 1985. *Igreja, ideologia, e classes sociais*. Petrópolis: Vozes.

Foster, R. 1999. "The Commercial Construction of 'New Nations.'" *Journal of Material Culture* 4(3):263–282.

Foweraker, J. 1981. *The Struggle for Land: A Political Economy of the Pioneer Frontier in Brazil from 1930 to the Present Day*. London: Cambridge University Press.

Frankfort-Nachmias, C., and D. Nachmias. 2000. *Research Methods in the Social Sciences*. New York: Worth.

Galvão, E. 1955. *Santos e visagens: Um estudo da vida religiosa em Itá, Amazonas*. São Paulo: Companhia Editora Nacional.

Gerbner, G. 1967. "An Institutional Approach to Mass Communication Research." In L. Thayer, ed., *Communication: Theory and Research*, 429–451. Springfield, IL: Charles C. Thomas.

Gerbner, G., and L. Gross. 1976. "Living with Television: The Violence Profile." *Journal of Communication* 26:173–199.

Gerbner, G., L. Gross, M. Eleey, M. Jackson-Beeck, S. Jeffries-Fox, and N. Signorielli. 1977. "Television Violence Profile no. 8: The Highlights." *Journal of Communication* 27(2):171–180.

Gerbner, G., L. Gross, M. Morgan, and N. Signorielli. 1980. "The 'Mainstreaming' of America: Violence Profile no. 11." *Journal of Communication* 30(1):10–29.

―――. 1986. "Living with Television: The Dynamics of the Cultivation Process." In J. Bryant and D. Zillmann, eds., *Perspectives on Media Effects*, 17–40. Hillsdale, NJ: Lawrence Erlbaum.

Gerbner, G., L. Gross, N. Signorielli, M. Morgan, and M. Jackson-Beeck. 1979. "The Demonstration of Power: Violence Profile No. 10." *Journal of Communication* 29(3):177–196.

Giddens, A. 1991. *Modernity and Self-Identity: Self and Society in the Late Modern Age*. Stanford, CA: Stanford University Press.

Gillespie, M. 1995. *Television, Ethnicity and Cultural Change*. London: Routledge.

Ginsburg, F. 2005. "Media Anthropology: An Introduction." In E. Rothenbuhler and M. Coman, eds., *Media Anthropology*, 17–25. Thousand Oaks, CA: Sage.

Globo. 2011. "Institucional." [Online]. http://redeglobo.globo.com/TV/0,,96 48,00.html.

Goffman, E. 1974. *Frame Analysis: An Essay on the Organization of Experience*. New York: Harper and Row.

Granzberg, G., and J. Steinbring, eds. 1980. *Television and the Canadian Indian: Impact and Meaning among Algonkians of Central Canada*. Winnipeg: University of Winnipeg Press.

Greene, J., V. Caracelli, and W. Graham. 1989. "Toward a Conceptual Framework for Mixed-Method Evaluation Designs." *Educational Evaluation and Policy Analysis* 11(3):255–274.

Gustafsson-Wright, E., and H. Pyne. 2002. "Gender Dimensions of Child Labor and Street Children in Brazil." October. Working Paper 2897, World Bank Policy Research.

Hall, A. 1997. *Sustaining Amazonia: Grassroots Action for Productive Conservation*. Manchester: Manchester University Press.

Hall, S. 1981. "Encoding and Decoding." In S. Hall, D. Hobson, A. Lowe, and P. Willis, eds., *Culture, Media, Language*, 107–116. London: Hutchinson.

―――. 1982. "The Rediscovery of 'Ideology': Return of the Repressed in Media Studies." In M. Gurevitch, T. Bennett, J. Curran, and J. Wollacott, eds., *Culture, Society and the Media*, 56–90. London: Methuen.

―――. 1992. "The Question of Cultural Identity." In S. Hall, S. Held, and T. McGrew, eds., *Modernity and Its Futures*, 273–326. Cambridge: Polity Press.

Hamburger, E. 1999. "Politics and Intimacy in Brazilian *Novelas*." PhD dissertation, University of Chicago.

―――. 2005. *O Brasil antenado: A sociedade das telenovelas*. Rio de Janeiro: Jorge Zahar Editor.

Hamilton, A. 2002. "The National Picture: Thai Media and Cultural Identity." In F. Ginsburg, L. Abu-Lughod, and B. Larkin, eds., *Media Worlds: Anthropology on New Terrain*, 152–170. Berkeley: University of California Press.

Harris, M. 1970. "Referential Ambiguity in the Calculus of Brazilian Racial Identity." *Southwestern Journal of Anthropology* 26(1):1–14.

Hebdige, D. 1979. *Subculture: The Meaning of Style*. London: Methuen.

Hecht, S., and A. Cockburn. 1990. *The Fate of the Forest: Developers, Destroyers, and Defenders of the Amazon*. New York: HarperCollins.

Hecht, T. 1998. *At Home in the Street: Street Children of Northeast Brazil*. London: Cambridge University Press.

Heckenberger, M., J. Petersen, and E. Neves. 1999. "Village Size and Permanence in Amazonia: Two Archaeological Examples from Brazil." *Latin American Antiquity* 10(4):353–376.

Heckenberger, M., A. Kuikuro, U. Kuikuro, J. Russell, M. Schmidt, C. Fausto, and B. Franchetto. 2003. "Amazonia 1492: Pristine Forest or Cultural Parkland." *Science* 301(19):1710–1714.

Hemming, J. 1978. *Red Gold: The Conquest of the Brazilian Indians*. Cambridge, MA: Harvard University Press.

Hendrickson, M. 2006. "Child Labor in the Brazilian Amazon: An Ethnographic Approach." M.A. thesis, Middle Tennessee State University.

Herold, C. 1988. "The 'Brazilianization' of Brazilian Television: A Critical Review." *Studies in Latin American Popular Culture* 7:41–57.

Hirsch, E. 1989. "Bound and Unbound Entities: Reflections on the Ethnographic Perspectives of Anthropology vis-à-vis Media and Cultural Studies." In F. Hughes-Freeland, ed., *Ritual, Performance, Media*, 208–228. London: Routledge.

Hobert, M. 2005. "The Profanity of the Media." In E. Rothernbuhler and M. Coman, eds., *Media Anthropology*, 26–35. London: Sage.

———. 2010. "What Do We Mean by 'Media Practices'?" In B. Bräuchler and J. Postill, eds., *Theorising Media and Practice*, 55–76. Oxford: Berghahn.

Hoineff, N. 1996. *A nova televisão: Desmassificação e o impasse das grandes redes*. Rio de Janeiro: Editora Dumara.

Hood, S. 1987. *On Television*. London: Pluto.

Horkheimer, M., and T. Adorno. [1947] 1969. "The Culture Industry: Enlightenment as Mass-Deception." In the *Dialectic of Enlightenment*, 120–167. New York: Continuum.

Hughes-Freeland, F. 2002. "Television, Politics, and History." *Current Anthropology* 43 (4):680–682.

Hurley, H. 1936. *Traços cabanos*. Belém: Gráficas do Instituto Lauro Sodré.

IBGE (Instituto Brasileiro de Geográfia e Estatística). 1999. "What Color Are You?" In R. Levine and J. Crocitti, eds., *The Brazil Reader: History, Culture, Politics*, 386–390. Durham, NC: Duke University Press.

———. 2001. *Censo demográfico e censo econômico*. Rio de Janeiro: IBGE.

———. 2010. *Censo demográfico e censo econômico*. Rio de Janeiro: IBGE.

Joyce, S. 2010. "Race Matters: Race, Telenovela Representations, and Discourse in Contemporary Brazil." PhD dissertation, University of Iowa. http://ir.uiowa.edu/etd/525.

Katz, E., and T. Liebes. 1984. "Once upon a Time, in Dallas." *Intermedia* 12(3):46–72.

Kehl, M. 1980. "As novelas, novelinhas, e novelões: Mil e uma noites para as multidões." In E. Carvalho et al., *Anos 70*, 49–57. Rio de Janeiro: Editora Europa.

———. 1981. "Um só povo, uma só cabeça, uma só nação." In *Anos 70*, 5–29. Rio de Janeiro: Editora Europa.

Kelly, A. 1984. "Family, Church, and Crown: A Social and Demographic History of the Lower Xingu River Valley and the Municipality of Gurupá." PhD dissertation, University of Florida.

Kemper, R., and A. Royce, eds. 2002. *Chronicling Cultures: Long-Term Field Research in Anthropology*. Walnut Creek, CA: AltaMira Press.

Kiemen, M. 1954. *The Indian Policy of Portugal in the Amazon Basin, 1614–1693*. Washington, DC: Catholic University Press.

Kilborn, R. 1992. *Television Soap Operas*. London: B. T. Batsford.

Kitzinger, J. 2004. *Framing Abuse: Media Influence and Public Understanding of Sexual Violence against Children*. London: Pluto.

Klagsbrunn, M. 1993. "The Brazilian Telenovelas: A Genre in Development." In A. Fadul, ed., *Serial Fiction in TV: The Latin American Telenovelas with an Annotated Bibliography of Brazilian Telenovelas*, 15–24. São Paulo: University of São Paulo.

Kottak, C. 1967. "Race Relations in a Bahian Fishing Village." *Ethnology* 6:427–443.

———. 1991. "Television's Impact on Values and Local Life in Brazil." *Journal of Communication* 41(1):70–87.

———. [1990] 2009. *Prime-Time Society: An Anthropological Analysis of Television and Culture*. Walnut Creek, CA: Left Coast Press.

Kraidy, M. 2005. *Hybridity, Or the Cultural Logic of Globalization*. Philadelphia: Temple University Press.

La Pastina, A. 1999. "The Telenovela Way of Knowledge: An Ethnographic Reception Study among Rural Viewers in Brazil." PhD dissertation, University of Texas at Austin.

———. 2001. "Product Placement in Brazilian Prime Time Television: The Case of the Reception of a Telenovela." *Journal of Broadcasting & Electronic Media* 45(4):541–557.

———. 2004. "Seeing Political Integrity: Telenovelas, Intertextuality, and Local Elections in Rural Brazil." *Journal of Broadcasting & Electronic Media* 48(2):302–326.

———. 2005. "Audience Ethnographies—Media Engagement: A Model for Studying Audiences." In E. Rothenbuhler and M. Coman, eds., *Media Anthropology*, 139–148. Thousand Oaks, CA: Sage.

La Pastina, A., D. Patel, and M. Schiavo. 2004. "Telenovela Reception in Rural Brazil: Gendered Readings and Sexual Mores." *Critical Studies in Media Communication* 21:162–181.

Leal, O. 1986. *A leitura social da novela das oito*. Petrópolis: Vozes.

Liebes, T., and E. Katz. 1991. *The Export of Meaning*. Oxford: Oxford University Press.

Lima, D. 1999. "A construção histórica do termo caboclo: Sobre estruturas e representações sociais no meio rural amazônico." *Novos Cadernos do Naea* 2(2):5–32.

Lima, S. 1992. "Preconceito Anunciado." *Revista Comunicações e Artes* (São Paulo), no. 27.

Lima, V. 1993. "Brazilian Television in the 1989 Presidential Election: Constructing a President." In T. Skidmore, ed., *Television, Politics, and the Transition to Democracy in Latin America*, 97–117. Baltimore: Johns Hopkins University Press.

Lins da Silva, C. 1985. *Muito além do Jardim Botânico: Um estudo sobre a audiência do Jornal Nacional da Globo entre trabalhadores*. São Paulo: Summus Editorial.

———. 1993. "The Brazilian Case: Manipulation by the Media?" In T. Skidmore, ed., *Television, Politics, and the Transition to Democracy in Latin America*, 137–144. Baltimore: Johns Hopkins University Press.

Lopes, M. 2009. "Telenovela como recurso comunicativo." *Revista MATRIZes*: 3(1):1–23.

Lopez, A. 1995. "Our Welcomed Guests: Telenovelas in Latin America." In R. Allen, ed., *To Be Continued . . . Soap Operas around the World*, 256–275. New York: Routledge.

Lozano, J., L. Frankenberg, and N. Jacks. 2009. "Audiências televisivas Latin-Americanas: 15 anos de pesquisa empírica." *Revista MATRIZes* 3(1):167–196.

Lull, J. 1986. "Ideology, Television, and Interpersonal Communications." In G. Gumpert and R. Cathcart, eds., *Inter/Media*, 597–610. New York: Oxford University Press.

———. 1988. *World Families Watch Television*. Newbury Park, CA: Sage.

———. 1990. *Inside Family Viewing: Ethnographic Research on Television's Audiences*. London: Routledge.

Machado-Borges, Thais. 2003. *Only for You! Brazilians and Telenovela Flow*. Stockholm Studies in Social Anthropology, 52. Stockholm: Stockholm University.

Mader, Roberto. 1993. "Globo Village: Television in Brazil." In T. Dowmunt, ed., *Channels of Resistance: Global Television and Local Empowerment*, 67–89. London: BFI Publishing.

Magee, P. 1986. "Plants, Medicine, and Health Care in Amazônia: A Case Study of Itá." M.A. thesis, University of Florida.

Mankekar, P. 1999. *Screening Culture, Viewing Politics: An Ethnography of Television, Womanhood, and Nation in Postcolonial India*. Durham, NC: Duke University Press.

Martins, J. 1985. *A militarização da questão agrário no Brasil*. Petrópolis: Vozes.

Mattelart, M. 1986. *Women, Media, and Crisis: Femininity and Disorder*. London: Comedia.

Mattelat, M., and A. Mattelart. 1990. *The Carnival of Images: Brazilian Television Fiction*. New York: Bergin and Harvey.

Mattos, S. 1982. *The Impact of the 1964 Revolution on Brazilian Television*. San Antonio: V. Klingensmith.

———. 1984. "Advertising and Government Influences on Brazilian Television." *Communication Research* 11(2):203–220.

———. 1990. *Um perfil da TV brasileira: 40 anos de história, 1950–1990*. Salvador, Brazil: A Tarde.

McCombs, M., and D. Shaw. 1972. "The Agenda-Setting Functions of the Mass Media." *Public Opinion Quarterly* 36: 176–187.

———. 1993. "The Evolution of Agenda-Setting Research: Twenty-Five Years in the Market Place." *Journal of Communication* 43(2):58–67.

Meggers, B. 1971. *Amazônia: Man and Culture in a Counterfeit Paradise*. Chicago: Aldine.

Miller, Darrell. 1974. "Amazon Town." M.A. thesis, University of Florida.

———. 1976. "Itá in 1974." In C. Wagley, ed., *Amazon Town: A Study of Man in the Tropics*, 296–325. New York: Oxford University Press.

Miller, Daniel. 1992. "*The Young and the Restless* in Trinidad: A Case of the Local and the Global in Mass Consumption." In R. Silverstone and E. Hirsch, eds., *Consuming Technology*, 92–102. London: Routledge.

————. 1995. "The Consumption of Soap Opera: *The Young and the Restless* and Mass Consumption in Trinidad." In R. Allen, ed., *To Be Continued . . . Soap Operas around the World*, 213–233. New York: Routledge.

Moraes Rego, O. 1977. "Feitorias holandesas da Amazônia." *Revista de Cultura do Pará* 26–27.

Moreira-Neto, C. 1992a. "Os principais grupos missionários que atuaram na Amazônia brasileira entre 1607 e 1759." In J. Hoornaert, ed., *História da Igreja na Amazônia*, 63–12. Petrópolis: Vozes.

————. 1992b. "Reformulações da missão católica na Amazônia entre 1750 e 1832." In J. Hoornaert, ed., *História da Igreja na Amazônia*, 210–261. Petrópolis: Vozes.

————. 1992c. "Igreja e cabanagem, 1832–1849." In J. Hoornaert, ed., *História da Igreja na Amazônia*, 262–295. Petrópolis: Vozes.

Morley, D. 1980. *The Nationwide Audience*. London: British Film Institute.

————. 1981. "The Nationwide Audience—A Critical Postscript." *Screen Education* 39:3–14.

————. 1986. *Family Television: Cultural Power and Domestic Leisure*. New York: Comedia.

Murray, J., and S. Kippax. 1978. "Children's Social Behavior in Three Towns with Differing Television Experience." *Journal of Communication* 29:31–43.

Nascimento, S. "Usina hidroelétrica de Belo Monte: O campo de forces no licencianto ambiental e o discurso desenvolvimentista dos agentes politicos." PhD dissertation, Nucleo de Altos Estudos Amazônicas—Universidade Federal do Pará, Belém.

Necchi, S. 1989. "Brazil: A Mogul's Muscle." *Columbia Journalism Review* 28(4):6–7.

Nightingale, V. 1993. "What's 'Ethnographic' about Ethnographic Audience Research?" In G. Turner, ed., *Nation, Culture, Text: Australian Cultural and Media Studies*, 164–177. London: Routledge.

Nugent, S. 2007. *Scoping the Amazon: Image, Icon, Ethnography*. Walnut Creek, CA: New Left Press.

Oliveira, O. 1991. "Mass Media, Culture, and Communication in Brazil: The Heritage of Dependency." In G. Sussman and J. Lent, eds., *Transnational Communications*, 200–213. London: Sage.

Oliveira, P. 1991. "Ribeirinhos e roçeiros: Subordinação e resistência camponesa em Gurupá, Pará." M.A. thesis, University of São Paulo, Campinas.

Ortiz, R., and J. Ramos. 1989. "A produção industrial e cultural da telenovela." In R. Ortiz, S. Borelli, and J. Ramos, eds., *Telenovela: História e produção*. São Paulo: Brasiliense.

Ortved, John. 2009. *The Simpsons: An Uncensored, Unauthorized History*. New York: Faber and Faber.

Ott, B., and C. Walter. 2000. "Intertextuality: Interpretive Practice and Textual Strategy." *Critical Studies in Media Communication* 17:429–436.

Pace, R. 1992. "Social Conflict and Political Mobilization in the Brazilian Amazon: A Case Study of Gurupá." *American Ethnologist* 19(4):710–732.

————. 1993. "First-Time Televiewing in Amazônia: Television Acculturation in Gurupá, Brazil." *Ethnology* 32(2):187–205.

————. 1995. "The New Amazons in Amazon Town? A Case Study of Women's Public Roles in Gurupá, Pará, Brazil." *Journal of Anthropological Research* 51(3):263–278.

————. 1998. *The Struggle for Amazon Town: Gurupá Revisited*. Boulder, CO: Lynne Rienner.

————. 2004. "Failed Guardianship or Failed Metaphors in the Brazilian Amazon? Problems with 'Imagined Eco-Communities' and Other Metaphors and Models for the Amazon Peasantries." *Journal of Anthropological Research* 60:231–259.

————. 2006. "O abuso científico do termo Caboclo? Dúvidas de representação e autoridade." *Boletim do Museu Paraense Emílio Goeldi: Ciências Humanas* 1(3):79–92.

————. 2009. "Television's Interpellation: Heeding, Missing, Ignoring, and Resisting the Call for Pan-National Identity in the Brazilian Amazon." *American Anthropologist* 111(4):407–419.

Parker, E., ed. 1985. *The Amazon Caboclo: Historical and Contemporary Perspectives*. Studies in Third World Societies, 32 (June). Williamsburg, VA: Department of Anthropology, College of William and Mary.

Peterson, J., and D. Peterson. 1995. *Eat Smart in Brazil*. Madison, WI: Ginkgo Press.

Peterson, M. 2003. *Anthropology and Mass Communication: Media and Myth in the New Millennium*. New York: Berghahn.

Pfaffenberger, B. 1992. "Social Anthropology of Technology." *Annual Review of Anthropology* 21:491–516.

Pinheiro, L. 2001. *Visões da cabanagem: Uma revolta popular e suas representações na historiografia*. Manaus: Editora Valer.

Pires, J., and G. Prance. 1985. "The Vegetation Types of the Brazilian Amazon." In G. Prance and T. Lovejoy, eds., *Key Environments: Amazonia*, 109–145. New York: Pergamon.

Postill, J. 2010. "Introduction: Theorising Media and Practice." In B. Bräuchler and J. Postill, eds., *Theorising Media and Practice*, 1–32. Oxford: Berghahn.

Porto, M. 1994. "Idéias & fatos: Telenovelas e imaginário político no Brasil." *Cultura Vozes* 6:83–93.

————. 2005. "Political Advertising and Democracy in Brazil." In L. Kaid and C. Holtz-Bacha, eds., *The Sage Handbook of Political Advertising*, 129–144. Thousand Oaks, CA: Sage.

Prado, R. 1987. "Mulher de novela e mulher de verdade: Estudo sobre Cidade Pequena, mulher e telenovela." M.A. thesis, Universidade Federal do Rio de Janeiro, Museu Nacional.

Rajagopal, A. 2001. *Politics after Television: Religious Nationalism and the Reshaping of the Indian Public*. Cambridge: Cambridge University Press.

Ramos, R. 1987. *Gra-finos na globo-cultural e merchandising nas novelas*. Petrópolis: Vozes.

Reis, R. 1998. "The Impact of Television Viewing in the Brazilian Amazon." *Human Organization* 57(3):300–306.

———. 2000. "'A Gente se Fala Depois da Novela': An Ethnography of Television Viewing in the Brazilian Amazon." *Boletim do Museu Paraense Emílio Goeldi—Antropologia* 16(2):109–275.

Ribeiro, D. 2000. *The Brazilian People: The Formation and Meaning of Brazil.* Gainesville: University Press of Florida.

Roberts, J. 1995. "Expansion of Television in Eastern Amazonia." *Geographical Review* 85(1):41–49.

Rogez, H. 2000. *Açaí: Preparo, composição e melhoramento da converção.* Belém: Editora da Universidade Federal do Pará.

Roosevelt, A. 1991. *Moundbuilders of the Amazon: Geophysical Archaeology on Marajo Island, Brazil.* San Diego: Academic Press.

———. 1994. "Amazonian Anthropology: Strategy for a New Synthesis." In A. Roosevelt, ed., *Amazonian Indians from Prehistory to the Present,* 1–29. Tucson: University of Arizona Press.

Ross, E. 1978. "The Evolution of the Amazon Peasantry." *Journal of Latin American Studies* 10:193–218.

Royer, J. 2003. "Logiques sociales et extractivisme. Etude anthropologique d'une collectivité de la forêt amazonienne, etat du Pará, Brésil." PhD dissertation, Université Paris III-Sorbonne Nouvelle, Institut des Hautes Etudes d'Amérique Latine.

Salazar, M., and A. Glasinovich. 1998. *Child Work and Education: Five Case Studies from Latin America.* Aldershot: Ashgate.

Santos, E. 2008. "A construção de espaços públicos na política educacional em Gurupá." PhD dissertation, Universidade Federal do Pará Núcleo de Altos Estudos Amazônicos–NAEA, Belém, Brazil.

Santos, R. 1980. *História da Amazônia (1800–1920).* São Paulo: TAO.

Schwartzman, S., D. Nepstad, and A. Moreira. 2000. "Arguing Tropical Forest Conservation: People versus Parks." *Conservation Biology* 14(5):1370–1374.

SESPA (Secretaria de Estado de Saúde Pública). 2006. *Levantamento de dados dos atendimentos do Hospital Municipal de Gurupá do ano de 2006.* Belém: SESPA.

Sheriff, R. 2001. *Dreaming Equality: Color, Race, and Racism in Urban Brazil.* New Brunswick, NJ: Rutgers University Press.

Silveira, I., D. Kern, and H. Quaresma. 2002. "Reconstruindo uma ocupação." In P. Lisboa, ed., *Caxiuanã: Populações tradicionais, meio físico e diversidade biológica,* 59–76. Belém: Museu Paraense Emílio Goeldi.

Singh, A., A. Belaisch, C. Collyns, P. De Masi, R. Krieger, G. Meredith, and R. Rennhack. 2005. *Stabilization and Reform in Latin America: A Macroeconomic Perspective of the Experience Since the 1990s.* Occasional Paper No. 238. Washington, DC: IMF.

Singleton, R., and B. Straits. 1999. *Approaches to Social Research.* Oxford: Oxford University Press.

Slater, C. 1994. *Dance of the Dolphin: Transformation and Disenchantment in the Amazonian Imagination.* Chicago: University of Chicago Press.

Smith, E., and M. Wishnie. 2000. "Conservation and Subsistence in Small-Scale Societies." *Annual Review of Anthropology* 29:493–524.

Soares, N. 2004. "Like a Mururé: Social Change in a Terra-Firme Community on the Amazon Estuary." M.A. thesis, University of Florida.

Sodré, M. 1977. *O monopólio da Fala*. Petrópolis: Vozes.

Sparks, G. 2006. *Media Effects Research*. Belmont, CA: Wadsworth.

Sponsel, L. 1995. "Relationships among the World System, Indigenous Peoples, and Ecological Anthropology in the Endangered Amazon." In L. Sponsel, ed., *Indigenous Peoples and the Future of Amazonia*, 264–293. Tucson: University of Arizona Press.

Straubhaar, J. 1981. "The Transformation of Cultural Dependence: The Decline of American Influence of the Brazilian Television Industry." Ph.D. dissertation, Tufts University.

———. 1982. "The Development of the Telenovela as the Pre-eminent Form of Popular Culture in Brazil." *Studies in Latin American Popular Culture* 1:138–150.

———. 1983. "Estimating the Impact of Imported Versus National Television Programming in Brazil." In S. Thomas, ed., *Studies in Communication*, vol. 1, 34–45. Norwood, NJ: Ablex.

———. 1989. "Television and Video in the Transition from Military to Civilian Rule in Brazil." *Latin American Research Review* 24(1):140–154.

———. 1991. "Beyond Media Imperialism: Asymmetrical Interdependence and Cultural Proximity." *Critical Studies in Mass Communication* 8:39–59.

———. 2003. "Choosing National TV: Cultural Capital, Language, and Cultural Proximity in Brazil." In M. Elasmar, ed., *The Impact of International Television: A Paradigm Shift*. Mahwah, NJ: Lawrence Erlbaum.

———. 2007. *World Television: From Global to Local*. Los Angeles: Sage.

Straubhaar, J., O. Olsen, and M. Nunes. 1993. "The Brazilian Case: Influencing the Voter." In T. Skidmore, ed., *Television, Politics, and the Transition to Democracy in Latin America*, 118–136. Baltimore: Johns Hopkins University Press.

Subervis-Vélez, F., and O. Oliveira. 1991. "Negros (e outras etnias) em comerciais da televisão brasileira: Uma investigação exploratória." *Comunicação e Sociedade* 10(17):79–101.

Szalai, A., ed. 1972. *The Use of Time: Daily Activities of Urban and Suburban Populations in Twelve Countries*. The Hague: Mouton.

Telles, E. 2004. *Race in Another America: The Significance of Skin Color in Brazil*. Princeton: Princeton University Press.

Tichi, C. 1991. *Electronic Hearth*. New York: Oxford University Press.

Treccani, G. 2006. "Regularizar a terra: Um desafio para as populações tradicionais de Gurupá." PhD dissertation, Universidade Federal do Pará-NAEA, Belém.

Tufte, T. 1993. "Everyday Life, Women and Telenovela in Brazil." In A. Fadul, ed., *Serial Fiction in TV: The Latin American Telenovelas with an Annotated Bibliography of Brazilian Telenovelas*, 77–101. São Paulo: Universidade de São Paulo.

———. 2000. *Living with the Rubbish Queen: Telenovelas, Culture and Modernity in Brazil*. Luton: University of Luton Press.

Verner, D. 2004. *Poverty in the Brazilian Amazon: An Assessment of Poverty Focused on the State of Pará*. World Bank Policy Research Working Paper 3357. Washington, DC: World Bank.

Vink, N. 1988. *The Telenovela and Emancipation: A Study of Television and Social Change in Brazil*. Amsterdam: Royal Tropical Institute.

Volosinov, V. 1973. *Marxism and the Philosophy of Language*. New York: Seminar Press.

Wagley, C. [1953, 1968] 1976. *Amazon Town: A Study of Man in the Tropics*. New York: Oxford University Press.

Weinstein, B. 1983. *The Amazon Rubber Boom, 1850–1920*. Stanford, CA: Stanford University Press.

Wesche, R., and T. Bruneau. 1990. *Integration and Change in Brazil's Middle Amazon*. Ottawa: University of Ottawa Press.

White, M. 1992. "Ideological Analysis and Television." In R. Allen, ed., *Channels of Discourse, Reassembled*, 161–202. Chapel Hill: University of North Carolina Press.

Wilk, R. 2002a. "'It's Destroying a Whole Generation': Television and Moral Discourse in Belize." In K. Askew and R. Wilk, eds., *The Anthropology of Media*, 286–298. Malden, MA: Blackwell.

———. 2002b. "Television, Time, and the National Imaginary in Belize." In F. Ginsburg, L. Abu-Lughod, and B. Larkin, eds., *Media Worlds: Anthropology on New Terrain*, 171–186. Berkeley: University of California Press.

Williams, T. 1986. "Background and Overview." In T. Williams, ed., *The Impact of Television: A Natural Experiment in Three Communities*. New York: Academic Press.

World Wildlife Fund. 2010. "Gurupá Várzea." http://worldwildlife.org/eco regions/nt0126.

Index

9 780292 762046